WILLIAMS · RON · · · RT ·
USON JENKINS · JO · AS · RICK MONDAY · I
UKOW · IVAN DeJE · VE GOODMAN · LEE S
E SANDBERG · HARRY CARAY · STEVE TROUT · JIM FREY · BOB DEI
SON · VANCE LAW · DON ZIMMER · GREG MADDUX · DOUG DASC
IGGLEMAN · DOUG GLANVILLE · BRANT BROWN · PAT HUGHES
· DERREK LEE · RYAN DEMPSTER · RYAN THERIOT · BOB BRENLY
YD · ERNIE BANKS · BILLY WILLIAMS · RON SANTO · DON KESSIN
ANDY HUNDLEY · FERGUSON JENKINS · JOE PEPITONE · MILT PA
LL MADLOCK · MIKE KRUKOW · IVAN DeJESUS · BILL BUCKNER ·
KEITH MORELAND · RYNE SANDBERG · HARRY CARAY · STEVE TR
ON DUNSTON · ANDRE DAWSON · VANCE LAW · DON ZIMMER ·
AC · GLENALLEN HILL · JIM RIGGLEMAN · DOUG GLANVILLE · B
OD · CARLOS ZAMBRANO · DERREK LEE · RYAN DEMPSTER · RYAN
ANDY PAFKO · VINCE LLOYD · ERNIE BANKS · BILLY WILLIAMS ·
OLTZMAN · BILL HANDS · RANDY HUNDLEY · FERGUSON JENKINS
ENAL · RICK REUSCHEL · BILL MADLOCK · MIKE KRUKOW · IVAN
DY DAVIS · LARRY BOWA · KEITH MORELAND · RYNE SANDBERG · H
CK SUTCLIFFE · SHAWON DUNSTON · ANDRE DAWSON · VANCE L

WHAT IT MEANS
TO BE A CUB

THE NORTH SIDE'S GREATEST PLAYERS
TALK ABOUT CUBS BASEBALL

FOREWORD BY
ERNIE BANKS

BOB VORWALD

TRIUMPH
B O O K S

*To the Ballplayers—thank you for your excellence on the field,
for giving so generously of your time, and for all the wonderful stories
and memories you shared for this project.*

This book is available in quantity at special discounts for your group or organization. For further information, contact:

Triumph Books
542 South Dearborn Street
Suite 750
Chicago, Illinois 60605
(312) 939-3330
Fax (312) 663-3557
www.triumphbooks.com

Printed in U.S.A.
ISBN: 978-1-60078-277-0
Design by Nick Panos
Editorial production and layout by Prologue Publishing Services, LLC
All photos courtesy of AP Images unless otherwise specified

CONTENTS

"Mr. Cub" Ernie Banks belts out the 2,500th hit of his Hall of Fame career against the St. Louis Cardinals' Bob Gibson at Wrigley Field on September 19, 1969.

a book titled *Mr. Cub*, and it stayed with me. It's a big part of my life because everywhere I go there's always somebody who says, "There's Mr. Cub." Not many players get named after the team. Stan Musial is not "Mr. Cardinal." There's no "Mr. Giant." It is very special.

We were on the road for about two weeks, and I was sitting with Jerry Kindall, who played with the Cubs. We were sitting on the plane, and after you are on the road for a while when you lose a lot of games, you get down a bit. So I said, "We're getting back to the Friendly Confines." The writers were right there, and it kind of stuck. It became a big thing with the team, with the philosophy of the organization, with the Cubs' culture, and the people who come out there. It's a friendly place, and we just tied in with the atmosphere of Wrigley Field. It's friendly, it's family, it's fun. It's all of that. It's a wonderful place to play.

FOREWORD

What It Means to Be a Cub

MY FIRST DAY AT WRIGLEY FIELD was almost like the Peggy Lee song "Is That All There Is?" I walked in and looked at the bleachers and vines and wondered about it. Everybody was telling me about going to the major leagues and joining the Cubs. I walked in and saw Phil Cavarretta and the other players taking infield drills, so I joined right in. I was focused on base-ball, so it wasn't a big deal to me at the time.

The Wrigley family used the park to advertise the team. It was, "Come out to Wrigley Field for sunshine and fresh air, and you'll see a major league game besides." They wanted to advertise things that were true, and the park was going to be there; they didn't want to advertise a particular player in case someone was sick or hurt and couldn't play that day.

I started out as a shortstop, and I always tried to think of myself as average and be an average person. I might do it, but I wasn't going to brag about it. When I won the MVPs, I didn't brag about it. I think I was almost embarrassed about it. Why me? We didn't get into the World Series, and I didn't think I had done anything special. Now, as I reflect on it, there were so many great players in the league—like Stan Musial and Hank Aaron—but it was I who won those MVP awards. It's something I cherished, but it didn't make me any better than any other folks.

There was a writer named Jim Enright who used to write for the *Chicago American*. He just told me one day, "You're Mr. Cub." I said I didn't believe in all that. He said, "Well, you are." And I said, if you do that, then every year he should have somebody else on the team who had done well and achieved something be "Mr. Cub." He said, "No, you're Mr. Cub." We did

Wrigley is about family, it's about friends, and it's about competition. It's about memories, and I truly enjoyed playing there and now going there. It's such a big part of my life, and every once in a while instead of going to see my psychiatrist, I just want to go to Wrigley Field and walk around. It's a wonderful place to be. People come there to look back and enjoy their memories. You walk back in there and flip back to when you were young.

When I first arrived, it was a new experience for me to visit with Jack Brickhouse and the rest of the announcers who were part of our family. When I was a rookie, I spent all my time just listening. It was difficult for me to be interviewed at first. It took a long time for me to get used to it. Jack was so nice to me, and I started to realize how many different people could see me play thanks to WGN. We were different than most teams in those days because we had so many games on TV.

I know I've been called a Pollyanna about running around smiling all the time, but that's who I am. I picked it up from Buck O'Neil when we were with the Kansas City Monarchs. I know my reality, and I know up from down. I want to live above and beyond. I still want to learn every day. My life is about growing, and I've learned so much about that from all the people I met at Wrigley Field through the years.

For my 500th home run, it was exciting working up to that. I didn't think about it that much, though there was a lot of talk about it. People were pulling for me to do it. My daughter was getting a little irritated that it took so long. She said, "Dad, hit the home run so we can get the media off of our backs." I told her, "All right, Jen, I'll get it over with." I knew that Cubs fans, for that one day, would all be very happy and have a great memory for the rest of their lives. That day, May 12, 1970, against the Braves in the second inning, I hit the home run. I was overjoyed and shared the moment with so many people. I realized the impact of it and what it meant to people. Jack Brickhouse was there, and he was so enthusiastic about it. I still play that tape and hear him saying, "Oh, it's outta here! Wheeee, attaboy!" It kind of lifts up my spirits. It's one thing when I do get down, I play that Jack Brickhouse tape of my 500th home run. I was overjoyed by it. I learned from that. Sports and the Cubs are just one thing that can make people very happy, not just for a moment. People tell me they were at that game all the time.

Cubs fans span generations. I see so many people who saw me play when they were 10 years old, and now they are 50 and maybe have grandchildren. They share their memories and love coming to Wrigley Field. That's why

Wrigley is a source of wealth and joy across generations. There's something about that first visit to Wrigley Field for anyone.

Billy, Ronnie, Fergie, all those guys, we played together for so long that we formed a special bond. We shared those struggles in winning and losing, but also our children being born and going to weddings and things that were greater than baseball. We connected and stayed that way after we were done playing. It's a most unique bond, and we really care about each other.

Having the statue at Wrigley Field is a great honor, and I am just so pleased that Jesse Jackson, John McDonough, the Cubs organization, and the fans bestowed this honor on me. It's different, and it's hard for me to believe I've done anything to deserve a statue. In Chicago, people here like to honor their heroes, and that is often the athletes. Chicago is amazing, and the more I thought about it and shared it with my kids, I thought, *This is amazing.* Even when I'm not here, I'll be here!

—Ernie Banks

Ernie Banks was playing with the Kansas City Monarchs of the Negro Leagues when the Cubs signed the young shortstop as a free agent on September 8, 1953. Banks finished second in the voting for Rookie of the Year in 1954 and had a breakout year in his second full season, hitting 44 home runs and driving in 117. After "only" 28 homers in 1956, Banks started a streak of four straight 40-plus homer seasons with 43 in 1957. Banks hit his peak in 1958, when he led the National League with 47 homers and 129 RBIs, then posted 45 homers and a league-leading 143 RBIs in 1959. He was named the Most Valuable Player in the league both seasons, then followed with a 41-homer year in 1960. In 1962 he made the move to first base and continued to be a model of consistency at the plate, averaging 27 homers and 93 RBIs for the decade of the '60s. Banks retired after the 1971 season and finished his career with 512 home runs. He was an All-Star for 11 seasons and won a Gold Glove at shortstop in 1960. Mr. Cub is the team leader in games played (2,528), at-bats (9,421), extra-base hits (1,009), and total bases (4,706). On August 8, 1977, Banks was inducted into the Baseball Hall of Fame. His No. 14 was the first-ever retired by the club on August 22, 1982. Banks was named to the Major League Baseball and Cubs All-Century teams in 1999, and on March 31, 2008, the Cubs unveiled a bronze statue of Banks that stands just outside Wrigley Field.

ACKNOWLEDGMENTS

To be able to work on a book like this, you not only stand on the shoulders of giants, but you also have to be able to reach down, tap them on the arm, and ask for a bit more help. This is far from the entire list of people I could thank, but as always, Jack Brickhouse put it best when he said in his Hall of Fame induction speech, "You know who you are, and you have my undying gratitude."

Thank you so much to all the individuals whose stories follow. Each of them shared his time and memories, and I can't thank them enough.

Jack Rosenberg wrote that speech for Brick, and I want to thank Rosey for giving me my start at WGN in 1982. He continues to be a valuable mentor and resource on all matters regarding baseball, life, and to a much lesser degree, the Internet and modern technology. Rosey is one of a kind, and I learn more than I can remember from him every time we're together. His memories and advice were a great help.

Marty Wilke of WGN-TV made this undertaking possible. When I laid out my plan to do a book and television special using interviews with Cubs past and present, Marty was an enthusiastic backer. I want to thank her for her unyielding support.

Thank you to everyone in the Chicago Cubs organization. Senior VP Mike Lufrano and media relations director Peter Chase with the Cubs are great friends and offered their encouragement when I outlined my plan for this undertaking. Jason Carr was a huge help in arranging for time with some of the the current Cubs, and Dani Holmes makes our life at the ballpark easier every day. Joe Rios has always been a great resource when it comes to hunting down ex-Cubs, both during the season and at the Cubs Convention. Katie Marta graciously provided assistance with the seventh-inning guest conductors.

Randy Hundley and Lori Socki were outstanding hosts at Randy's Fantasy Camp in Mesa, Arizona. Their hospitality and willingness to help at every turn gave me the chance to spend time with a number of Cubs legends, plus experience a week on the baseball field I'll never forget. My still-aching body simply won't let me.

Len Kasper and Bob Brenly are as good a team as anyone calling baseball today, and their willingness to share stories, offer advice, and put up with disruptions in the booth are very much appreciated. Every time those two open their mouths, I get a little smarter.

Marc Brady, Doug Stanton, Jon Walgren, Skip Ellison, and the WGN baseball crew were a huge help throughout this project. Their creativity and organization allowed me to use valuable crew time each game day to sit down with many of the men whose stories are told here. Jeanette Rivera-Rosa and Bridget Gonzales keep the WGN production department up and humming along and make all our days easier.

Jim Tianis, Joe Pausback, Wyn Griffiths, Mike Clay, and Greg Gressle are all wonderful cameramen who offered up their time to sit with me and record as many of these interviews as possible when we were at the ballpark. I can't thank them enough for their patience and outstanding work.

There are numerous people at Wrigley Field who are always ready with a smile and word of encouragement each day. No one is more emblematic of these people who bring the ballpark to life than press box usher Keith Schram, whose love of the Cubs and baseball inspires me each and every day.

Steve Byrd and the gang at STATS, LLC deserve special mention here, as well. Without STATS PASS as a reference guide, I'd still be digging for info.

Several of the interviews here were not conducted by me, and I want to thank the individuals who were kind enough to grant me permission to use them. It's important we never forget Steve Goodman, and no one knows that better than NBC's Mike Leonard, who shared his interview with Steve. Kevin Bender talked to Jack Brickhouse for the *Ball Talk* documentary and was kind enough to send it to me after I contacted him out of the blue. Tim Sheridan's time with Vince Lloyd spawned *The Voice of Summer*, and parts of that interview are included in this book.

When I visited Triumph Books for the first time in February 2007, Mitch Rogatz and Tom Bast didn't throw me out. Instead, they listened to my proposal and with Steve Green's help, we published *Cubs Forever* a year later. When Mitch, Tom, and Don Gulbrandsen offered me the opportunity to work with Triumph again, I jumped at the chance. Don's editorial guidance on *What It Means to Be a Cub* has been a godsend, and I can't thank the entire staff at Triumph enough for all their help.

Finally, I want to thank my family. My parents, Bob and Barb, made sure a visit to Wrigley Field was an annual rite for our family, and sisters Val, Elaine, Sandy, and Maureen all endured a house where the game was always on the radio or TV. Jack, Michael, and Mark are the three best sons a man could hope for. Guys, I can't thank you enough for letting me share my stories with you each night and for all your encouragement. My wife, Karen, may not agree with the concept of extra innings, but her patience and support allow me the chance to spend time with this game I love so dearly.

INTRODUCTION

THEY PLAY MOSTLY DAY GAMES in the second-oldest ballpark in baseball. There is limited parking, the stadium is small, and the team hasn't won a World Series in more than 100 years. Yet, somehow, the Cubs are one of the most popular and beloved franchises in any league.

The fascination with the Cubs has never been bigger. The team sells out almost every home game and has tens of thousands of fans in attendance at every road game. Despite the heartbreak of near misses in '69, '84, and '03, Cubs fans remain optimistic and support their team at every turn. Playing at the Friendly Confines of Wrigley Field and on television across America on WGN, the Cubs occupy a special place in baseball's landscape.

In *What It Means to Be a Cub*, the men who are the fabric of the franchise talk about their memorable experiences with Chicago's National League ballclub and explain their part in building one of the most unique relationships in sports between a team and its fans. There has been far too much focus in recent years about the men who "didn't get it." This is the story of those who do.

Ernie Banks left the Negro Leagues and instilled a permanent, positive attitude of hope while becoming the face of the franchise. Ron Santo overcame life-threatening ailments to share his passion on the field and in the broadcast booth. Billy Williams let his bat do the talking and rode his quiet grace to Cooperstown. Fergie Jenkins threw strike after strike, inning after inning, en route to six straight 20-win seasons. Ryne Sandberg lifted two split-fingered fastballs into the left-field bleachers and became a national hero. Greg Maddux was brilliant early and late, and never forgotten during the years he got away.

Others were fixtures in the Cubs' lineup through the years, while becoming endearing heroes for their reliability and effort. Don Kessinger learned how to switch-hit on the fly to earn a spot at shortstop and anchored the middle of the diamond with his good friend Glenn Beckert for nine seasons. Randy Hundley and Jody Davis paid huge physical tolls for their insistence on being behind the plate almost every day. Keith Moreland didn't care what position he played as long as he could get on the field. Rick Sutcliffe and Andre Dawson were each spectacular in their debut year with the Cubs, but it is their perserverance in the face of injury and clubhouse leadership that marked them as Cubs legends. Bill Buckner went through hours of preparation to get his legs ready to play but managed to answer the bell almost every day and win a batting title.

For many, the spotlight has never been nearly as bright, but the fire inside has burned every bit as intensely. Outfielder Doug Dascenzo shrugged off questions about his size to become a brilliant defensive outfielder and unexpected bullpen savior. The steady drumbeat of Jack Rosenberg's typewriter was his only on-air presence during four decades of Cubs television broadcasts, but his stories, wit, and commitment to excellence helped establish the simple elegance of the televised games you see today. Bill Hands never reached the heights of fellow starter Fergie Jenkins, but his tenacity and drive made him a valuable workhorse and 20-game winner. Steve Goodman has been gone for a quarter century, but his voice and music ring joyously throughout the park after every Cubs win.

These Cubs are part of the national extended family where hope reigns supreme, hard work is rewarded with lifelong adulation, and the yearning for a championship is shared by players, staff, and fans alike. Their stories are told at a time when the Cubs are at a bit of a crossroads, with new ownership taking over and postseason expectations at an all-time high. The "Lovable Losers" tag was shed a long time ago, and recent seasons have given rise to signs of impatience and frustration that used to be foreign to Wrigley Field.

Those expectations are seen as a sign that the team is doing things right. "I don't take it lightly, and that's enabled me to roll with the punches. I get a lot of credit and get talked about very favorably when we're doing well. I take a lot of grief when we're not, I understand that," said Cubs general manager

Jim Hendry. "That never goes into the play of the importance of what I feel we owe our great fans, not only in Chicago but all over the country, and the responsibility that I have of trying to somehow, some way, win this thing one time." Manager Lou Piniella concurred. "One thing about it is the fans care," he said. "That's the most important thing. If you have fans that don't care, that's a problem. The other thing is that you can get on a roller coaster, but we have expectations."

Nobody has been a part of those expectations more than Cubs legend and broadcaster Ron Santo. "These fans have supported the Cubs forever," he said. "They believe in next year and they don't lose their allegiance, even when they move. It's amazing. Everybody laughs about it, but Cubs fans really do believe in next year." That belief is why former Cubs first baseman Eric Karros proclaimed that every player should get to play on the North Side for at least one season.

We believe. The tales and memories that follow will help you remember why.

The
FORTIES

JACK BRICKHOUSE

BROADCASTER

1940–1981

ICAME TO CHICAGO IN 1940 to work for WGN Radio thanks to one of the all-time greats, Bob Elson, who put the good word in for me. I started as a part-time sports broadcaster. In those days WGN Radio, as well as other stations in the city, was broadcasting both the Cubs and the White Sox. Those were the days when we would do the home games, but the road games were done by ticker. The good old Western Union ticker has been very well-publicized since President Reagan started talking about his days as a sports announcer back in Iowa.

Sometimes, it gave you a chance to sound like a genius. Here comes the tape, Cavarretta singles to right, scoring Jones. Well, you could say, "You know the last time Cavarretta was up, the pitcher got him out on an inside pitch, and I bet if he tries to do that this time, Phil will be ready for him, so don't be surprised if Phil swings and hits one into right field. Here comes the pitch—oh, there it goes! A base hit to right by Cavarretta!" We'd do things like that. Sometimes, you would work sound effects in there. We had a lot of fun in those days, but you not only did ballgames, you did dance-band things at night, man-on-the-street interviews, and it was all great background.

How do you make a dull game exciting? You do try, and what you do is look for positives. Any game has a number of positives in it. I have always maintained that you can root for the home team at the local level and maintain reportorial integrity. The way you do that is to give credit where credit is due on both sides. If Stan Musial of the Cardinals makes a great play, give him all the credit in the world. If you do beat them, it's great, and your victory is sweeter because you beat a great effort. If you lose, it's no dishonor to lose to a great performance. I've taken the position that this is entertainment, and people want to be entertained. They don't want a lot of complaints on their broadcast. They're trying to get away from a week of worry and complaining and that sort of thing.

I've been known for an expression on a home run, "Hey, hey!" How did it develop? Hank Sauer hit one out one day at Wrigley Field, and on my monitor in the booth, the crew flashed full-sized letters that said "HEY HEY." I had been doing this on home runs without realizing it and had fallen in love with the expression. The minute I saw this I knew what they were telling me, and the question was should I leave it in? There's nothing wrong with being identified with a call, so we left it, and it kind of caught on, I guess.

The 1969 season was certainly the most talked-about Cubs season in my history, even more so than the 1945 pennant-winner. The Cubs had a nine-game lead in August and lost it to the Mets, but let's not forget one thing: the Mets stepped up and won that pennant. The Mets played ball when it counted the most. In the meantime, the Cubs were exhausted. Leo Durocher, according to the people I've talked to, mishandled the ballclub. Leo should have rested certain fellows, and he didn't. He had a tired ballclub, and they were too tired to keep up the pace the last month. If you talk to the boys on the ballclub, they will tell you they did give their best effort, and they did, but their best effort wasn't enough, because they were too tired. I saw a couple of guys dragging that bat behind them on the ground up to the plate, it almost seemed like. It's unfortunate that it happened, but the Mets stepped up and won it.

We had ourselves a memorable year. Santo, Kessinger, Beckert, Banks were the infield. We had Jimmy Hickman out there, Billy Williams, and several guys in center, including Don Young, and the catcher was Randy Hundley. We had Fergie Jenkins, Bill Hands, and other pitchers like Kenny Holtzman. We had ourselves a pretty interesting ballclub.

My favorite Cub of all time was Ernie Banks. Ernie was the kind of fella who could be so contagious; his enthusiasm was so great that he could take you along with him. Here's a fella who was so happy to be in the major leagues, you couldn't find words to describe it. He was that way both on and off the field. Ernie Banks was the greatest single goodwill ambassador for

3

Jack Brickhouse, who broadcast for WGN Radio and TV since 1948, works his final game for the Cubs at Philadelphia's Veterans Stadium on October 4, 1981.

baseball I've ever known. Ernie also had another quality. You know kids are a lot smarter than we think they are. They have an instinct for knowing when an adult likes them or when they are faking it. Ernie had this wonderful sincere love for children, and he could make a little boy or girl feel the reason he came to the park that day was just for them.

There was a time when I absolutely hated Billy Williams, because anybody who could swing like that and have a waistline like that, I was so jealous of him! The fact is that Billy Williams has always been one of my favorite people. When he came up to the big leagues, he was a withdrawn type. He was not outgoing at all. I think Billy had a little bit of a suspicion about northerners, but whatever it was, he was a little tough to bring out. Billy credits Rogers Hornsby with helping him a lot.

I called eight no-hitters. My first no-hitter was by Sam Jones in 1955. The Cubs were playing the Pirates, and the score was 4–0 in the ninth inning when Mr. Jones proceeded to walk the bases full. Stan Hack, the manager, came out because Frank Thomas was up and they had a couple of other heavy hitters on deck. If somebody swats one, it's all tied up. Hack was concerned about the ballgame, not the no-hitter. People were afraid they were going to see Jones lifted and started to boo. Hack left him in, whereupon Mr. Sam Jones proceeded to strike out the side, and that was my first no-hitter. When I saw Hack afterward, I asked him what he said to Jones when he went out there. He said, "I told him to get the blankety-blank ball over the blankety-blank plate or your blankety-blank tail is out of here."

The last Cubs no-hitter I did was in 1972, when Milt Pappas came within one pitch of a perfect game. He had a ball-two, strike-two count on Larry Stahl and was one pitch away from a perfect game. Bruce Froemming was the plate umpire, and the next pitch could have gone either way. Froemming called ball three, and Pappas gave him that Greek glare. The next pitch was in almost the same spot, and Pappas was almost insane. He's the only guy I ever saw get a no-hitter and still be angry. He lost his perfect game.

Ernie Banks' 500th home run was one of the most memorable home runs I've ever seen. He was batting against Pat Jarvis for the Atlanta Braves, and all of the media and fans had been waiting for this home run. Sure enough, it came on a line drive into the seats, and Ernie finally had his 500th home run. That's one of the highlight moments we play all the time. Pat Jarvis later became sheriff of a county near Atlanta, Georgia, so every time we went down there, we had to warn Ernie to be careful because Jarvis was going to have him arrested once he got to town down there.

People ask, what's the longest home run you ever saw? Dave Kingman hit one that was a tape-measure job over the left-field wall, but the longest home run I ever saw was hit by Roberto Clemente. If you take a look at the scoreboard [in center field], it was still going about halfway up the board when it went by. That had to be almost 500 feet and was a fantastic home run.

There is a difference between the Cubs fans and the Sox fans, and it certainly is a difference of opinion. They are both great fans. Chicago fans are among the greatest fans in the whole world, they really are. I think in the final analysis, if both clubs were to play .500 ball, I think the Cubs would outdraw the White Sox most of the time, not all of the time, but most of the time. Some people have tried to label this a Cubs town, but that's not true. The Sox also are very much a part of this town. Like Cubs fans, Sox fans are the most loyal in the world. It's a little bit like a national election where you

5

have straight Democrats and straight Republicans and in the middle, independents. Whichever club is doing better is going to get those independents. Where does it become fashionable to see a ballgame this year?

Was it frustrating to have all those losers all those years? Not really. I don't think the word is *frustrating*, it's more being unhappy for them, because they are such great guys and such great fans. They deserve so much more. Even though this city hasn't had its share of team winners, it has had its share of individual performances, the likes of which were amazing.

My greatest moment would have to be when I went into the Hall of Fame in 1983. I'm lucky enough to have been elected to nine different Halls of Fame, but that one is the one I'll never forget. That was my moment. I was informed in January by Bowie Kuhn that I was going to go in the following July. I sat on this all summer long, and finally we went to Cooperstown. Before I went up there, I got a handwritten note from Ted Williams, which really thrilled me. The *Sporting News* had a cocktail buffet on the patio the night before the ceremonies, and I was standing talking to Joe DiMaggio. Some fellow came up and asked for an autograph, then Joe said, "Wouldn't you like to have the autograph of another Hall of Famer, Jack Brickhouse?" Then it hit me. It finally sank in. I was in the same lodge as those guys? It finally hit home. What a moment.

I've been called an institution and a legend and all that sort of thing. I've gotten a lot of publicity, and I keep taking those things down to the bank, but they still want a mortgage. I guess what I'm trying to say is that anybody who gets too serious about that sort of thing is making a mistake.

Jack Brickhouse was behind the mike when WGN-TV went on the air April 16, 1948, and would remain the eternally optimistic chronicler of the Chicago Cubs into five different decades. He was an announcer for all seasons who called every sport imaginable and yet was as comfortable broadcasting from the Vatican as he was announcing a professional wrestling bout. He was best-known, though, as the voice of the Cubs, sharing his happy totals each afternoon from the Friendly Confines. Jack signed off at the end of the 1981 season and was elected to the Baseball Hall of Fame in 1983. He remained a Chicago fixture until his death in 1998, and the foul poles at Wrigley Field are adorned with "Hey Hey" in his memory. (This interview was conducted by Kevin Bender in 1988 for the documentary *Ball Talk* and is used with his permission.)

ANDY PAFKO

OUTFIELDER/THIRD BASEMAN

1943–1951

STARTING OUT, it's been so long I almost forgot about it, but it sure does bring back some memories. I was a 21- or 22-year-old kid who came out of the minor leagues, and I finished the season with the club in '43. Then I found myself in a World Series in 1945—it was pretty hard to believe.

To me, I have a lot of good memories about playing for the Cubs. Unfortunately, they went downhill after I left. I was really disappointed when I left the ballclub. I thought I was set for a long time to be playing as a member of the Cubs, but the trade at the time disappointed me. I went to a great ballclub in the Dodgers, and I wound up my career playing in my home state of Wisconsin, where I got to play in a couple more World Series, but I have pleasant memories of Chicago.

They used to call me "Prushka." Charlie Grimm was my manager at the time, and he had lots of nicknames for all the players. Bill Nicholson was "Swish," and Cavarretta was "Fill-a-Buck," so I got the name of "Prushka." How he got that I don't know. It stuck right away, even with guys I played against.

We clinched the pennant against Pittsburgh that year on the next-to-last day of the season, and I drove in the winning run. It was the first time I ever had any champagne. Boy, it tasted good.

We opened the 1945 World Series in Detroit. Hal Newhouser was the first starter for Detroit, and he had pitched great that year. That first game was

7

probably the best World Series game of my career—I think I got three hits and threw out a runner at third base.

Just to be able to play in the World Series was a big event. I had a younger brother stationed in France at the time, and he was having a heck of a time trying to convince his buddies that his brother was playing in the Series! I played in other Series, but that first one, to get there for the first time in Chicago in front of such loyal fans. I'll never, ever forget that.

I spent most of my career as an outfielder, but I was at third base in 1948 and still made the All-Star team. I never felt comfortable at third, because I was so close to the hitter. In the outfield, all you had to do was chase down fly balls. The infielder can go ahead and have all those smashes right at them.

When I was traded in 1951, we were playing in Wrigley Field for a three-game series against the Dodgers. The second game came along, and we were having batting practice when Don Newcombe came out of their dugout and hollered at me, "Hey, Pafko, you're gonna be a Dodger tomorrow!" Naturally, my ears perked up because I had never thought anything about it. We played the ballgame, and I went home where my wife Pat had made dinner. All of sudden, the phone rang, and it was Wid Matthews of the Cubs. He said, "Andy, we just made an eight-player trade, and you are going to the Dodgers." Well, my wife started to cry. She was all shook up, and of course I was disappointed. I packed my bags and headed to the ballpark the next day. I went to Wrigley, into the home clubhouse to clear all my gear out, walked across the field to the other clubhouse, and then I was a Dodger. One day I'm a Cub, the next day I'm a Dodger. It was unbelievable.

8

At first, I was shocked. I was hoping to play here for a number of years. I was disappointed, but the way it turned out, I went to a great Dodgers ballclub. Eventually, I got over it. I'd rather have been traded in the offseason when you have time to adjust and think. Here I was, traded in the middle of a series. You can imagine what went through my mind. I don't think I slept a wink that night. After I got to Wrigley Field, I didn't go home after the game. I had to go to St. Louis with my new club. It turned out for the best.

The Dodgers ruled the roost in those years, and they were the class of the National League, just like the Yankees were in the American League. It was an honor to play with guys like Jackie Robinson and Pee Wee Reese. I was born and raised in Boyceville, Wisconsin, so to play with the Braves in the World Series was a great thrill at the end of my career.

Cubs All-Star Andy Pafko (right), poses with the Brooklyn Dodgers' Jackie Robinson
and boxer Ezzard Charles at Wrigley Field prior to a game on May 16, 1951.

The longest home run I ever hit was at old Braves Field in Boston. Over the wall there were railroad tracks, and a freight train was coming by just as I hit a ball out of the park. It landed in a coal car and went from Boston to New York. I was in *Ripley's Believe It Or Not* for a home run that went over 200 miles. Mickey Mantle and those guys had nothing on me!

I was involved in one of the most famous plays in baseball history in 1951. My Dodgers team faced the New York Giants in a playoff, and I was in left field when Bobby Thomson hit his famous home run at the Polo Grounds. I can still see that ball flying over my head. The irony was that he was later my teammate with the Braves, and we became great friends. We often talked about that game, and I always told him, "Bobby, you owe me a lot of meals because you took a lot of money out of my pocket." It couldn't have happened to a nicer guy, though. He was great.

What a career for me—I played for the Cubs, Dodgers, and Braves and got to play in a World Series with all of them. When I think of Ron Santo and Ernie Banks, who never got that break, I feel very lucky.

I was elected to the Cubs All-Century Team in 1999, and I was humbled by that honor, to be remembered like that in my lifetime. When I think about my time with the Cubs, I am overwhelmed. I'm a Cub at heart. I'm just like all the other Cubs fans—I pull so hard for them to win. It always feels good any time I can get back to Wrigley Field. It's a great baseball town here. If anybody ever deserved a pennant, it's these wonderful, wonderful fans.

After coming to the majors in 1943, "Handy Andy" Pafko hit 12 homers and drove in 110 runs to help the Cubs win the pennant in 1945. In 1948 he hit 26 homers and topped the 100 RBI mark again with 101. Pafko's 36 homers in 1950 were his career high, in a year when he struck out only 32 times. Pafko represented the Cubs on the National League All-Star Team four straight years, from 1947 to 1950. The Cubs made one of the worst deals in the team's history in midseason 1951, when Pafko was traded to the Brooklyn Dodgers along with Wayne Terwilliger, Rube Walker, and Johnny Schmitz for Eddie Miksis, Joe Hatten, Bruce Edwards, and Gene Hermanski. In 1999 he was named to the Cubs All-Century Team as an outfielder.

The FIFTIES

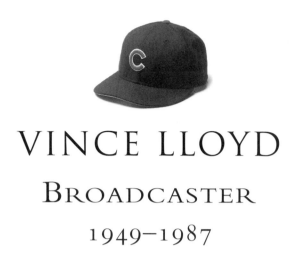

VINCE LLOYD

BROADCASTER

1949–1987

I WORKED ON WGN-TV doing both the White Sox and Cubs, whichever team was in Chicago, for 10 years. The White Sox went to the World Series in 1959. I hadn't been in town all that long, and I thought this wasn't too bad to see a World Series every few years. When I retired, it was still the only Chicago team to get into a World Series.

I first met Jack Brickhouse when I was in Peoria. He had been at the same station I was with. He came down for something, and I put him on the air, then we had a few drinks together. He'd come down every once in a while, and we'd yak. One night, I got a phone call after we did a sports show, and it was him calling from Chicago, wanting me to come up to WGN. I said, "Jack, I appreciate the offer, but I like it here, and my wife likes it. We both like Peoria very much." I said thanks, but no thanks.

He called again a couple nights later, and I turned him down again. The station manager called. This was in September, and they wanted me to come up and do Big Ten football and work with them on boxing, wrestling, basketball, and any sports that came up along the way. When I told my boss about it, he told me to go ahead. He told me they had made a mistake, and the board of directors had voted to give back the television license and go into FM. He told me to go to Chicago and learn all I could about television so if they got their television license back, I could come back and set up the station.

Vince Lloyd broadcast sports for WGN Radio and TV from 1949 to 1987, and became the radio voice of the Cubs alongside Hall of Famer Lou Boudreau for the last 23 years of his career.

Photo courtesy of WGN-TV

13

The first year doing Big Ten football and basketball, boxing, and wrestling, I had a ball. I called my wife and said, "I think I want to stay." She wasn't very happy about it, but she finally came up in September of '49 with our baby son. We stayed 38 years and just had a ball. Brick was a lot of fun, being together, we shot some golf and had a few beers along the way. When we got the Cubs on radio, they hired Lou Boudreau as the color guy, and he and I got pretty close. There was a hotel next to the Tribune Tower that had a heck of a good gym. We'd play basketball, and he would kill me. We'd play badminton, and he was so quick with his hands. We'd work out at noon for an hour or so and became good friends.

In 1965 our radio play-by-play guy, Jack Quinlan, was killed in a car accident going from Chandler to Mesa at a fork in the road. He started to go the wrong way and cut across and didn't see a big semi-trailer truck and was killed instantly. They talked me into taking his place.

That was the first year I came out to Mesa to do spring-training games. I finished up maybe three weeks before spring training ended, then did the whole season with Lou Boudreau. In fact, I wasn't going to do it at all, but what convinced me was that Lou gave me a phone call at home. He and I had been close friends for years, and he said, "If you don't take the job, I'm quitting." I said, "Lou, c'mon." He said, "No, I mean it. Either you do it or I'm leaving." That kind of convinced me. When I came out to spring training, he met me and had a place for me. We became as close as brothers.

Lou had as good a baseball mind as I ever encountered. As a player and a manager, he knew the game inside-out. There were some things about his record that always stuck with me. In 1948, when he managed and played shortstop for the Cleveland Indians, they won the pennant and went on to win the World Series. That whole season, he came to the plate more than 670 times and struck out only nine times! Now, you see guys who strike out that much in a week. We'd talk baseball 'til 2:00 or 3:00 in the morning on the road.

Lou would say as a hitter to always look for the guy's best pitch, that way you wouldn't be fooled. No matter what the count was, look for his best pitch. Good advice, but how many guys take it? Hitters tend to look for the pitch they want. He put himself into a game one time as a pinch-hitter with the bases loaded, two outs, and two strikes on the hitter, then banged one off the wall to win the game.

We probably had as good a crew as any station in the country. There wasn't any backstabbing. If you needed somebody to help you out for an assignment or speaking engagement, they were happy to do it. If you needed some money, sure. We had a lot of fun together, especially on the road when we were playing night games. We never brought our golf clubs with us, but we'd know guys at different country clubs around the country. A lot of them were from Chicago, and we'd give them a call, and they'd say, "Yeah, come on out and bring some guys with you." We always had a dozen bets going, though I never knew who was keeping track of them.

I remember the first year I traveled with the ballclub. We got into L.A. at the beginning of a road trip at about midnight. There must have been 50 fans at the airport to greet us! We had a terrible ballclub, lousy. We were in last place. When we got to the hotel downtown, there were another 45 or 50. At that hour of night! They had gotten the schedule, knew we were going to be there, and were there to greet the guys and show their support. That's always baffled me that the fans are so loyal and enthusiastic.

They have a great marketing team at the ballclub, and that carries over to Mesa. They have a new ballpark there, and to see that park jammed with fans is a wonderful sight. I know the ballplayers appreciate it. Money or no money, if they are not getting the support of their fans, it makes a big difference. The

14

first time some of the new guys experience that, it really hits them. I've talked to a lot of guys who played briefly with the Cubs and went on to other teams, and they still loved Wrigley Field and being with the Cubs, and spring training set it off.

Ernie Banks is just as outgoing, cheerful, happy, and friendly as he ever was. I hope that never changes, and I think it never will. He was a great spirit-lifter for the ballclub and the guys who played with him. For fans, he was an absolute idol. He always signed autographs. He'd come out of the batting cage, the fans would be around the dugout, and he'd go right over. Now you can't do that anymore, but he'd go right away to sign autographs and have pictures taken with them. In the players' parking lot after the game, he might stand there for a half hour or 45 minutes signing autographs for people and talking to them. He was a great booster of morale for fans and for the ballclub.

When Ron Santo first came up, he was going to be a catcher, and I think Lou Boudreau talked him into being a third baseman. He'd been quite an athlete in Washington, a good football and baseball player. He never had any speed and couldn't run a lick, but he had good quickness. He had a great pair of hands and a powerful arm. I've seen him throw runners out at first base from foul territory, 15 feet behind third base, and fire that thing on a rocket to first, a line drive. Never an arcing throw, just a straight line-drive throw all the way across. He could hit. He should be in the Hall of Fame, but he never played on a ballclub that got into the playoffs and never got into a World Series, of course. Had he done so, there would have been a lot of writers who would have seen him in his early days and would have said, this guy is a Hall of Famer. Brooks Robinson got that advantage, and he was great, too.

15

Fergie Jenkins was the best Cubs pitcher I ever saw. When they got him in a trade, he was a relief pitcher. After they used him a few times in relief, they decided to give him a start. I'd say that was a pretty good decision. The complete games he pitched were phenomenal, and he hated to be taken out of a game early, just hated it. At that time, most pitchers had a different feeling. You never heard a guy say, "I hope I can go six or seven innings." They expected to go nine innings. You had two thoughts in mind—you go the complete game, which is what you're getting paid for, and you win. Now they figure if they give you five or six innings, they've done their job. It's a different philosophy.

Billy Williams was as good an all-around player as I've ever seen. The first time I ever heard of him and Ron Santo was from Rogers Hornsby. He was a good friend and spent some of his time scouting for the Cubs. He lived a block or two away from me, and I hadn't seen him for a week or so. I went to the ballpark, and he was sitting in the press box. I said, "Rog, where've you been?"

"Oh, they had me doing some scouting," he said.

"Did you see anybody good?" I asked. We had a terrible ballclub.

"Yeah, I saw two guys," he said, "and they should bring them up right now. They can hit with anybody here except Banks."

"Who are they?" I asked.

"One kid's name is Santo," he said. "They have him catching, but he ought to be playing third base. The other kid is an outfielder named Williams, and he's a beautiful hitter. They ought to bring both of them up now."

They didn't bring them up until September. I told them both the story, and they both got a kick out of it.

The '69 season was a great one. You could see the team developing for a couple of years after Durocher took over. He worked 'em and put together a good team. You could see it in spring training that this was going to be a hell of a ballclub. In '69 the Cubs had a good shot at winning it, but were short a center fielder and a relief pitcher and lost it to the Mets. It was a hot summer, one of the hottest Chicago ever had.

Billy Williams played every single game, and I asked him how he did it. He would shower and sit in the clubhouse for about a half hour so he wouldn't have to fight traffic. Then he'd go home and have dinner with his wife and kids and spend the night at home resting. He said he did that all through the hot weather so he'd be sure to be able to play the next day. The record games streak that he had [for the National League] was later broken, but that's how devoted Billy Williams was.

It was a hot summer. I think Randy Hundley lost about 25 pounds, catching every day, and he couldn't afford to lose it. He might have weighed 175—I could put my hands around his waist by the time that summer was over, he got so thin. But he still played, and he never asked for a day off.

It was unforgettable to see Sandy Koufax pitch his perfect game. The guy was a great pitcher, and that wasn't any fluke. He'd been a good basketball player, too. That was probably as unforgettable an event as I ever covered. Our pitcher Bob Hendley was so good that night. He gave up a single, the only hit that night. There were a lot of great players on both sides. That would probably be my most memorable broadcast.

16

Vince Lloyd joined WGN in 1949 and spent the first years of his Chicago career broadcasting Cubs and White Sox baseball, boxing, wrestling, and many other events alongside Jack Brickhouse. In 1961 he made history by being the first broadcaster to interview a sitting U.S. president during a game, when he talked with John F. Kennedy at the White Sox–Senators season opener. After Jack Quinlan's death, Vince moved over to the radio booth, and from 1965 to 1987 his recognizable South Dakota baritone was the voice of the Cubs on WGN Radio. Vince Lloyd died on July 3, 2003. (This interview was conducted by documentary producer Tim Sheridan at Vince's home in Green Valley, Arizona, in 2002. The complete interview is available on the DVD *The Voice of Summer*.)

JACK ROSENBERG

Sports Editor, WGN

1953–1994

IN THE FIFTH GRADE, we had to write a paper on what you wanted to do when you grew up. I lived 180 miles from Chicago, and my theme was that I wanted to be a sportswriter for the *Chicago Tribune*. I came to Chicago in 1953. I had met Jack Brickhouse at a couple of banquets in Peoria, where he was already legendary. My boss, Kenny Jones, the sports editor of the *Peoria Journal*, knew that I wanted to go to Chicago, and he was great friends with Jack. Between the two, they arranged an interview for me with Arch Ward, the legendary sports editor of the *Chicago Tribune*. He told me he had a job for me at $100 per week. I told him I was already making $110 in Peoria and was supporting my mother. He said, "The only thing that counts in the workplace is if you're in the right place when the lightning strikes. Go home and think about it for a few weeks."

While I was waiting and thinking, Jack Brickhouse called me and said, "Hey, kid, it's Brickhouse. I know you want to work for the *Tribune*, but WGN-TV and Radio is also part of the *Tribune*, and I have an opening here. I'd like you to come here and join us." I told him I'd never been around a radio or TV station, but he told me it was no problem. I came to Wilmette, and we were together for three hours. At the end of the session, he offered me a job at $85 a week. I told him I had just turned down $100 from Arch Ward, but he assured me not to worry about the starting salary. Three weeks later, I was at WGN. In 1994 they threw me a retirement luncheon, and I told everybody how proud I was that in over 40 years, I had managed to more than triple my salary!

Every little move we made was new. We had no restrictions, and nobody was worried. If you made a mistake, so be it. Things like how many cameras to use all had to be worked out through trial and error. When I started, a lot of people still did not have television sets. We were feeling our way around, and I think the thing that really helped is that we were like a family. Even the players knew this was something new on the horizon. The fact the medium was in its infancy brought all of us closer together.

We had friendships there and were together all the time. Everybody was young, vibrant, and eager to be a part of it. Admittedly, it was black-and-white television, and we didn't have the visuals you have now, but as the technology changed, we changed with it. Jack Jacobson, Bill Lotzer, and Arne Harris were the directors, and they were all brilliant in their own right. Our cameramen and engineers were unbelievable, because they all felt a stake in things. It was a joy to be part of television at the outset of the medium, an incredible feeling.

I would get to the ballpark about 10:00 AM and go into the clubhouse and talk to everyone to get any tidbits I could get. I was looking for human interest stories, because statistics were given to us by the PR people. After visiting the clubhouse, I would go out to the batting cage and dugouts for about an hour and a half. After talking with someone, I would take out an index card and make notes of all the little things I picked up. Jack, Vince Lloyd, Jim West, Milo Hamilton, all our guys were also doing the same thing.

Once the game started, I had my trusty typewriter to type up notes for Jack. I didn't know it then, but the sound of my typewriter became familiar to fans over the years, because they could hear the click-click-click in the background. Jack and I had it down to a science, because I would give him one or two lines, and he would weave it right into the telecast. You could never tell he was reading it.

We all came down the road together at WGN Sports. Weddings, births, graduations, bar mitzvahs, funerals, everything in the broad spectrum of life brought us together. The station was and is a family station, and all of us at WGN Sports were family. You don't know how many times I hear, "When I was a little kid…" and I say, "You ran home from school to see the last few

19

Jack Rosenberg worked as the WGN sports editor for more than 40 years and was the cofounder of the Tribune Cubs Radio Network. *Photo courtesy of the Bob Vorwald*

innings of the Cubs game." I hear that story, even in retirement, over and over. It's gratifying to look back and know that we had a hand in getting it started originally.

WGN had never done a no-hitter, but on May 12, 1955, the station was celebrating its 1,000th baseball telecast, and Sam Jones was on the mound. After walking the bases loaded to start the ninth inning, he struck out the side to complete his no-hitter. He was known as "Toothpick," because he always seemed to have one, and a couple days later Harry Creighton, our color man, gave Sam a gold toothpick on the *Leadoff Man*.

Those Cubs teams may have been called "lovable losers," but anybody who thinks they didn't want to win as much as the teams of today is mistaken. They had the same intensity and willingness to sacrifice for their teammates.

In 1969 we couldn't believe what was happening to the Cubs or to us. Every day you could hardly wait to get to the ballpark, because this was it after so many years of futility. Opening Day went into extra innings with the Phillies, and Willie Smith hit a home run to win it. I can still hear Jack's

"Hey, hey!" all these years later, and it has been replayed thousands of times over the years. It just got the Cubs going, and you could almost feel it out there. They started to widen the lead and then August 19, Kenny Holtzman, who was normally a strikeout pitcher, threw a no-hitter against the Braves without a strikeout. At that point, the Cubs were eight or nine games ahead.

Then, all of a sudden, some say the Cubs wore out. Leo Durocher used the same lineup almost every day, and people can still recite it to this day—Kessinger, Beckert, Santo, and the rest. The Mets started their move right then. They moved into first place in early September, and by the time it was over, they won the pennant by eight games. That was a big swing, and the Mets went on to win the World Series. It was devastating. We just figured it was our year, but it wasn't.

Jack Brickhouse was unbelievable as a coworker and as a friend. He knew no strangers. He always had time for everyone. He would sign anything and was an incredible personality. Jack was one of the great after-dinner speakers and had so many stories to tell. He was a phenomenal human being, and I'll never forget him. He stood up as an usher at my wedding, and he had never been to a Jewish wedding before. At the end of the ceremony, when I shattered the glass as the groom, Jack jumped about three feet in the air, and for the rest of his time, he would say, "I thought somebody took a shot at me!" He was a happy-go-lucky man with extraordinary talent and a tremendous voice.

Jack got a call from the Hall of Fame in 1983, notifying him that his dream had come true: he had been named to the broadcasters' wing at Cooperstown. He was ecstatic and asked me to write his speech. I told him it would be an honor. I convinced him to keep the speech to three minutes and handle all the thank-yous with this line: "Countless people have brought me to this pinnacle. You know who you are, and you have my undying gratitude." The one he really liked was, "In the fantasy of my dreams, I have imagined I would one day broadcast an all-Chicago World Series, the Cubs against the Sox. The Series would go seven games with the seventh game going into extra innings, then being suspended because of darkness at Wrigley Field." He wound it up with, "I realize now I have rounded third base and scored standing up. Thank you very much." When he came off the dais, the old-time New York sportswriters slapped him on the back and told him he might have given the best-ever speech at Cooperstown. He told them, "Go over and tell Jack Rosenberg. He wrote it." How could I ever forget that?

Ernie Banks came to the Cubs in September 1953, so his first full season was my first full season. We were friends from the beginning. In the early years, Ernie was very, very quiet. You could talk to him, but he was shy beyond belief. As time went along, you could see the metamorphosis. His confidence grew, not only as a hitter, but as a man and a personality. He had that great laugh and smile. When they called him "Mr. Cub," it was not a misnomer. He did things with his bat and with his personality that were unbelievable. Ernie would always do his annual saying, such as, "The Cubs Will Come Alive in '65," or, "The Cubs Will Be Fine in '69." It got to be a tradition on our spring-training show. Ernie Banks will be part of the scene at Wrigley Field forever.

Being a Cub is an extra-special part of a lifetime for anyone who has been a part of it. The players, in particular, will never, ever see a time when the adulation and the fun is at such a fever pitch. To be a Cubs player is to walk into a restaurant and suddenly have people applauding. The players have become part of people's lives. Anyone who is associated with that team has a certain kinship that is indescribable. Win or lose—preferably win—there is nothing quite like it in the world of sports.

22

My recollection of Cubs baseball will probably always start with the '69 team that was a very special group. I saw them repeatedly standing by the home-plate wall until it was time to go out and play. They always found time. When they would get done with a game, they would come out and stand for an hour or more signing until everyone got what they wanted. You hear so many players now who will waive their no-trade clause to go to the Cubs. The city has embraced the team forever. An occasional boo is part of baseball, but generally speaking, this city has been incredible with its treatment of a group of athletes that are very well paid, but much respected and much beloved.

Jack Rosenberg spent more than 40 years at WGN as sports editor and later helped found the Tribune Cubs Radio Network. He mentored scores of broadcasters throughout the years. In 1990 he persuaded WGN Radio to hire both Ron Santo and Bob Brenly for the analyst job, launching two memorable broadcasting careers. He worked on the NFL, Big Ten, White Sox, Bulls, Blackhawks, and countless other telecasts, but his lasting legacy will be the quiet clatter of his typewriter in the background, furnishing Jack Brickhouse with quips, information, and stories throughout every Cubs game.

The
SIXTIES

BILLY WILLIAMS
OUTFIELDER
1959–1974

I SIGNED TO PLAY BASEBALL IN 1956 and spent a couple years in Ponca City, Oklahoma. Later on, I got all my scouting reports, and they basically said, this kid will go as far as his bat will take him. The guy who signed me, Ivy Griffin, wrote "ML" on the form where it said "classification he could reach." He saw something real good at the time he signed me.

Ronnie Santo and I go back to 1959 in San Antonio and the minors. I was already with the team, and he got signed out of Washington. When he stepped on that field, we became attached to each other at that time. We played there together, at Dallas–Ft. Worth, Houston, and then all the years in the majors together with the Cubs.

When we were at San Antonio, John Holland was the general manager of the big club, and he sent Rogers Hornsby around to scout all the minor league teams and take stock of the players in the Cubs system. When he came to San Antonio, they put us through a full workout with hitting and fielding. After that workout, Rogers gathered the team in the stands, and we were expecting he'd tell us what to work on. He was a Hall of Famer, a great hitter, and a former manager, so we were respectful of whatever he had to say. Then he told a few guys, "You'd better go find another job right now, because you have no future in baseball." I was sitting right next to Ronnie when Rogers came to us. "Williams," he said, "you could play in the big leagues right now." That meant a lot to me because I was in Double A right

On Billy Williams Day, June 29, 1969, Williams broke Stan Musial's NL record for consecutive games played (895) and had five hits, including two doubles and two triples, as the Cubs swept a doubleheader against the Cardinals, 3–1 and 12–1.

then. "Santo, you could hit in the big leagues right now, too. You two would do a good job." We were the only two guys he liked, and when he went back to Chicago, he met with Holland. John said, "Rogers, what kind of players do we have out there?" Rogers told him, "You got Williams and Santo who can come up and play right now. I suggest you get them up here and release everyone else you have on your Double A team right now." Rogers was great to me and tutored me over the years. When he saw me heading down to the batting cage, he would drag a chair down there and sit to watch me hit. At Wrigley Field, he'd be sitting right behind home plate and would remind me to keep my eye on the ball. Something must have worked!

You know it's always easier to get here. There's an old saying, "It's easy to get to the big leagues, but it's tough to stay." I think you find yourself after about two years. The first year, in '61, I had 25 home runs and drove in 86 runs as a young kid coming up from Triple A. I think my confidence came from when Mr. Holland saw that I'd had a good year in Triple A, and he just told the coaches to put me in left field and leave me out there. Luckily, I was hitting third, and Ernie was hitting behind me. He was hitting 40 home runs, so I saw a lot of fastballs!

26

When I went to spring training the next year, there was talk about the sophomore jinx. When you came to the big leagues and had a good year, the next year the pitchers figured you out, and you didn't have that kind of year. Going to spring training in the outfield, there were about five or six guys in left field. I think they were saying, this guy is a fluke, hitting 25 home runs on the major league level. There were about five guys out there, and so I put some good numbers on the board in '62, and the following year I went out there and there were about two. I put some more good numbers on the board in '63, and when I went out there the following year, I had left field to myself.

When you talk about the College of Coaches, I know it was something Mr. Wrigley wanted. A lot of guys had fun with it. But the coaches didn't have too much fun with it, because four guys would be on the big-league level and four guys would go to the minor leagues. The only advantage of that was when a coach went to the minor leagues, he got to see some of the young players. They would go down for about a month, then come back to the big-league club. There was no advantage to the rotation up here. Everybody wanted a different style of play. Some wanted to hit and run, some wanted to hit the ball out of the park, some wanted to change the lineup around. Everybody got a chance to be the head coach, and I guess that satisfied Mr. Wrigley.

I was gifted with a quick bat. I could wait until the ball was almost in the catcher's glove, then swing, and still hit the baseball. By doing that, I didn't block off left field. I wanted to see the ball as long as I could. That was something I really worked on. When I was just starting in D ball, every time the team went on the road, they left me in Ponca City, Oklahoma. Just before the team would come back, I'd take a lot of batting practice and hope they would let me pinch-hit. I got five straight pinch-hits at one point, then the following year I got the chance to play. I worked on fundamentals such as taking a short stride, taking my hands back four to six inches, and I stayed with those things. I wasn't a guy who was into changing my stance or changing my swing all the time. I had a good swing and stayed with it. I had a Vern Stephens S2 model bat, and I kept that through the years. I got the last hit of my career off Dick Drago with that bat.

When I came to bat, I had this little thing where I would spit out my half-stick of gum, and most of the time, I'd hit it into the other team's dugout. I would do that as a little psychological thing for me, because I'd tell myself, if I could hit that little piece of gum, I should be able to hit that big baseball. Now sometimes that wasn't true, especially if Koufax was pitching, but I worked at seeing the ball with good results. Guys would say, "Did you know what was coming?" I didn't, but my stride was short, and I had a balanced swing. By doing that, I didn't pull the ball too much, only if it was inside. My goal was to stay with the pitch. On an outside pitch, you can stay with it a little longer and really hit it solid. I never tried to hit a home run, but 426 of them just happened to leave the yard.

27

We brought Leo Durocher in, and things started to turn around. We went to San Francisco and got a starting pitcher in Bill Hands and Randy Hundley, who was our catcher. Fergie Jenkins came in that year. He was in the bullpen as a relief pitcher, but Leo saw something in him and made him a starter. Right then, we had three good players on our ballclub. When Leo started, that was the only time we trained in Long Beach, California, the one year in 1966. I was living in Los Angeles at the time and was going back and forth to Long Beach. That particular spring, we were all over the place. I think we went into the season tired and finished last. But you could see the ballclub beginning to jell—in '67 and '68 we started winning ballgames. I can remember one time, Leo was standing behind the batting cage, watching a young kid throw, and he said, "This guy can win in the big leagues right now." The guy out there throwing was Kenny Holtzman. That particular year, when we really made a good splash, he was in and out of the service, but he won a lot of ballgames just coming in on Sundays to pitch.

We had Ernie, who had moved to first base from shortstop. I thought Don Kessinger was a determined player because in spring training, he was a right-handed hitter. Leo knew he could play shortstop. He said that if he made himself a switch-hitter, he could come to the big leagues. Kessinger did that, and I thought that was great for us, because he filled a void. Glenn Beckert was the life of the party, and we had a lot of fun. He was a great player at second base. In a way, I think it's unfortunate that he was here, because Kenny Hubbs was our second baseman, and when Hubbs got killed in an airplane accident, John Holland made a trade with Boston and got Beckert with the ballclub. We traded for Jim Hickman from the Dodgers, Adolfo Phillips came over from Philadelphia along with Fergie, and of course, I was in left field.

At third, Ron Santo was always a fighter. He enjoyed being the captain and was a holler guy who didn't want to lose. I was right behind him in left field, so I saw how good he was. He wasn't fast, but he was quick. There's nobody in baseball other than maybe Brooks Robinson who could come in and make that off-balance throw on a dribbler or swinging bunt. He worked at it, and people forget that he signed as a catcher.

Billy Williams Day was June 29, 1969. I had hurt my foot before and had to work hard so I didn't miss the game. When I got to the ballpark, there were 10,000 or 15,000 people waiting to get in. It was a doubleheader with the Cardinals, and they tell me they turned away another 10,000 or 15,000. The first game, I got a base hit and wound up scoring the winning run. For the ceremony, I had my mother here. I told her to make sure not to faint. During the ceremony, they ran out the car, they ran out the boat, and all the guys on the team were standing around. It was great, and I had a lot of fun. In the second game, I got a single, double, triple, and I needed a home run for the cycle that day. Going up to the plate, I knew what I had to do, and the fans knew it because they were chanting my name. That would have really topped it off, but I struck out. As I headed back to the bench, they gave me a standing ovation, and I always said I was the only guy who got a standing ovation for striking out. We won both games, though. By the time I got home and hit the Barcalounger they gave me, I was dead asleep. I'll tell you, it was a beautiful day.

Ken Holtzman threw a no-hitter later that year, and I remember the wind was blowing in so hard that day. Henry Aaron came up in the seventh, and

Holtzman left something inside, and Aaron got all of it, but again, the wind was blowing in. As I went back, I said, "Boy, this ball is way out of here." Then the wind began pushing it back, and because I kept my eyes on the ball and knew the outfield at Wrigley, I thought I might have a chance to get it. I saw fans in the back of the bleachers looking like they might get it, but the only way I was going to get it was to wedge myself in that corner in the alley. When I caught that ball, I was sideways with my back to the left-field foul pole. That few extra feet made all the difference. The no-hitter was intact. It was really something, because Aaron had gone into a little trot coming around first base. He really thought the ball was hit out of the ballpark.

I had a ton of fun that year. I couldn't afford to buy a home someplace else and live in Chicago, so I stayed in Chicago, and of course, I've been here ever since, except when I went to Oakland. Being here in Chicago, you walk around in this city and have so many people walk up to you and tell you about the fun they had in 1969. It didn't turn out the way we wanted it to, but it was a fun year. We had a great time, we had a great run, and I like to think we didn't lose it; the Mets just won it. They played great baseball that particular year. I found out from that, if you've got good pitching down the stretch, you win the pennant. If you've got four or five starters going pretty good, throwing strikes, getting people out, you can win a pennant on the big-league level.

The people who were here during those years had a great time. Of course, in '69 we drew 1.6 million fans. I think everything derived from that. We showed the people who came to the ballpark the fun they could have. At Wrigley Field, they didn't open the upper deck until the weekend. They would only get about 6,000 or 7,000 people. But we began to play good baseball and excited the people. Every time we went on the road, simply because of the superstation, everybody saw us, we were household names. So it was good for us and good for WGN. It was a great year.

I played 1,117 games in a row and am really proud of that. Number one, it means I was good enough to be in the lineup every day. The second thing is that I was consistent enough that the manager always thought I was going to help the ballclub. I went through three stages. At first, I was afraid somebody would take my job in left field. The second stage was being aware of the numbers. I knew Stan Musial had the National League record, and I thought I could pass it and get to 1,000. The third stage was that I wanted to be in the lineup to help my team win, and I would be letting them down if I didn't. If I was in the lineup, I knew I would do something to help my team win.

29

There were great players everywhere, and they had about five or six studs on some clubs. When I made it to Cooperstown and the Hall of Fame, I saw a lot of the guys whom I played against. I saw Juan Marichal, Gaylord Perry, Bob Gibson, Sandy Koufax—I had to face all of them, as well as the late Don Drysdale. It was a golden era of baseball. I don't think you will see as many players, as many good players on one ballcub as you did back in that era, the late '50s to the early '70s. You saw some great players. Too bad we had to face those guys, we could have put up some good numbers! They were great pitchers, they were competitors, and of course, Sandy Koufax was a tough pitcher and was one of the guys I hated to face. You talk to anyone, and they will all say the same thing: Sandy Koufax was dominating.

Getting into the Hall of Fame was great. When you play the game of baseball, people say, "He might be a Hall of Famer." You plant it in your mind, but you are never sure. That was so far away when I was actually playing the game. In 1987, when I got the call after waiting about six times before I got in, I remember sitting at home when the phone rang. I got a call around 5:00 PM from Jack Lang, who called guys who made it in the Hall at that time, and he said, "Billy, if I call you between 6:45 and 7:00 tonight, that means you're in the Hall of Fame." That was the longest wait ever. I was staring at the clock, and when the phone did ring, my wife Shirley would quickly tell people to get off the line. About five minutes to 7:00, the greatest voice I've ever heard through the years said, "Billy, this is Jack Lang calling from New York." Right away, I knew I had made the Hall of Fame. I went in with Ray Dandridge and Catfish Hunter. It was so exciting, and the first thing I wanted to do was hug Shirley and my kids, then I wanted all the people in the area to come over to the house. We celebrated at the house, then they took me to a hotel for a press conference. It's a thing where I was excited to be in the Hall, but it really hit me when we flew to Albany and there were vans there to pick us up. When I saw the Hall of Fame logo on the side of those vans, I said, "We're really getting close now." I got a jolt when I was up on the podium and they called my name: now it was time to do my speech. I looked around and saw the greats of the game like Musial, Mays, Banks, Williams, Koufax, and that's when I knew all the hard work—all the sweat, all the things I had done to make myself a better player—was worth it. It all wound up with me in the Hall of Fame, and that is really great.

It's a special relationship I have with those guys I played with during those years. Not a month goes by that I don't talk to Glenn Beckert. Don Kessinger calls. I check in with Ronnie to see how he's doing. I see Ernie and Fergie, or we talk on the phone. It was a fun to play together for so long.

When you come to the Cubs Convention, you see not just Cubs fans who are 40 or 50 years old, but also kids who are 10 or 11 and are fans because their parents were fans. When you talk about Kessinger, Banks, Beckert, Santo, Jenkins—these guys were all together for seven, eight years in a row. There were only 2,500 fans in the ballpark in those early days. When we would walk to and from the clubhouse on that left-field line, we got the chance to meet lots of people. It's been great over the years. Most of our guys couldn't afford a home in two cities, so they moved to Chicago. It worked out for all of us who did that because we were here with the fans who supported us for so many years.

My wife Shirley and I got married in 1960. We met in high school, and I've said to her, "Can you believe after so many years growing up in Alabama that we would be here and have residency in Chicago, Illinois?" I didn't know where Chicago was growing up! It's been a lot of fun. I can't imagine that I've been here for so long, but I'm still having fun, I'm still enjoying it. I love coming out to the ballpark, and I really like to see a good baseball game.

"Sweet Swinging" Billy Williams was the 1961 National League Rookie of the Year. He averaged 27 homers and 94 RBIs for the next nine seasons but took his game to another level in 1970, with a .322 average, a career-high 42 homers, 129 RBIs, and a league-leading 137 runs and 205 hits. In 1972 he won the batting title with a .333 average while slugging 37 homers and driving in 122. Williams was a six-time All-Star and played in 1,117 consecutive games, then a National League record. In 1974 Williams was traded to Oakland for Manny Trillo, Darold Knowles, and Bob Locker. He played two seasons for the A's and finished his career with 426 homers, 1,475 RBIs, 1,410 runs, and a .290 average. Williams was inducted into the Hall of Fame in 1987, and the Cubs retired his No. 26 the same year. He was named to the Cubs All-Century Team in 1999. Williams works for the Cubs as a special assistant to the president and attracts a crowd of players from both teams any time he steps behind the batting cage to hold court before a game.

RON SANTO

THIRD BASEMAN
1960–1973

BROADCASTER
1990–Present

I GREW UP IN SEATTLE, where we had a Triple A team, the Rainiers, and I worked there at the stadium in high school. I was a batboy, and my senior year I was the clubhouse boy. I played high school ball and was selected to go to New York for the Hearst all-star game. I had a lot of teams after me. I watched *The Game of the Week* on Saturday—that was the only baseball we got each week. When the Cubs were on, there was something about Wrigley Field and those fans. There was something about Ernie Banks, too. They would take the close-up, and you could see him wiggling his fingers on the bat, and then—boom! Ernie Banks and Wrigley Field had a lot to do with my ending up with the Cubs, because I had higher offers from other teams. I took the lowest offer with the Cubs, but I was in the big leagues a year later. I picked the Cubs because I thought there was something special there, and today it is still special here.

The first guy up there who spoke to me was Ernie. I would say that I didn't have what you would call an idol, but there was something about Ernie that I loved. When I met him, it was the best. I came up on Sunday, June 26, 1960, and I was sitting in the dugout, watching Roberto Clemente hit in old Forbes Field. I was all by myself, and Ernie came and sat next to me. He said, "Are you nervous?" I said, "Oh, yeah!" He said, "Well, you have to look at Bob Friend and Vernon Law." Law was a 20-game winner, and Friend was an 18-game winner. Ernie told me to look at them like they were just two other Double A pitchers. I told him, "Ernie, that's easy for you to say!" I don't think I hit a ball out of the cage, I was so nervous.

The first time up, Friend threw me a curveball, and I backed off. Smokey Burgess was their catcher and got in my ear and said, "That's a major league curveball, kid." I stepped out and got back in the box. They threw me a fastball, and I lined it up the middle, and the world just came off my shoulders. I ended up going 3-for-7 in the doubleheader, drove in five runs, and we ended a nine-game losing streak. I broke in beautifully.

Then I got here to Wrigley Field, and I'd seen it on TV, but I'd never been here. I got in the locker room and got dressed. I was walking out, and Ernie was walking with me. We were walking down, I was looking, and it was empty. I swear I was walking on air. There was this feeling that I've never had before, and the electricity, the atmosphere, and nobody in the stands! That's how I felt. Anytime you go on the road and the season goes on, you get tired. As soon as you get back and walk on this field, you are up here. It moves you to another level.

We got better as it went along. We ended up getting Kessinger, Beckert, Hundley, and guys like that, and then Fergie came along. It was a team that came together and was coming together in '66, even though we finished 10th. In '67 we were third, '68 third, and then '69 we led from the get-go. That spring of '69, we knew this was going to be our year. To prove the fact, we got off to an 11–1 start.

The heel-clicking started on June 22. Jim Hickman was up to the plate. It was the first game of a doubleheader. We were down by one run in the bottom of the ninth inning. There was one man on base. Hickman hit a home run, and when he came around, I was pounding him on his head because I was so excited, and I ran down the left-field line. I don't even remember doing this, that's how excited I was, and I went up in the air and I clicked my heels one time. We went into the clubhouse, and it was just wonderful.

I got home, and I always turned on WGN-TV to watch the highlights. The first thing, even before the news came on, was me clicking my heels. And I said, "I did that?" I couldn't believe it. The next day I came into the clubhouse, and Leo came down to me and said, "Can you continue to click your heels?" And I said, "Well, what do you mean?" He said, "After a win, if you could still do that, that would be great." It was so exciting that year, '69, the way we started off and the excitement, and I said, "Well, I think so." He didn't realize I had a cleat cut in one of my ankles from where I had clicked my heels. From that moment on, just at home, I would go up and click my heels after a win. The fans were all waiting for me after the game to go down the left-field line to our clubhouse. Then I used to take Berteau Street when I left, and I'd see kids come along my car and be clicking their heels. It was fantastic. I got a card from two elderly people, and each of them had a leg up on a coffee table. They had tried to click their heels, and both of them broke their ankles, but they sent me a card.

34

Ron Santo (10) jumps up and clicks his heels on his way to the clubhouse after a 5–4 Cubs win over Pittsburgh on June 23, 1969, at Wrigley Field. His ninth-inning sacrifice fly drove in the winning run.

I thought in '69 we were the best team in the National League, and I thought the best team in baseball was the Orioles, and that's the match-up I thought we'd see in the World Series. The Mets not only beat us, they beat Atlanta in the playoffs, and then beat the Orioles in the World Series.

I never did enjoy going to New York. In 1969 I was getting death threats, and they had security with me. I was sent a letter that said I'd be shot in New York, so when we got there, they wouldn't let me leave the hotel. Leave it to my roomie, Glenn Beckert, to get me. I woke up the next morning, and he was gone, but there was a big sign over his bed with an arrow pointing down that said, "Beckert sleeps here"!

They couldn't get rid of Shea Stadium fast enough for me. A few years ago, we were there at the beginning of the season, and it was cold. The broadcast booths there were like concrete bunkers—small and with low ceilings. Anyway, it was cold, so we had the overhead heaters on, the kind that glow red. I was standing up for the national anthem, and all of a sudden, Pat Hughes turned to me and said, "Do you smell something burning?" I reached up, and my hairpiece was smoking. I got it out, and it looked like someone had taken a divot out of it, but Pat was nice enough to say it looked okay.

The bond with that team never will go away. In 1969 there were no free agents. Ernie, Billy, and I were together for 12 years. The other guys, we had been together nine years. Not only were we close on the field, we were close off the field; all the wives knew each other. We spent time on cruises in the winter. It was a close-knit family.

Those Cubs fans in '69 were our friends. When I played pro ball, we needed fans. All of us would come down from the left-field foul line where our clubhouse was and sign autographs. We had a personal thing with our fans, and still have. I think that's a big reason that the fans remember the '69 Cubs, because we related to them. We cared about them. We cared about going out and getting the job done, and of course, they were very disappointed. Everybody was disappointed. That particular year, I moved into a new home, and I had all the furniture except a dining room table. I told my wife not to worry, we'd be in the World Series, and that would pay for it. Well, that dining room table was never covered by that.

I think my legacy isn't going to be just about baseball. What I've accomplished being a diabetic in baseball is something. A lot of my fellow diabetics couldn't understand how I got through 15 years of major league baseball and was able to put up the numbers I did. In my day, we didn't have a glucometer

35

where you could test your sugars. I had to go out there every day and play that game the way I felt, if my sugars were up or my sugars were down. It was later in my life when the side effects kicked in.

My son Jeff gave me a gift that I cannot believe, and that's [the film] *This Old Cub*. I didn't know how it was going to turn out, but it was such an inspiration. It made me feel good, because people are going to remember me for the way I treated them and how they treated me. That's what it is all about. I can say one thing—positive thinking has a lot to do with overcoming a lot in life. You have a tendency to drop down and give up, but you can't do it. Diabetes can beat you, but if you fight it, you can definitely beat it.

The first thing I said when I learned I was diabetic was, "Can I play baseball?" I had just signed a professional contract, and that's what I asked my doctor. He was just an M.D., there weren't a lot of specialists yet, and he said, "Ron, I have no idea. I haven't dealt with that." Then I went to the library, which is probably the only time I was there during high school, and read about diabetes. It talked about causing blindness, hardening of the arteries, gangrene, and finally said the average life expectancy after the onset was 25 years. I was 18 years old, and that's what really got me more than anything else. But again, I said, I'm gonna play with it.

I wanted to hide it. I went to spring training my first year and stayed with the big-league club 'til the last cut. Then I went to Double A and got through it with a good year, and two months into the season the next year, I was in the big leagues. My feeling was that if I didn't stay in the big leagues, they would say it was because of the diabetes, because nobody at that point had played with it. I didn't want anyone to feel sorry for me. I had told the Cubs' doctor, "Please, I'm counting on you to get me through this. I am not telling anybody in the organization until I make my first All-Star Game." I made it at the age of 23, then I came out to the organization, but not to the fans. My general manager, John Holland, didn't understand. He said, "What is that?" And I told him I was just learning, too. I knew what I had to do, and then finally in my 10th year I came out publicly.

So much has happened. I don't think there was any money raised for research until about 1974, and then the federal government got involved along with charities. The key word there is *research*, and that's why I'm proud to be with the Juvenile Diabetes Research Foundation, because 85¢ on the dollar goes to research. The technology, my two artificial legs, surviving my surgeries, all that happened because of the advances made

Santo throws out the ceremonial first pitch prior to the Cubs' home opener at Wrigley Field on April 5, 2002. After his All-Star career as the Cubs' third baseman, he joined the WGN Radio broadcast team as color analyst and remains one of the most popular former players with Cubs fans.

possible by research. I'm not going to say it's easier to live with, but it is getting better.

When they called me to interview for the radio job in 1990, I had never looked at myself as a broadcaster. My first year, if it hadn't been for Bob Brenly and Thom Brennaman, I'd never have gotten through it. When my first year was over, I walked in to see [WGN Radio general manager] Dan Fabian and said, "This just isn't me, but I appreciate the chance." He said, "Ron, I want you to listen to a tape." We went into his office, and he turned a tape of me on. I said something constructive and then had something funny to finish, and he said, "That's you. That's why we hired you. You have to be you, but you're trying to be somebody else. Be you. We want you to be you." And from that moment on, I just kind of relaxed. I'm me. I'm a fan. I hate bad fundamental baseball. The moans and groans—I don't even realize I do that on the air. After a game, when I'm driving home, and they say, "This is what Santo had to say about the play," *boom*, you hear me going crazy and I can't believe that's me. That's how I get my emotions out as a fan, saying, "This is bad." On the opposite side, I get excited when we hit a home run. When Pat Hughes started with me, I felt bad on those. But I told him, "You be you, and I'll be me." And Pat is great about that. I'm a Cubs fan in that booth, and the fans feel like I feel. They're part of me, because I want this team to win so badly. I don't know what will happen when we do, but I sure want to be here. It's going to be exciting.

On the Brant Brown play [a dropped fly ball in the ninth inning to lose a key game against the Brewers in September 1998], it's hard for me to even remember saying, "Oh, no!" After that, I remember just dropping my head and watching Jeromy Burnitz running. When Brown dropped the ball, I was hoping we could get Burnitz at home or hold him at third. I was devastated. I didn't realize I made that call. The next morning in Houston, I got a call from Arizona, and a radio station woke me to have me on. The guy said, "Ron, that was one of the all-time great calls." I said, "What?" I was still hurting. They played it for me, and it was the first time I'd heard it. When I did hear it, I thought somebody died! The radio host started to laugh and told me he was a Mets fan. I told him if he thought that was funny, he might think this was funny, and I hung up on him. I went in the clubhouse before we even left Milwaukee that day and hugged Brant and told him not to worry, that it would be okay. I've made mistakes, and I know what he felt.

My jersey retirement in 2003 was the biggest day of my life. I thought *God, I would love to have that*, but you never talk about it. I assumed that I would have to be in the Hall of Fame to have my number retired, so I was so surprised when Andy MacPhail, Jim Hendry, and John McDonough told me about it. Ernie Banks and Billy Williams were with me, and that meant a lot, because we played so many games together. When they told me they wanted to retire my number, I couldn't come down from feeling 10 feet tall. McDonough and the marketing department did such a great job. There's a lot of jerseys retired in a lot of ballparks, but there are only six here: Billy, Ernie, Ryno, Fergie, Greg, and me.

The wonderful thing about it was that we had already clinched. I didn't want my day to interfere with them winning it. Forget my day, let's win and then do it. It was heart-wrenching. It was so beautiful. That day, I was so excited and emotional the whole time. I looked down and saw Randy Hundley and Glenn Beckert pulling up the flag, and that was wonderful. I didn't know if I could even get through my speech, but the fans always bring out the adrenaline in me. When I got to the mike, I didn't know what I was going to say, but it just came out. I said, "This is my Hall of Fame, that flag right there is my Hall of Fame."

I'm proud of what we've done. When you look at 1969, when I first came up in 1960 when I was 20 years old, we were drawing maybe 600,000. It started to build after Leo came in '66, and in '69 we drew close to 1.7 million. I think that team is the one that started all the great Cubs fans. The Cubs fans, I found out early, never lose their allegiance. It's their kids, and their kids' kids, and that's the way it's been.

These fans have supported the Cubs forever. They believe in next year, and they don't lose their allegiance, even when they move. It's amazing. Everybody laughs about it, but Cubs fans really do believe in next year. Now, there are definitely higher expectations for this ballclub every year.

The Cubs fans deserve a win. They know their baseball, and they sure love the team. It's just a wonderful relationship I have with them, because personally, I was told very young by my mother, always treat people the way you want to be treated. I've always done that. I've never said I couldn't sign. If I couldn't sign, I tell them why. If I walk down the street and somebody says, "There goes Ron Santo," I turn around and say hi, have a conversation, that's what it's all about. It doesn't take much time to stop and make somebody happy. I love it. I just really love being around people.

39

Ron Santo has had two extended stints as part of the Cubs family—14 seasons as a player, and 20 more and counting as a radio broadcaster. Santo the player was signed by the Cubs as a free agent prior to the 1959 season. He joined the big-league team in 1960 and grabbed the third base job he would hold for the next 14 seasons. From 1963 to 1970, Santo averaged 29 homers and 105 RBIs while establishing himself as the premiere defensive third baseman in the National League. On December 11, 1973, he was traded to the Chicago White Sox, where he played one season before retiring. His career numbers include 342 home runs, 1,331 RBIs, nine All-Star Games, and five straight Gold Gloves—all while playing with diabetes. In 1990 Santo rejoined the Cubs as an analyst for WGN Radio, where his passion for the game, baseball knowledge, and sense of humor entertain Cubs fans across the nation every day. In 1999 he was named to the Cubs All-Century Team, and his No. 10 was retired by the Cubs on September 28, 2003.

DON KESSINGER

SHORTSTOP

1964–1975

I CAME UP WITH THE CUBS at the end of the 1964 season, and 1965 was my first full year. It's kind of a frightening experience, actually. You look around, and in my case, I was looking at Ernie Banks, Billy Williams, and Ron Santo, then playing against Mays, McCovey, Aaron, and the lot. There were times when I'd think, *What am I doing here?* After a while, you settle in and realize that you can contribute to the team at that level, and it becomes a lot more fun then.

I remember I played in my first game at the end of the 1964 season. As hard as it is to believe, I don't remember a whole lot about it. I do know there weren't a whole lot of people at the Cubs games by that time in September, and we were playing the Dodgers, but that's about it.

In 1965 I was fortunate enough to be put into the lineup and play. I never had to experience that deal where you wait your turn, so to speak. I was very fortunate in that sense. There's nothing like going out there and starting a ballgame every day, hearing the national anthem, and looking at the other team. If you don't have a few butterflies, you're not ready to play. I honestly believe that.

When Leo Durocher came in, it was different. I only played one year before Leo. When he came in, probably the biggest difference early on was a lot more media attention and things like that. That was Leo, and he commanded that. He was a great story, and there was a lot more attention on our

Cubs shortstop Don Kessinger watches his throw to first base after forcing Pete Rose of the Reds at second during a 6–4 win at Wrigley Field on April 30, 1972.

ballclub. The biggest difference from a playing standpoint was that in 1965 we had finished eighth in a 10-team league. So the first thing Leo said was, "I'll guarantee you this is no eighth-place ballclub." He was right—we finished 10th. We were not very good. We were a bad ballclub.

Another thing that happened when I got to the Cubs was that I got the nickname "Pete." I had never been called that before or since, but I think what happened was when I came up, Pat Pieper, the public address announcer, asked John Holland, our general manager, my first name, and Holland told him it was Pete. Well, once that went out, of course my teammates picked up on it, and so did Leo when he came.

I give Leo a lot of credit. He put Glenn Beckert and me out there. We were young guys going out there to play every day, and we took our lumps, but we learned a lot. Beck is a great guy, and we've been friends for a long time. We spent some years there, especially those early years as rookies, and we would come to the park before anyone else. We would take our ground balls and work on the double play, where the other guy wanted the throw, all of those types of situations. We would do that 20–30 minutes every day prior to all our home games. It just became a communication deal where we knew what each other was thinking.

It was an unbelievable feeling to see it come together. As I said, in 1966 we were a bad ballclub, but in 1967, halfway through the year, we went into a first-place tie, and we couldn't get out of the ballpark because the fans wouldn't leave. I think we were there for two hours after the game. I cannot explain that feeling. We had a great relationship with our fans. I don't know what it was, but that group of guys felt a closeness to Cubs fans. We were really excited.

In 1968 we had been a good ballclub and contended, so we went into '69 believing that we had a real shot at winning. From Opening Day until mid-September, we led the league. I will always believe we were the best team in baseball that year, but we didn't win the pennant. I really believe that the teams in 1970, '71, and '72 were probably every bit as good as the '69 team, and we finished second several times. I just think if we had been able to win in '69, we might have won two or three of the next five years. It was a tough deal for us. It was the best of times, and it was the worst of times. It was the most fun I've ever had in baseball, yet the last month was the most disappointing.

On Opening Day that year, I was in the dugout when Willie Smith hit his home run to win the game. There's a difference and excitement in the yard on Opening Day, and when Willie hit that, we just felt it was a sign of things to come. We were very good and felt like we had the players to do it. As soon as he hit it, we knew it was gone, and we all ran on the field. We were grown men playing a kids' game, and that kid comes out in those moments.

During Ken Holtzman's no-hitter, I remember when Hank Aaron's shot went over my head, I figured it was gone. Billy Williams did a great job playing that ball, because the wind was blowing in, and where the fence curves is where he stayed with it and caught it. Kenny had pitched a fabulous ballgame, and Billy made a fine play. It didn't look like it because he was right under it when he caught it, but it was because he stayed with it. On the last out, I was anticipating Aaron would hit the ball to me. He was a pull hitter, and I thought it would be at me. Fortunately, he hit it to Beckert, and he made the play for the no-hitter.

I was in no-hitters on each side. In the dugout, you know it, and everybody knows it. It's one of those things that you just don't talk about. You might not say anything to the pitcher about it, but you're aware of it. As innings go on and on, you become more aware of it. The thing is, you know if you make an error, it doesn't take the no-hitter away, but it does give one more man a chance to get a base hit. You don't want to give an out away, and you're very conscious of that.

I always hoped they'd hit the ball to me. I tried to concentrate and think on every pitch in every game. I was always trying to be ready to have to make a great play on every ball, not that I was just going to catch it, but I'd be ready to make a great play. I felt if I could do that, I would always be ready to make any play.

With the Mets, we were up eight or so games when they really made their run. They won a phenomenal amount of games down the stretch. The whole thing came to a head that first weekend in September, when we went into Shea Stadium for a two-game series, two and a half games ahead of them. It was an electric atmosphere with their fans going nuts. That was when the black cat ran across the field—the cat didn't have much to do with it, but Seaver and Koosman did! The play where Tommie Agee was safe at the plate was a big one. We thought we had a shot at him at the plate, and Randy Hundley thought we got him. A player doesn't react the way Randy did unless you thought you really had the out. You may contest a call, but you don't react like that unless you think you got him.

It was not only a wonderful year, but a wonderful four or five years. Everybody focuses on '69 as the year, but that team that was together was one of the best teams in baseball. My memories are of the relationship we had with each other and the fans. It was a joy to come to the ballpark with what was going on there.

I was really skinny then, and I never had any problem getting into shape in spring training. I used to hear people say the only negative to having spring training in Arizona was that it was hard to lose weight. I never had that problem. Today's players make enough money that they don't do anything during the off-season but stay in shape. They work out year-round, and that's marvelous. In our day, players didn't make that kind of money, and we had another job in the off-season, so there was more of coming to spring training needing to get into shape.

I can think of a lot of games that meant something extra to me. In that 1969 season, there were times down the stretch when I still think about things that happened that might have cost us a game. Personally, in 1971 I went 6-for-6 in a game against the Cardinals. When I left that morning, I told my wife that maybe today would be a good day to give me a day off, because Steve Carlton was pitching. I had played every inning of every game, and I was about 0-for-three-years against him. Then, I went to the park, and it turned out to be a day where I got six hits. My sixth hit led off the tenth inning of a tie game, and I scored the winning run, so it was a fabulous day.

I knew that I was going to be traded at the end of the 1975 season. It was time, I guess. I had a cup of coffee in St. Louis then was traded to the Chicago White Sox. When I was told I was going back to Chicago, I was thrilled because Chicago had been so good to me. I had no idea what my acceptance would be on the South Side, but they were great to me.

It's difficult to describe the thrills you get playing at Wrigley Field. It's such a unique ballpark, and I think every player enjoys coming to Wrigley. The nice, new ballparks are great, and I don't take anything away from them, but there's something special about walking into Wrigley. There's a lot of ghosts in Wrigley Field and a lot of memories there, things you've heard from the past. The thing that is really special for the Cubs players is the closeness of the fans. The fans are right down there next to the action, and there is more interaction with them than at other parks.

44

Chicago sports fans are fabulous. You just couldn't beat the Cubs fans. I went to the White Sox my last three years, and they treated me like a king. They were great to me, so I have nothing but love for all the Chicago baseball fans. When you are fortunate enough to play here, you see how wonderful they really are.

I watch games today, and I'm kind of drawn to the shortstops, because that's where I played. Today's players are so talented. Let's face it—they are bigger, faster, stronger, and can do many things better. They are great athletes. Whether they have a better love for the game, I don't know about that. They sure can't love it any more than we did. Today's guys, though, can do wondrous things, and they are really great athletes.

We knew our batting order when we went to spring training. That's different than now. It wouldn't have been that way if the rules in place now were in place then, but they weren't. We were together and we really enjoyed each other. We played together for a lot of years through some bad times and some really good times. There was more of a bond with that group than any other group I've ever been with.

I go to Randy Hundley's camp now when I can. What's fun for us is being able to see the campers have fun. We were blessed to be able to live this life for a lot of years, and to see these guys who have followed our careers come out and have a great time for a week emulating us is a great time for us.

I am a Cub and I'll always be a Cub. I appreciate my time on the South Side, but people always recognize me as a Cub.

Sure-handed Don Kessinger came to the Cubs after starring in both baseball and basketball at the University of Mississippi. After a short stint in the minors, he emerged as the Cubs' starting shortstop in 1965 and held down that position until he was traded to the St. Louis Cardinals after the 1975 season. After one and a half seasons with the Cardinals, he was traded to the Chicago White Sox, where he played from 1977 to 1979 and spent part of the 1979 season as a player/manager. He holds the team record of 1,618 games played at shortstop and won Gold Gloves after the 1969 and 1970 seasons. Kessinger played in six All-Star Games for the National League, making the team from 1968 to 1972 and again in 1974. His 6-for-6 day in 1971 tied a team record.

GLENN BECKERT
SECOND BASEMAN
1965–1973

I REMEMBER MY FIRST GAME as a Cub very well. It all started the night before the game, and I called my dad in Pittsburgh and told him I was a nervous wreck about the game. He told me I would be okay and to calm down. I asked him if that was the last thing he had to say to me, and he said, "Son, I've got one other thing to tell you. Don't embarrass your mother." Then he hung up the phone!

It was about 34 degrees at Wrigley Field, and I had to face Bob Gibson of the St. Louis Cardinals. He whiffed me, and I never even saw the pitches. Going back to the dugout, I thought maybe I should call home, because I might be going back there pretty soon. I did get a swinging bunt down the third-base line for my first hit.

The first time my mother and dad ever came to Wrigley Field, it was against Pittsburgh. For some reason, Leo Durocher liked me and got my parents great tickets to the game. I got the game-winning hit, and when I went back, my mother and dad had tears in their eyes. Pretty soon, I had tears in my eyes. It was pretty special. We were a farming-type family. My father was a florist, and my uncle and grandfather worked on the farm growing vegetables. To have them there was a great day for me.

That team was really put together beginning in 1966. Fergie Jenkins came over, Kessinger and I were young players, and we also picked up Bill Hands and Randy Hundley. We knew that talent was beginning to blend together.

It was a good time in baseball. There was a tremendous amount of talent in the game and much more depth in pitching throughout the league. Every team had at least three solid starters, and you rarely see that anymore. Seaver, Koosman, Nolan Ryan, that's who you would see in a series with the Mets, for example. Baseball was different then. You'd have the same team year-in and year-out. Seven or eight of us were together for nine years, which is impossible now. People knew who was on the team each year because there was no free agency to pull you apart.

In 1969 we knew we had some good talent on the team, and it was just a matter of putting it together. Leo Durocher deserves a lot of credit for developing that team. He changed the attitude of the whole Cubs organization. Before, it was okay to go out and hopefully finish .500, but he demanded winning. That's what we did right through the first five months of the season. We won on Opening Day in 1969 on a Willie Smith homer, and I have to admit I was in the dugout freezing. That win set us off on the right track. That was a big ballgame to win, and you could see the momentum starting. The '69 team was bringing the Cubs out of the doldrums and establishing the new idea of being a contender. Again, I give Leo Durocher a lot of credit for putting the team together. We had a good infield with Santo, Kessinger, Banks, and myself.

Holtzman's no-hitter was a great day. The grass was really high. It had been wet, and they didn't have the chance to mow it. And the wind was blowing in, too. Kenny was loose and was not superstitious, so you could talk to him. I still get kidded about bobbling the ball on the last out, but I was determined to block it at any cost. You have to remember, Hank Aaron hit maybe two balls my way in the seven years I played against him. I was hollering, "Be ready, Ronnie, be ready, Kess," because he was a dead pull hitter. Then, of course, he picks the last out of a no-hitter to hit the ball to me. I know, it looks like I stumbled. No way was that ball getting through me. I knew he wasn't running well, so I had time. I know it didn't look good, but I got the job done.

The excitement was everywhere in town, and people were all talking about the Cubs. You couldn't wait to get to the ballpark and see the big crowds. I remember games in '65 and '66 where the only people there were the ushers working. In '69 it was a happening.

The Mets' staff really came together, then they had guys playing at a really high level. Swoboda was making all those diving catches, and I remember

Glenn Beckert played second base for the Chicago Cubs from 1965 to 1973 and made the National League All-Star team four consecutive seasons (1969–1972).

they told him he should wear a helmet. When we went to play them in New York in September, that was not a good time. The play that hurt was the one where Tommie Agee was called safe at home. He was out, and he will admit it. Don't forget, right before that trip, we had a ninth-inning lead against the Pirates, and Willie Stargell hit a home run to beat us. That was a big loss, and we went on that trip feeling down before we got to New York. I don't know why we ran out of gas. The Mets beat us and had a great pitching staff that nobody had heard of then. It was one of those things.

For five months, it was a wonderful time to be a Chicago Cub. The city loved us, and it was really something special. To this day, people recognize us and love us, even though we lost. Only in Chicago would you see our team recognized like that. We all went down together. I don't know if we were worn out and that Leo might have used a few extra players. We played our hearts out, we did our best. Even though we lost, we created a lot of interest in Chicago about the Chicago Cubs. We had the Bleacher Bums come out. They were jumping on the field—that's part of the reason they put the basket up in the outfield. We made friends with them, and they came on some trips with us. They were part of the team.

Ron Santo was my roommate for nine years on the road. He never held anything in. If he was upset about anything, it came right out of his mouth. In 1965, my rookie year with the Cubs, we were playing in San Francisco. Ronnie was hitting probably .327, and I was stuck right around .200. Back in those days, if you were a rookie, you carried all your luggage with you because you might not be going back to Chicago. One morning, I saw Ronnie giving himself an injection in the bathroom. It was the first time I saw it, and I didn't know anything about his diabetes. I said, "Ronnie, we have to have a talk. Something's wrong. You're hitting over .300, and I'm struggling to stay at .200. Where's the needle? I want to give myself the same injection." He laughed at me and we always hit if off. He'd ask me, "Am I okay? Am I good roommate?" I'd say, "Yeah, but the way I got assigned to you is there was a drawing, and you weren't told about it. I got the short stick and ended up with you."

49

He still tells the story about the night Sandy Koufax threw a perfect game against us. I've been known to say a lot of things at the wrong time. He struck me out in the first inning, and I hated that. Before, I had hit a line drive down the left-field line that missed being in by maybe an inch. I thought, *Jeez, I had that one.* So Santo said, "Rooms, what's he got?" I said, "We've got him tonight. He's not throwing anything." Well, a perfect game is a lot to throw! Santo tells that story all the time, but I can't get out of it. It's the truth.

I had great teammates. Fergie Jenkins was great. You know every now and then your arm hurts you, but Fergie never said a word about it. He always took the ball and pitched. It's remarkable that six years in a row he won 20 games. I think that is something that will stick around for awhile, because now they pull the pitcher out in the sixth inning, and here come the relievers. As far as Fergie goes, he definitely deserves to be in the Hall of Fame. I'm glad he's there.

Billy Williams was one of the best hitters I've ever seen. I was fortunate enough in my playing career to bat in front of him. By him hitting behind me along with Santo and Ernie Banks, they were not going to worry too much about me, because I'm not a home-run hitter. I knew I was going to get a good fastball, usually down the middle. I picked up on that, and things worked out good for me.

I played on the same team with three members of the Hall of Fame, and that's something. I don't know a lot of teams that has happened to. There's a fourth that should be in, and that's my roommate, Ron Santo. He definitely should be in.

I give a lot of credit to Don Kessinger. We knew each other's style, where we would play, how we would move on it, where to throw the ball on a double play. That knowledge certainly helped. I was traded to San Diego, and I knew we were in bad shape when I got there and the shortstop didn't speak English and I didn't speak Spanish.

I played nine years at Wrigley Field, and it was a great thrill. Walking in still brings the goosebumps out in me. The majority of the ballparks are new now. If you say to someone, "Have you ever been to Wrigley Field?" they always say, "I've been there once, and I'll never forget how beautiful it is, and I want to go back." That's Wrigley Field.

I still come back to the Cubs Convention every year. No other team has this support, and sometimes I'm baffled. I don't know what created this. The Cubs haven't won the title since 1908. It's this great charisma, and I love it. I had fun singing the stretch, but it's scary. I wasn't even allowed to sing in college when my fraternity was in the song contest. It was a great thrill. At my age, it's nice to be invited anywhere!

I was not only fortunate to play in the major leagues but to play with such great friends for so many years. We're all getting to the age now of going to the hospital and getting surgeries for our repairs, so maybe we'll always meet up in a retirement camp somewhere. Most of us go to Randy Hundley's camp every chance we get in the winter. There something about putting on the uniform that takes you back, and we talk just as crazy as we used to.

From 1965 to 1973 Glenn Beckert was a fixture for the Cubs at second base. No. 18 batted second in the Cubs lineup each year and was selected to four consecutive All-Star teams, from 1969 to 1972. In 1968 he led the league in runs scored and was annually one of the toughest hitters to strike out. He won a National League Gold Glove at second base in 1968. Beckert had a breakout year in 1971, when hit .342 to finish third in the National League. He had hitting streaks of 27 (1968), 26 (1973), and 20 (1966) games in his career.

KEN HOLTZMAN

PITCHER

1965–1971 ★ 1978–1979

Nineteen sixty-six was my first full year in the majors, and I was made a starter by new manager Leo Durocher in spring training. Our team was young and certainly had no pennant race experience. We lost more than 100 games and, amazingly, I led the team in wins, strikeouts, et cetera, even though I had a losing record. At the end of this very difficult losing season, I was anxious to finish and return to Champaign to continue my education at the University of Illinois. It just so happened that my last start of the season was to have been against the first-place Dodgers at Wrigley Field. Since a Jewish holiday was going to occur on this date, I asked Leo Durocher if he could move my start back one day so that I could attend services, and he readily agreed. My parents were in town for the weekend and, as it turned out, we all went to services together, and they attended the game the next day. When they realized that Sandy Koufax would be the Dodgers' starter, they got very excited, and my dad was pumped, because he held Sandy in very high regard, as did everybody where I was from

Even though I wound up winning the game 2–1, which turned out to be Sandy's last National League loss, my most vivid memory was when he struck me out in the seventh inning. Sandy wasn't that great a hitter, and I had struck him out earlier on an 0–2 curve that just buckled his knees. He kind of glared at me, as if to say, I didn't have to embarrass him by throwing a curve ball when a simple fastball would have sufficed. I didn't think anything more of it until I came to bat later, and he threw me three fastballs in a row, which seemed to get faster each time. The last one had to be over 100 mph, because I barely saw it, and I just went meekly back to the bench. I learned a valuable lesson that day and still remember it vividly, even to this day.

Nineteen sixty-seven was a pivotal year for the Cubs and for me, as well. It turned out to be the first time in many years that a Cubs team finished in the first division, and it also marked the emergence of Fergie Jenkins and Bill Hands as great pitchers. These two gentlemen had more to do with my education as a pitcher than anyone. They were not only great pitchers but went out of their way to help me learn the art as well as the science of being a major league pitcher. My time in the military was quite hectic, but it seemed every time I came back to pitch on a weekend, the Cubs would score a lot of runs and therefore make it a lot easier on me. After the season, I remember Mr. Holland wanted me to come to Chicago to talk about my contract for the next year. He offered me a $1,000 raise, and I asked him how he arrived at that number, since I was undefeated and had a good ERA and other stats. He said that to preserve the club payroll structure, he could only pay me what a nine game–winner would make! I told him I only pitched 12 games because of my military involvement, but he was adamant, and I had to sign for what he offered. What would that be worth today?

52

On my first no-hitter in 1969 against Atlanta, the wind was blowing in a lot. I didn't strike anybody out in that game, which was a rarity. One of the reasons was that once I got a three-run lead after Santo hit a three-run homer right away, I was just going to go out there and throw strikes. I wasn't going to try and fool around with the wind blowing in, even if I gave up a lot of fly balls, yeah, you might give up one home run, but if you don't walk anybody and throw the ball over the plate, you had a pretty good idea that you might be successful, and that's what happened. I was throwing strike after strike after strike. I wasn't trying to fool anybody to get a strikeout or anything like that. I wasn't really in any trouble in any inning. I didn't have a lot of walks or anything, so I really didn't have to try for a strikeout. I just went and threw 99 percent fastballs and tried to move it around a little bit, and they kept hitting the ball at everybody. Our team made a few really good defensive plays, which happens in every no-hitter, and I caught a lucky break on Hank Aaron's fly ball in the seventh when Billy Williams made the great catch.

I had pitched long enough to recognize the crack of the bat and the trajectory of the ball. When you throw a pitch like that, especially to a guy like

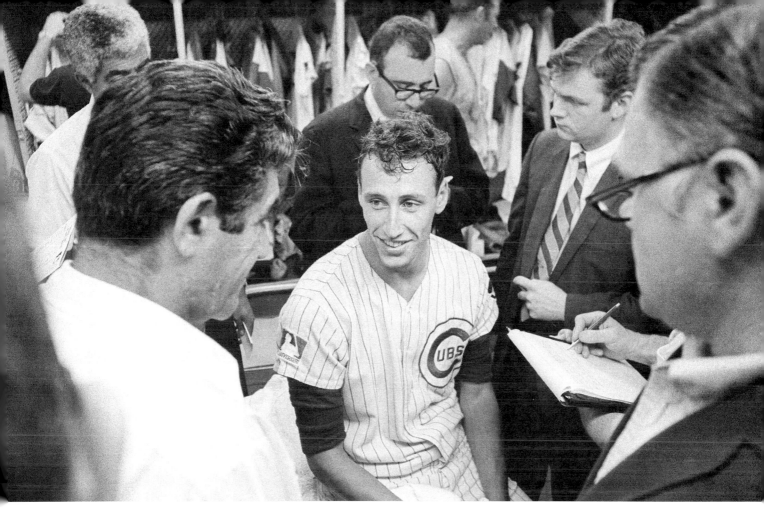

Cubs southpaw Ken Holtzman talks to reporters in the Wrigley Field clubhouse
following his first major league no-hitter, a 3–0 victory over the Atlanta Braves on
August 19, 1969.

Hank Aaron—okay, well now the score is 3–1. But then it got up, and the
wind was not only blowing in, but pushing the ball down. Billy kept drift-
ing over to this little recess, which is like another four feet. He waited and he
kind of drifted, then he jumped up and caught it. I can remember looking
up, and I thought, *This is kind of weird*, because I really thought Hammer got
it, and then it blew back in. I didn't know what to make of it. I was concentrating so hard on pitching the game and pitch after pitch and everything like
that. I can remember at the time, I said, "You know, there's something special going on in this game, and I can't explain it." You just go ahead and pitch,
but when that happened, I did think maybe it was a special day.

Aaron was also the last hitter of the game. I had a 3–0 lead, there were two outs in the top of the ninth, and the crowd was going absolutely crazy. I couldn't hear myself think, and Geno Oliver back there, he just wanted me to stay away from him. He may get a hit, but let's stay away from him, you know. I've still got to try and win the game. So I threw it as hard as I could and kept it away, and he hit a ground ball at Beckert. I turned around when he hit it, he didn't really hit it that hard, and Beck is shaking, he's nervous, boy. I don't think he wanted that ball hit to him. He kind of double-clutched at it a couple of times. Finally he put his glove on it, and knowing Beck, I was lucky he didn't throw it into the fourth row. He was only 20 feet away from Ernie, but he got it over there.

As far as challenging Hank in that situation, I'm supposed to pitch nine innings. Why would I want to walk him? That's just the way you had to pitch the game in order to complete the game. That's the way we thought. I'm trying to win the game and go nine innings. If I get a no-hitter that's great, but that's not the reason I'm out there.

During 1969 I had to fulfill reserve requirements just as I had in 1968. I had to leave the team occasionally for up to two weeks at a time when my unit was activated. Nineteen sixty-nine was quite a year, and I know it still remains very vivid in the minds of many Cubs fans. The park was filled every day, and for five months we were the toast of the town. Eventually, it all came tumbling down as the Mets overtook us and went on to win the World Series. I lost 15 pounds during that summer and was literally exhausted by the end of the season. It was certainly my most disappointing season, but I learned some valuable lessons that would serve me well when I went to Oakland and had to pitch many postseason games.

My second no-hitter at Cincinnati in 1971 was a hot night. During this season, I was called to active duty again, and this time it really screwed up my rhythm and timing, and I had to struggle every start to try and reestablish my control. During this game, I felt very strong, but didn't have exceptionally good command, so I threw about 95 percent fastballs. The most memorable occurrence happened when Johnny Bench tried a surprise bunt in the seventh or eighth inning, and it just rolled foul at the last second. It would have been an easy hit, of course, but he wound up flying out. Also, Lee May was the final out of the game, and I later played with him in Baltimore. He gave me one of his bats that he said he used in that game. What a terrific and classy guy!

When I asked to be traded after the 1971 season, I told Mr. Holland that I didn't have any preferences (of course, in those days one didn't have a choice), but I would like to go to a contender. When he called me in St. Louis to tell me that he had traded me to Oakland, I suddenly realized that I was going to a different league with new players and a distant city. It was, at first, a little overwhelming, but then I remembered that Oakland had a young team which had won their division and had some very exciting players. Obviously, it was the turning point of my career as I wound up being a part of one of the 10 best teams of all time. Looking back, as much as I loved Chicago and playing for the Cubs with their loyal fans and beautiful park, the trade to the A's was the ultimate break of my life. While it's true that I am still associated with the Cubs by many fans (90 percent of the baseball cards that I'm asked to sign are of me in a Cubs uniform), it is the time I was with the A's that really defined my career.

I owed Leo a lot for taking a chance on a 20-year-old to step right into the starting rotation and completely remaking a pitching staff. We played cards on planes and in hotels, and I enjoyed his stories about when he played in the '20s and '30s with Babe Ruth, and others. Toward the end of my run with the Cubs, we started to drift apart, primarily because of how he handled a lot of my starts. I was the type who never wanted to come out of a game, even if I was losing or getting hit hard. I always wanted to stay in, and sometimes I resented him taking me out in favor of a relief pitcher. We had some shouting matches in his office after several of these occurrences, and it never really got resolved until I was eventually traded. In retrospect, I'm glad I played for him because he did have a vast knowledge of the game and was an important figure in the game's history, which I've always respected.

Wrigley Field is unique in that it's so storied. It just has this mystique. Even today when I go to Wrigley Field to watch a game, I'm struck by it. I've been fortunate enough that they've invited me back to sing "Take Me Out to the Ballgame" three times. There's something about walking into that park that's like the same day when I walked in, in 1965 for my first time that I ever saw it. It's like a green oasis in the middle of the city, and it's in a great neighborhood. There's just something special, and I hope that it always stays that way.

'Til the day I die, probably, I'll be associated in a lot of people's minds with the Chicago Cubs, and that's fine. That's who I was drafted by in the first free-agent draft, that's who I spent the first seven years of my career with, and my final two years. I played nine years with the Cubs. Nobody loves the

55

city or the organization more than I do. In between that, I was on four different world championship teams, one of which I believe is one of the three or four greatest teams that ever played, and yet, I'm never associated with that. I don't really mind that. The Cubs are such a unique experience and opportunity to play when you're in the major leagues. First of all, you're playing in a very historic park, which has a lot of emotional significance for a lot of people in Chicago, because they associate their lifetimes with that park, there's the span of their years as measured against the memories of that park and their team. The Cubs, WGN, and the park are such an embedded part of the culture of the city that it's hard to be disassociated with it, and I understand and kind of welcome that. It's okay if people forget about the rings. I mean, I know I've got the rings, but then again some of my happiest times were the years I spent in Chicago.

Ken Holtzman was picked by the Cubs out of the University of Illinois in the 1965 amateur draft. As a rookie in 1966, the left-hander led the Cubs with an 11–16 record. Due to National Guard obligations, Holtzman appeared in only 12 games in 1967 but posted a perfect 9–0 mark. He went 17–13 in 1969 and hurled a no-hitter against the Atlanta Braves, all while shuttling between the team and his military commitments. On June 3, 1971, he threw his second no-hitter, this one at Cincinnati against the defending National League–champion Reds. Holtzman was traded to the Oakland A's for Rick Monday after the 1971 season and became a key part of three straight World Championship teams, winning 19, 21, 19, and 18 games as the A's won the AL West four straight years. He was 4–1 with a 2.55 ERA in eight World Series games for Oakland. After pitching with the Yankees in 1977, Holtzman was traded back to the Cubs in the middle of the 1978 season. He finished 6–9 in 1979 and retired after the season.

BILL HANDS

PITCHER

1966–1972

I DIDN'T KNOW MUCH ABOUT the Cubs when I was traded there. I had played against some of their guys in the minor leagues like Kenny Hubbs and some of those guys at Salt Lake City. I grew up a New York Giants fan, so I was happy to be a Giant, but I was sitting in the wings there because they had Juan Marichal, Gaylord Perry, Jack Sanford, Ron Herbel, and others. I was waiting for my opportunity, so once the shock of being traded wore off, I was very happy.

Leo came to the Cubs with a reputation, but I never had any problems with him. You could tell he was all business, and it was going to be a tough work ethic and mindset. I really think the Cubs needed him. The Cubs had been the "lovable losers" for a number of years, including when they had the College of Coaches and all of that stuff. They were almost a joke. I'm not taking any potshots at anyone when I say that, it was just an abnormal situation. When the Wrigleys hired Leo, it gave some stability to the whole organization. Joe Becker came over as pitching coach, and we had Pete Reiser and Joey Amalfitano as coaches, all of them good guys.

The Cubs had the famous Brock-for-Broglio trade before I got there. They had some older guys like Larry Jackson, Curt Simmons, and Robin Roberts, which I really liked. The older pitchers were really helpful to all of us—Holtzman, Jenkins, Rich Nye, Joe Niekro—we all benefitted from

Right-handed starting pitcher Bill Hands was acquired by the Cubs along with Randy Hundley in 1966. Over seven seasons he amassed 92 wins with the team, including a 20–14 record and 2.49 ERA in 1969.

them. Ernie had been there a while, Santo and Williams for a little bit, then Kessinger and Beckert were new, too.

We knew our job as starting pitchers was to take the ball 35 or 40 times a year. I don't think we knew any different. Leo was always hesistant to go to the bullpen, anyway. I was a hard thrower as a young guy, and I toiled for a long time in the minor leagues. I didn't throw as hard when I got to the big leagues. I wasn't the most talented guy in the world, but I worked hard and tried my best.

I did throw inside. That was kind of the way I pitched. My slider was my out pitch, and for that to be effective, I had to pitch inside to right-handed hitters, in particular, and make them aware of the ball on the inside part of the plate. You have to get in their kitchen, and I got a lot of guys out on the inside part of the plate, because my ball ran in. I don't call myself a head-hunter, but Leo had his way of playing, which was five years later from when he had managed the Giants and over 30 years after he played with the Gashouse Gang. The game was different then, and you did knock guys on their ass.

When I was first coming up, a guy I couldn't get out was Joe Morgan. He was a .240 hitter with the Houston Colt .45s and Astros at that point, but I couldn't get the little guy out, and people would look at me like, "Who's he?" Years later, they found out who he was, but I had a real tough time with him, and he was as tough a guy to get out as anyone. Left-handed hitters were difficult for me, certainly Willie McCovey. He was fearsome, because if you threw the ball away he would hit it back through the box so fast you couldn't react. If you didn't get it in real good, he would either take the first baseman's head off or knock it over the wall. Those were two guys who really stand out. I guess you could say there were a lot of guys who had my number! I faced Hank Aaron a lot, and I think I gave up four of his 755 homers. I had some success against him, though.

My catcher, Randy Hundley, and I were good friends. We had played together one year in Triple A Tacoma. Our kids played together, and we were roommates for a number of years. We thought along the same lines, and he knew that when he caught me I wouldn't shake him off very often. We were on the same page and got along very well.

It was always disappointing when one of your buddies got traded. I had a strong friendship with the late Joe Niekro, was good friends with Jimmy Hickman, and enjoyed Johnny Callison, who has since passed away. We had good relationships, and it wasn't just going to the ballpark every day. It was more than that. Playing in Chicago was more like a nine-to-five job. If you played somewhere else, it was mostly night games and a whole different routine you were in versus when we were home in Chicago.

Nineteen sixty-nine was exciting. It was exciting not only in Chicago, but we had piles of fans go to Cincinnati, St. Louis for sure, but not New York or California like they do now. We were on television every afternoon on WGN, and all the women did their ironing and watched the Cubs games.

59

I think the women were more rabid fans than the men, and I'm serious when I say that.

I was proud to win 20 that year. Any pitcher's personal goal would be to win 20 games. We all want to win, and you want to win the pennant. That was the idea. Aside from the team's success, you want to be successful yourself, and you were playing for next year's contract.

Nineteen sixty-eight was a pretty good year where we were a young team and making things difficult for everybody. In '69 we had a real good year, and it was the first time the Cubs had a winning record in consecutive years in a long time. We started the excitement as far as the Bleacher Bums, and it became cool to be a Cubs fan.

My thought process at Wrigley was to keep the ball down. Obviously, the wind blows in during the spring and fall. I don't think I changed my game plan at all throughout the season. We were always known for having slow infield grass. If you got the ball hit on the ground, chances are, no matter how hard-hit it was, one of our infielders was going to get to it. My strength was pitching down in the zone, and I didn't worry about somebody hitting a cheapie home run. If it happened, it happened. That was my basic game plan, keep the ball down and make them hit the ball on the ground.

My favorite game was probably beating Tom Seaver and the Mets 1–0 in Chicago in 1969. It wasn't my most dominant game, but it just happened to be a day I beat Seaver, who went on to win the Cy Young Award that year. He dominated us, and I was fortunate to keep them off the board. I remember it being a hot, sticky day in Chicago.

It was great being a Cub. I don't think there's any better place to play. My heart is still in Chicago.

Right-handed pitcher Bill Hands joined the Cubs in December 1965, when he was traded along with Randy Hundley from the Giants in exchange for Don Landrum and Lindy McDaniel. Hands won eight and seven games his first two seasons with the Cubs, then stepped up in 1968 with a 16–10 record and 2.89 ERA. Hands followed with an outstanding season in 1969, when he made 41 starts, pitched 300 innings, and went 20–14 with a 2.49 ERA. He went 18–15 in 1970 but was traded with Bob Maneely and Joe Decker to the Minnesota Twins for Dave LaRoche on November 30, 1972.

RANDY HUNDLEY

CATCHER

1966–1973 ★ 1976–1977

I WAS A KID PLAYING SHORTSTOP, and I loved pitching. I had this big curve-ball and would knock those hitters down and scare the pee out of them. But my dad didn't want me to pitch. I didn't like playing short, because it was too boring for me. The pitchers didn't get the ball over, and if they did and they hit it to me, it would likely go through my legs. I went to my dad one day and said, "Dad, I need to be where the action is." He said, "Well, come on, son." It was a very hot August afternoon. The humidity must have made it about 110 in Virginia. He said, "C'mon, I'm going to teach you the position." We started out of the house, and he stopped me at the front door and said, "Son, I'm going to teach you to be a one-handed catcher." He pointed his finger right between my eyes—I can still see that big finger pointing down on me—and he said, "If I ever see you put that bare hand up to catch the ball, I'm going to come and personally take you out of the game." I played games right here in Wrigley Field worried about my dad seeing me just get that hand too close to the mitt. Knock on wood, I never missed a ballgame because I had a foul hit my right hand. Back then, a lot of guys—Tom Haller, Tim McCarver, a number of guys—would come to me and ask, "What's this one-handed catching stuff?" It extended a lot of guys' careers. Nobody catches two-handed now.

The first time I ever came into Wrigley Field, I was with the Giants. I went out to loosen up in the outfield and ran in front of the right-field bleachers. I took one lap, and I stopped because they were all over my fanny! I thought, *Man, this is one rough place to play.* Once you get here and become part of the ballclub as I did, it's the greatest. When I got traded to the Cubs, they treated me great, and I loved playing there. You get to know them, and they feel part of you and you feel part of them.

In 1967 we went into first place for the first time in however many years. I never realized what the team flags on top of the scoreboard were for. I'd only look at the flags to see which way the wind was blowing, I didn't know

Cubs catcher Randy Hundley fouls a pitch back during a game against the Houston Astros at Wrigley Field on May 6, 1972. From 1966 to 1969, Hundley played in 612 games, including a high of 160 in 1968.

what they meant. After we won that day, all of a sudden I saw them take the flags down and put the Chicago Cubs on top, then I thought to myself, *You dumb hillbilly, where have you been all these years?* The people would not leave, and we had to come out of the clubhouse and tip our caps. That was a very memorable time for me.

In 1969 we knew we were getting better, but I don't think we realized we were as good as we were at the time. When Willie Smith hit the home run on Opening Day, that really put a charge in our ballclub. It started and went on from there. It lasted until early September or so, but it was wonderful to be a part of that team.

I missed Ken Holtzman's no-hitter that year. I didn't catch either one of his no-nos. I was injured with a severed tendon in my toe, so I was home watching it on TV. I was scared to death watching, because Hank Aaron had hit a ball I thought was a home run earlier when Billy Williams caught it. Aaron hit that last ball to Beckert, and he was able to make the play to get him. It was tense, and I didn't get to play in the game physically, but I was there mentally.

We went into New York with a small lead, and we knew the first game there would be key. We had a big lead, and every time we looked up at the scoreboard, the Mets had won. I'll never forget the game at Shea Stadium, and of course I remember tagging Tommie Agee out and the umpire calling him safe. That gave them momentum and put us on our heels a bit. I was there, and I know how hard I tagged Tommie Agee on the play. The ball went from the pocket of my glove up into the webbing. I can't jump as high anymore as I did after that play. I knew I couldn't bump an umpire or I'd get suspended, so that's why I tried to go straight up and down. Things started to go downhill after that. I was proud to have been on the 1969 ballclub and proud of what we did. The Mets played extremely well and won the championship by a pretty big margin when it was all said and done. I was still proud to have been a Cub and in that organization.

Ron Santo and I have had so much fun over the years. He's so excitable, and when you look at him the wrong way, he'll be right at you, "What are you looking at?" We never knew that he was diabetic for the longest time. I'll never forget a play in St. Louis where the ball was hit to him, he threw to first, and the runner was safe. Ronnie started hollering at the umpire at the top of his lungs, then all of a sudden went down to his knees and stayed there for a moment. Meanwhile, there was a big argument going on at first base, so no one noticed that he got up and went to our bench on the third-base line, grabbed and ate a Hershey bar real quick, and was right back on the field!

Since I had been with the Giants, I used to have fun talking to those guys when they came to the plate. I'd try to get in their heads and tell them we were going to knock them on their fannies if they got a hit off us.

One day we were playing at Wrigley Field, it was as hot as all get-out, and I had to go to the mound because Bill Hands was pitching. He had a 1–0 lead in the top of the ninth and got the first two outs, then walked the bases loaded. I figured it was time for me to go talk to him. I was going to calm him down and make sure he knew what we wanted to do with Hank Aaron in this time at bat. I said to him, "What are we going to do with Hank Aaron?" He threw his hands over his head. "I don't know, man, get back there and call something!" he said. I went back and called a curveball only to get the fastest fastball I'd seen all day. The ball went to the screen, and in came the tying run. So I called a fastball, and here came the curveball this time! Ball against the screen, another run in, and we lose the bloomin' ballgame. Jack Brickhouse had already named Hands as the player of the game and wanted to interview him after the ballgame. Jack asked Hands, "Who is the toughest player in the league for you to pitch to?" Hands came right back and said, "My catcher, Randy Hundley!" I didn't go to the mound much to talk to Bill after that.

64

Another day I hit a home run to win the game in the second game of a doubleheader against the Mets. I rounded second and headed for third only to find there was no base there. The grounds crew had already picked it up. I was wondering what in the world to do next, but Pete Reiser, our third-base coach, stopped me and made me stay right there until the grounds crew went back under our dugout and got a base. I touched it and then finally went home.

I was really upset when I was traded to the Twins. I didn't like it at all. I remember the year before I heard rumors that I would be traded that summer, and it totally affected my play. I didn't like that. When I came back in 1976, I injured my knee in my second at-bat with the ballclub, and that was really disappointing. I had to have my knee operated on again and really didn't get to play very much with the club. That part was very frustrating. I had an infection in my knee, so everything that could go wrong did, and I couldn't be a Chicago Cub.

One game that stands out, after I came back to the Cubs and had another knee surgery, is getting to play Opening Day and standing there for the national anthem. That was the biggest thrill for me, because nobody expected me to play again, so that was very exciting.

My group from that '60s era is really close. Years later, we're still close friends and maybe more so than when we played together. I've been very fortunate that way. I love these guys. When someone gets sick, you get worried about them. We played almost 10 years together as a group and have a real fondness for each other. Baseball players are a tough breed. When you play a 162-game schedule, you have to be tough. You can't go out there every day and feel 100 percent. I think our guys were all tough, and that's served us all later in life.

I can't even comprehend this ride. I love coming to the Cubs Convention and love being a part of the Cubs organization. The Cubs fans don't forget you and won't let you forget them, either. I'm very proud to have been a Chicago Cub and played with that organization, because I don't know any other place where you could have a relationship like you do with the Cubs.

Imagine a kid coming into Wrigley for his first game, coming through the gates, walking up the stairs, and looking out onto that field. How could you not be a Cubs fan after seeing that ballpark? As a player, it can get a little rough there when you're not playing well. I certainly experienced that when my son, Todd, was playing there. That was a little frustrating. I wish it had worked out better for him.

When you talk about the magic of the Cubs fans, one of the things is that the people are close to the field at Wrigley. No matter what seat you're in, even in the upper deck, you're right there. I think people feel a connection to the ballplayers, and believe me, I know the players feel a connection to the fans.

I started doing my fantasy camps in 1982. I was doing kids camps, and I had a friend who asked me if I'd thought about doing a camp with former players and people who would like to be ballplayers. I told him I had and thought I could make it like a spring-training camp and really make it work. If somebody had ever told me that camp would survive for two years, I'd have said he was nuts.

When we first started out, I was very concerned about people getting hurt. I couldn't imagine the camp running this long and as many people coming back as they do. I work very hard at having the right players come to

65

coach who can express the feelings and the ups and downs they've had in the game of baseball. Any of us who have played it know you're going to have ups and downs and things aren't going to go your way all the time. The campers are able to experience that for a week. It's a tough game and a great game.

It's hard to believe how much fun it is and how many laughs we have with each other. In the morning meetings, we rag on one another and tell stories that actually happened in the big leagues. We have all become family. I used to watch the 1984 team play and to now get to know those guys and be teammates with them has been fantastic for all the former players. I don't ever want to forget this.

It never gets old putting on a uniform. I love doing the camps and I love what everybody else is getting out of it. We were a family who enjoyed playing together, and to now let other people enjoy that with us has really been a fantastic experience all these years.

After being traded to the Cubs from the Giants after the 1965 season, Randy Hundley grabbed the starting catcher job in 1966, knocking out 19 home runs with 63 RBIs. He averaged an astounding 153 games behind the plate over the next four seasons and won a Gold Glove in 1967. He had 18 homers and 64 RBIs in 1969 and was selected to the National League All-Star team. He tore up his knee in 1970 and battled injuries for the rest of his career. Hundley was traded to the Twins after the 1973 season but returned to the Cubs for the 1976 and 1977 seasons. Injuries limited him to a handful of games each year, and he retired after the '77 season. Randy invented the baseball fantasy camp concept in 1982, and his Cubs fantasy camp is held every January in Mesa, Arizona.

FERGUSON JENKINS

PITCHER

1966–1973 ★ 1982–1983

Larry Doby was one of my heroes when I was growing up because I lived close to Michigan. Being from Canada, my dad would take me over to Tiger Stadium, and I saw Larry Doby hit some home runs. It changed my idea of wanting to become a hockey player in the NHL or a basketball player in the NBA into wanting to become a big-league ballplayer. After I watched him play, that became my goal, and I was very fortunate to get there.

My first major league appearance was in relief for the Phillies against the Cardinals, and I beat them in 12 innings. The first batter I ever faced was Dick Groat, and I struck him out on four pitches. Cookie Rojas drove in John Herrnstein with the winning run in that first win. The first home run I ever gave up was to Ron Santo in 1965, and it was a wind-blown fly ball into the bleachers. I remember my first Opening Day start I beat Jim Bunning 4–2 at Wrigley Field. You don't forget those things.

I got traded to the Cubs from the Phillies when I was very young, 23, going to be 24 that winter. I just think that every player wants to make a mark. I got my opportunity early in the season. Leo let me start. I won some ballgames. I did really well, and it just continued to flow. I put that string of games together and had some good ballplayers behind me—Santo, Kessinger, Beckert, Banks, Williams, you name the guys. When I pitched, they played hard for me. I think that's a plus. I went out there to try to win every game I pitched in, and these guys really played hard. This was a small ballpark back then. The only other small ballpark was Crosley Field. When teams came in here, the wind blew out or across or whatever, guys were looking to pad their averages or pad their home-run totals. We had Kenny Holtzman, Billy Hands, Rich Nye, myself, and Dick Selma, we tried to shut 'em down. That was our job.

I wore No. 30 with the Phillies, and when I got traded to the Cubs, [clubhouse manager] Yosh Kawano said I couldn't have that number because Kenny Holtzman had it. So he gave me 31, and I said fine. I was born December 13, so I told myself 31 was just 13 backward. At one time, Dave Winfield in San Diego was the only other player in the National League with that number. It wasn't real popular.

I think I had my struggles at the beginning. I'd consider myself more of a thrower than a pitcher when I first started in 1965. After I won 20 games for the first time, I became more of a pitcher. Learning the art of pitching is something you can't teach. It's self-control on your own, so after the '67 season I became a pitcher.

My father was kind of that inspiration. He'd say, "Son, if you go out there, you start what you finish." That's the kind of mindset I had. When I came to the Cubs, Leo Durocher kind of reinforced that. We didn't have a very strong bullpen, so lots of times he'd be walking past me in the dugout, and he'd say, "Hey, big fella, don't be looking for any help today," or, "We're going to give the bullpen a rest." This is the reason why I had a lot of complete ballgames.

68

I loved pitching, and I had a rubber arm. I didn't mind going out there. I recall once or twice on the road, I started three games in a week—Monday, Thursday, and Sunday. I did it. It's documented. The nice thing about it is I loved pitching and I loved to go out there and perform. As a pitcher, you had a four-man rotation and had to sit around and wait until you pitched again. It was a little different than pitching out of the bullpen.

Day baseball became a way of life for me here. Wrigley Field was an incredible place, and I'm glad I never played under the lights here. To come to Wrigley at 8:45 or 9:00 AM, get dressed, come out on the field, play a game, be done by 3:00, and then be able to get home was special. My kids grew up with me, and that was a nice part of it.

I enjoyed the hot, muggy weather. I got loose easily and would stay loose all day. Joe Becker was our pitching coach, and believe me, we ran every day. Thanks to that, I had lots of stamina and didn't mind the muggy weather.

Hall of Fame Cubs pitcher Ferguson Jenkins gets ready to uncork one to a Mets batter in the fourth inning of a game at Shea Stadium on July 8, 1969.

I always had good control, and I'm not sure how that evolved. I used to throw in the wintertime, and I worked at it and worked at it, throwing lots of strikes. After a while, I could pretty much throw a strike with any pitch I had. I threw four—fastball, curveball, slider, and change-up. I threw my splitter as a change-up and really had good success with it. Throw strikes, get ahead of the hitter, let the hitter do part of the work—that's what the game is all about. Make your defense work as much as you do.

We had a tough manager in Leo Durocher. He'd let me hit a lot of times in the seventh or eighth inning, maybe to push the runner around with a bunt or maybe even swing the bat to stay in the ballgame, and I enjoyed that part of it. It was a confidence level that he had with me, and I had in my team. So I played to win every time I went out there. I didn't look forward to losing. I wanted to win.

We had some good players. The teams here got better as we played. Leo wanted to have that happen. Leo came over here in '66. He made trades for certain individuals and brought guys in, and they became better ballplayers because of that. I enjoyed pitching in day baseball. I just think that if you love and enjoy where you play, you produce. If you don't like where you're at, it's time to move on.

Randy Hundley was the catcher most of the time along with Ken Rudolph. I just think we knew the players as much as we could. We had a game plan and tried to stick to it. I used to come right at hitters, I didn't walk anybody. I didn't try to walk anybody, and I think that was a part of my game I enjoyed more than anything else, challenging the hitter, making him put the ball in play. I gave up some home runs here and on the road, but I think when a hitter came to the plate, he knew I wasn't going to try and pitch around him. I was coming right after him.

I think Randy had his theory about getting hitters out. I think all the pitchers had their theories, too. We had a game plan and we all pitched different; no two pitchers pitch alike. Randy had to know our little idiosyncrasies about approaching, setting the hitter up, working him in the count, and trying to get him out as best we could. That was a plus, knowing the hitters, along with Randy knowing them, as well.

The Cubs' buzz was something that probably started in the 1960s when I came here. We had very small crowds, and we started winning. One of my favorite days was in 1967, when we went into first place for the first time in quite a few seasons. The crowd stayed, I think, because the Cardinals were playing the Mets, and the Mets ended up beating the Cardinals. I think 40,000 people stayed here for the outcome of that game. We beat the Cincinnati Reds that afternoon, and they put our *W* flag up. The crowd was pretty happy.

It started with the '68 ballclub. We were the first ballclub to draw 1 million people with the Cubs. Nobody was going to take Ron Santo's job at third base or Kessinger's or Beckert's or Hundley's. Ernie was at first base, and Billy Williams was our left fielder. That was a tradition, and under the management and tutelage of Leo, we were set. He believed in one starting lineup. He put it on the team door as you left the clubhouse, and if you couldn't go to the post the next day, you had to go to his office and tell him. This is the reason why guys played so many games in a row. If your name was posted there, you'd better be playing the next day. Don't let Leo down, don't let your teammates down, and that's the way it was. In 1968, the same year Gibson had his great season, I had a good season. I got shut out five times 1–0. If we had scored some more runs, who knows how many games I could have won that year?

The crowds got really big. I just think the fans started to understand that the organization was going to try to win a pennant. Nineteen sixty-nine was really not a Cinderella story, we were in first place April 15 and stayed there until September 10. The Mets got strong and overtook us, and unfortunately, we just didn't win that year.

We were so close-knit. Holtzman, Bill Hands, Beckert, Kessinger, Joe Pepitone, Milt Pappas, and so many guys enjoyed themselves here, again because of day baseball. You had something to do after the ballgame, because it wasn't like it was midnight and everyone had to head home to bed. We would go out and see shows together. There were some jazz clubs nearby, and Billy Williams loved jazz. Pepitone had a club here off Broadway, and we would go by there and have a few cocktails. That was a part of growing up here, and it was just so enjoyable to play here.

I played two years with the Harlem Globetrotters, which was kind of a ploy at the time. Because I'm a Canadian and they were traveling in Canada, they asked me if I would come and be part of their routine and act as the pitcher that always gave up the home run to Meadowlark Lemon. It went across so great the first 24 or 30 games, I ended up playing about 55 or 60 games the first year and about 85 the next year. I was part of the tour for those years, 1967–1968.

I used to chart games in the stands, we all did, and I was there for Kenny Holtzman's no-hitter against the Reds and the same for when Milt Pappas threw his. All this stuff about not talking to a guy on the bench is an old fallacy. We used to walk by and say stuff like, "C'mon, you've got one going, you can get it today." Everybody thinks they don't want to make you nervous, but in your mind, you know you are throwing a good ballgame, that the guys are playing well behind you, and that you can be part of history. The closest I came was a one-hitter against Baltimore one time.

Willie McCovey was one guy I did not want to see coming to the plate with men in scoring position. He was always dangerous. If you made the inside pitch, he'd pull it hard down the right-field line foul or just fair, but if you left it out over the plate, he would rip it right up the middle, and as a pitcher, you were just too close. For a couple years in the late '60s with McCovey and Willie Stargell, you could hear the ball go by you, and I'm glad one never hit me. They hit it hard.

You think about milestones: I know I struck out George Hendrick for my 2,000th strikeout and Garry Templeton for my 3,000th. I beat every team in baseball except the Cubs. There's some trivia for you—I won 284 games in the majors and beat every team but the Cubs and Texas.

72

It was a little tough when I was traded to Texas. There were a lot of rumors that I had a bad arm, and I told them I didn't have a bad arm. It was just one of those things. I got to Texas and won 25 games, then won 17 the next year. Then I got traded. You bounce around, and trades are what the game is all about. I played 21 seasons and never had a sore arm.

I came back in 1982, and there were lots of new players. Ryno was a rookie, Lee Smith, Jody Davis, and Keith Moreland were among the young players. I was kind of the senior guy at 38, and all those guys were 22 or 23. It was fun, and they gave me the nickname "Pops," which I didn't mind. But after a while, everybody calls you "Pops," and you say, "I'm not that old, guys!" The nice thing about it was coming back to Wrigley Field, where it all started.

For the Hall of Fame, you wait five years after you retire to be on the ballot. The first year I was eligible, they took Johnny Bench and Carl Yastrzemski, two pretty good ballplayers. The next year, they took Jim Palmer and Joe Morgan. Gaylord Perry was a pretty good friend of mine, and he was kind of ticked because Palmer won 268 games and Gaylord won over 300. I told him to calm down, that we'd go in together, and in 1991 we did. I went in with Gaylord and Rod Carew, and we were three pretty good ballplayers.

The biggest change in the game I see is no one throws a complete game anymore. There might be a few guys in the league who can throw one, but when we played, there were 25 or 30 guys who would throw 15 or more. The bullpen is so strong now, and it's all strategy. They want six good innings from a starter and that's all; bring in the set-up guys and the closer. The pitch count has something to do with that, too. I pitched plenty of games where I threw 140 or 150 pitches. I don't know if it's fair the way they do it now. Some of these young men are strong and can perform, but the management have it in their heads that when a guy nears 100 pitches, the bullpen has to be in the ballgame. I think if a guy is in a one-run game, the manager should do what they did to me and have the manager ask you how you feel. There's only a few guys who have that privilege now. The game revolves around the bullpen now.

I think one of the great things about Wrigley still is that it's a neighborhood stadium. You have to park adjacent to the fire station. Fans had a chance to really intermingle with us because we walked through the crowds either coming into the ballpark or leaving. I think that was a big plus for the ballplayers and the fans back in those early days.

The fans here are incredible. They love baseball and they love the competition. The people come out to the Cubs Convention every single year. It starts with the kids who are brought by their parents, and years later, they bring their own kids. I still have people who come up and show me their Die-Hard Cubs Fan Club cards. That's great. To play here in Chicago and have the fans love you as much as they do is a great distinction.

Having my number retired was great because I had a chance to play with these other athletes. Great guys, great ballplayers on the field and off the field, and I've known them for quite a few years, Billy, Ronnie, and Ernie especially in the '60s, and Ryno in the '80s. It was a great day for both Greg [Maddux] and myself. It's outstanding to see your number on that flagpole, because this is where my career basically started. Although I signed with the Phillies, this is where I got team support, fan support, and where I won most of my ballgames, in a Chicago uniform. I played with some great guys. I'd

73

like to be considered a great teammate and friend, and we just had a great time together for my years in Chicago.

Ferguson Jenkins came to the Cubs on April 21, 1966. Leo Durocher put Jenkins into the starting rotation that year, and in 1967 he broke out with the first of six consecutive 20-win seasons. The team's workhorse made 42 starts and threw seven shutouts for the 1969 Cubs on his way to a 21–15 mark. In 1971 Fergie won the National League Cy Young Award after his finest season. He led the league in wins (24), complete games (30), innings (325), starts (39), and posted a 2.77 ERA. After a 14–16 record in 1973, he was traded to Texas for Bill Madlock and Vic Harris, where he posted a 25–12 record and 2.82 ERA in his first season with the Rangers. Jenkins returned to the Cubs as a free agent in 1981 and retired before the start of the '84 season. His final career record stands at 284–226. In 1991 he was elected to the Hall of Fame. Jenkins was named to the Cubs All-Century Team in 1999, and the Cubs retired his No. 31 on May 3, 2009.

The SEVENTIES

JOE PEPITONE
OUTFIELDER/FIRST BASEMAN
1970–1973

WHEN I GOT TRADED from the Astros to the Cubs, believe me, I really wanted to get out of Houston. I knew that the Cubs had great ballplayers like Billy Williams, Ernie Banks, Fergie Jenkins, and Randy Hundley, so I knew I was going to a great ballclub. I knew they were going to be there. That's what I was looking for. I wanted a chance to go back to the World Series like I did when I was with the Yankees. I played hard for those guys. When I got to Chicago, I really wanted to bear down and play hard.

I had been traded from the Yankees, and in those days, being traded was really a putdown. I didn't want it. Then I heard I was going to Houston, and I figured it might be good. When I got there, all that was there was a hotel, and that was about it. There was nothing there but the Astrodome. I guess the Yankees wanted to send me far away, and they did. I didn't get along too well with the manager, but the players were great. I got out of there right away. I only played half a season in 1970, but I had 14 home runs while I was there.

When I found out I was going to the Cubs, it was the greatest feeling. When I was a kid, and they first came out with TV, the first games I saw were the Cubs. In New York, they would show them about once a month in black and white. I remember seeing Ernie Banks and how he held the bat. I was a wrist hitter also, and I would watch Ernie and how he curled the bat. I thought how much I would like to play for the Cubs. It was a great feeling to come

Joe Pepitone (right) sits in the dugout with his new manager, Leo Durocher, at Shea Stadium in New York on August 3, 1970. *Photo courtesy of Getty Images*

over and be with those ballplayers. Batting behind Billy Williams and playing with Ron Santo, that was a great team.

To tell the truth, when I got there, the Cubs had always been in second place. All the talk was about second place this, second place that. I remember Ernie Banks coming up to me and saying, "Pepi, what was it like to be in the World Series?" Wow! Ernie Banks was asking me, and I told him it was the greatest feeling in the world. You live for that, and the Yankees always won. The nerves are there, and it really makes the game good when you're nervous. You really bear down, and there is nothing like the World Series. Ernie would talk to me about it. Of course, I'd get mad at him when I would come in with a hangover, and he's say, "It's a good day for two!" That would really bother me. Ernie was a great guy.

Billy Williams became one of my closest friends and so did Fergie Jenkins. It seemed like every time Fergie was pitching, I'd hit a home run or two or drive in the winning run. I really played hard for Fergie. I did for the other guys, too, but there was always a little extra for Fergie.

Leo Durocher was my type of manager. He would stay out with me 'til 4:00 in the morning. He was great. He didn't know what to expect, because he had heard about me. He knew I could play the outfield, too. I didn't play for about a month, but right when I got here, he put me in. I think I met the club in Cincinnati, and he put me in a doubleheader. I probably went about 1-for-5, and it felt great. I started getting on a hot streak, and he was great to me. He didn't even mind when I bought a motorcycle and brought it into the clubhouse.

78

At the time of the big clubhouse meeting in 1971, I was one of Leo's bobos. He really liked me. Leo used to have Randy Hundley watch me all the time. Of all the people, he had Randy Hundley. It was like the preacher watching the devil! Randy and I became good friends, but he was always looking for me, because I would show up in the clubhouse at odd hours. One day, he came in and found me in the john and told me, "Pepi, Joe Amalfitano told me Leo is going to call a meeting. Don't say anything. Don't raise your hand and volunteer anything, because Leo really likes you. Don't get in his doghouse."

Sure enough, Leo had his meeting and he said, "You say what you want to say, and I'll say what I want to say and I won't get mad." The first guy who raised his hand was me, and he went crazy. I said to him, "Leo, [former Yankees manager] Ralph Houk doesn't treat everybody like you, treating everybody the same. He had guys he would pat on the backside and guys he would kick in the pants." He started yelling at me, called me a bum and said that he picked me up when nobody wanted me. Don't get me wrong, though, I loved Leo. He treated me well, and I had my first .300 season with him [1971]. He played me all the time, against both left-handers and right-handers, and I hit well for him. Leo was a good guy, but if you got in his doghouse, you stayed there. If it hadn't been for the writers, I would have never come out of it.

I loved playing at Wrigley. I loved playing at the old stadiums. The field was nice, and if the wind was blowing in, it was hard to get one out, but I could because I was a line-drive hitter. It was a great ballpark, especially with the Bleacher Bums. I played more football out there than I did baseball. They'd holler, "Hey, Pepi!" and I'd turn around and someone would throw me a football. It was great, and they were such great fans. Even if you had a bad game, they would still cheer you. They were for the Cubs, so if you were for the other team, they would find a way to get you.

I opened up a club, and all the Bleacher Bums were there. That was tough! It was called Joe Pepitone's Thing, and I really opened it up for myself. I just wanted a place to hang out with my friends. I wanted to have a little place. I started into it to help out a friend, and as soon as I did, he took off with the money. The place did really well, and there were lots of Cubs fans there, or course. I had Mario Andretti come down, Evel Knievel, all the football players from the other towns.

Something happened [in 1972] where I just didn't want to play, and I briefly retired when I was with the Cubs. I had just hit .300, and they put me on the B squad in spring training, and I had to work my way up. They had gotten on my case, and I said, "I don't have to play for that." That's just the way I was. I wasn't really making any money. [He returned to the club later in the season.]

Then Whitey Lockman came along, and I was gone. Certain people like you, and certain people don't. He had something against me, and that's just the way it was. I had a good year in 1972, but the next year I was in Philadelphia with the team, and they traded me to Atlanta. You can see why I didn't like Whitey Lockman.

It was hard to leave. When I was traded, I saw Billy and Fergie in the lobby, and they couldn't believe it. It was hard leaving the guys I'd really come to love. That was my third year in Chicago, and I lived there for another eight years. I stayed there with my club and really had a great time. I love Chicago and all those great people.

A game that really stands out in my mind was one against the Dodgers. Don Sutton was pitching, and I knew him. He had told me if I got a hit off him that year he would buy me a steak dinner. The first time they were in town, my first time up against him, I hit a grand slam off him on the first pitch. I ran around the bases and was hollering at him, "What can I get for that? A steak and some caviar?"

Batting behind Billy Williams was a thrill. I'd stand behind him and watch him spit in the air, then he'd hit it with his bat. When I tried it, I got spit all over my pants and uniform. Batting behind him was special, because I really thought he was one of the best hitters of all time. He was a great ballplayer.

Ron Santo should be in the Hall of Fame. Pee Wee Reese and Phil Rizzuto are in the Hall of Fame, and I love Phil, but compare Ron's stats with any of them. He's got over 300 home runs, lots of Gold Gloves, and made all those All-Star teams. I love Ronnie, and he was a good friend to me when I came over. We palled together as a couple of Italian kids and had a good time. It makes me crazy, because Ronnie really deserves it, much more than at least 30 percent of the guys in the Hall now.

With me, what you see is what you get. It has never changed. I'm a free person, and there's not a lot hidden about me. If I can't have fun, I don't want to do it. The way I played the game of baseball was that if I couldn't have fun, I couldn't do it. Today, even if I didn't have fun, I'd probably play just to get that 15 or 20 million bucks a year. But if I made that much money, I guess I'd be dead in about three days!

I love the Cubs. I've been going to Randy Hundley's camps for at least 20 years. To see guys like Glenn Beckert and Don Kessinger—all of those guys I played with—is great. I had good years in Chicago, and those guys all became my friends.

The Cubs acquired Joe Pepitone from the Astros in July 1970, and "Pepi" gave the Cubs a strong second half with 12 homers and 44 RBIs while playing both first base and center field. He hit over .300 for the only time in his career in 1971, finishing at .307 with 16 homers and 61 RBIs, despite battling a bad elbow. Pepitone retired briefly during the 1972 season and played in only 66 games that year. On May 19, 1973, he was traded to the Atlanta Braves and retired shortly after. Pepitone does community relations work with the Yankees and is a fixture at the Randy Hundley Fantasy Camp each winter.

MILT PAPPAS

PITCHER

1970–1973

I WAS WITH THE BRAVES at the time I was sold to the Cubs in 1970. Blake Cullen, the Cubs' traveling secretary, was a friend of mine. We had met many years before I came to Chicago, and every time I saw him, I'd say, "Hey, when are you going to bring me to the Cubs?" He told me that Leo always liked me, so when the time came that Atlanta gave up on me, Blake called and told me they were going to bring me to the Cubs. I was very, very happy. I knew I wasn't past my prime and was hoping I could get a new start with the Cubs and be able to show what I could do. It worked. I was extremely happy I was given the opportunity, because I sure wasn't being given the opportunity in Atlanta. I was glad to get out of there. Leo put me right into the rotation, and obviously I helped. The rest is history.

We pitched every fourth day, and the manager would tell us, "Don't look behind you." That meant we were out there for the duration and only if we were tired would they come and get us. Otherwise, you were there. That's the way we performed. It's a lot different than the guys today. We knew what our job was, and every fourth day we took the ball. We were professionals with a job to do, and that's what we did.

Leo was a manager who loved veterans. He was not a big fan of kids, because kids you had to tolerate, and with veterans, they were supposed to know what to do. He didn't have patience with younger players, which is why the Cubs were usually loaded with veterans.

Milt Pappas joined the Cubs in 1970 as a right-handed starting pitcher and had career highs with 17 wins in both 1971 and 1972. He capped the '72 campaign on September 2 with a no-hitter against the San Diego Padres.

I won 17 games each of my first two full years with the Cubs, and it felt good because I knew in my heart I wasn't done mentally or physically. The Braves weren't letting me do what I could do, which I didn't understand, but I was tickled to come to the Cubs and do the job.

I think one of the reasons so many fans still identify me with the Cubs is because of my no-hitter in 1972. A pitcher is aware of what's going on, and by the time you get to the seventh or eighth inning, the bench knows what is going on. That day, when I came in after the eighth inning and I still had the perfect game, I walked down the bench, and no one said a word. That was ridiculous, and I wanted my guys to get going, so I said, "Hey guys, I'm throwing a no-hitter," and that got them loose and laughing. Then I got tight because, where I was sitting in the dugout, the cops and ushers were gathering and making a racket, so I had to ask them to be quiet.

In the ninth, John Jeter hit a fly ball to the outfield, and when I saw our center fielder Billy North slip down, my heart sank down to my toes, and I thought, *There goes everything*. Thankfully, Billy Williams was hustling and made a running catch. I got Fred Kendall for the second out, and then Larry Stahl was a pinch-hitter.

I got ahead of him 1–2 right away. I was one pitch from the greatest thing a pitcher can do. Next pitch was a slider on the outside corner, ball two according to Bruce Froemming, who was umping behind home plate. Next pitch, another slider on the corner, ball three. All these pitches were right there, and I was saying, "C'mon, Froemming, they're all right there." Now comes the 3–2 pitch, again on the outside corner, and he called it ball four. I went crazy. I called Bruce Froemming every name you can think of. I was swearing at him in Greek. I knew he didn't have the guts to throw me out, because I still had the no-hitter. The next guy, Garry Jestadt, popped up to Carmen Fanzone, and I got the no-hitter, which was great. But those balls should have been called strikes.

When you look at the last pitch to Dale Mitchell in Don Larsen's perfect game, it's not even close, but there was a perfect game on the line. The thing that got me was that smirk on Froemming's face after the pitch. The next day, he actually asked me to sign a baseball, and I said, "I would be more than happy to, Bruce, and you know where you can stick it." That was the only time I ever pitched a no-hitter in all my years of Babe Ruth, high school, minor leagues, anything.

The next time I saw Larry Stahl, he told me he was rooting for me to get the perfect game and had decided he wasn't going to swing. I said, "I wish you would have winked at me or something to to give me some kind of sign." If he had, Randy Hundley and I wouldn't have been messing around with sliders on the outside corner in that situation. All three of those pitches were right there, though.

When I pitched at Wrigley, my approach wasn't too different. I was a sinkerball pitcher, so to me that was in my favor just like it was when I was in the American League pitching at Fenway Park with the short wall and Yankee Stadium with the short fence down the right-field line. It was about concentration to try and make sure I kept the ball down. Otherwise, you could get killed.

If anybody gave me trouble, it was the little guys that pestered me a lot. A guy like Matty Alou would hit a 10-hop ground ball to shortstop and beat it out. They gave me the most trouble. The big guys were going to get their hits, but my concentration was to make sure that base hit didn't cost me the ballgame. I faced a lot of great hitters like Clemente and Aaron and Mays in what I think was the golden era of baseball. The talent was just tremendous, but I had good luck with the big guys, making sure if they got a hit, it wasn't one that would cost me a game.

I wasn't a bad hitter. If they threw the ball in the strike zone where I was swinging, I got lucky a few times and connected. I enjoyed hitting and actually hit two home runs one day in Minnesota when I was with Baltimore. Any time a pitcher can hit somewhat, you've got a chance of staying in the ballgame a lot longer.

It was very frustrating not to be able to win a division with the Cubs. We knew we had good teams, but when it came down to the wire, I guess playing all day baseball was a burden and a chore. It took a lot out of the guys with the heat in the daytime of August and even September. That's what it was, and it was difficult for the same guys to go out there and compete every single day. Leo liked veterans, so those veteran guys we had were going to play every day, come hell or high water.

I was let go in 1974 when I felt I could still pitch. It bothered the hell out of me what Whitey Lockman did to me, releasing me a week before the season started, which was the worst time in the world you can release anybody. All the teams have their rosters set, so I was very, very upset. I had a really good spring that year. I was shocked by his letting me go. I found out later that being a player representative didn't help me, either. No other team other than the Padres contacted me to pitch for them, so I felt a bit blackballed. There was a movement afoot with the Cubs to break up the team because we hadn't been winning, so they thought it was time to do it, get rid of whomever they could and start all over again.

It was 36 years until another Cub threw a no-hitter, and I watched the game when Carlos Zambrano did it against Houston. That game was in Milwaukee, because Houston was being hit by a hurricane. Records are made to be broken, and I always figured if anybody was going to do it, it would be Carlos, and he did. I've still got the last one at Wrigley Field. He mentioned my name after the game, and I thought that was very kind of him to remember me in that situation.

I pitched with a number of teams, but most people remember me as a Cub. The near-perfect game didn't hurt, and all those games were on WGN. The Cubs' mystique was there then, and it is now. It's an amazing franchise, and those fans are just fantastic. They are the greatest fans in the world.

The Cubs purchased Miltiades Sergios Pappastediodis from the Atlanta Braves on June 23, 1970. He provided immediate help to the starting rotation, going 10–8 with a 2.68 ERA for the remainder of the season and followed with a 17–14 mark in 1971. Nineteen seventy-two was his best season as a Cub when he posted a 17–7 record with a 2.77 ERA. On September 2 that year, Pappas retired the first 26 San Diego Padres before walking pinch-hitter Larry Stahl on a 3–2 pitch. He retired the next batter to finish with a no-hitter, becoming the only pitcher in major league history to complete a no-no after having a perfect game broken up with two out in the ninth. He is also the only pitcher in major league history to lose a perfect game by walking the 27th batter. Pappas slumped to 7–12 in 1973 and was released on April 1, 1974. He finished his career with 209 wins and hit 20 home runs in his 17 big-league seasons.

RICK MONDAY
CENTER FIELDER
1972–1976

I STARTED WITH THE OAKLAND A's and grew up with that club. You could see that club was going to win. We had won the Western Division in 1971, then lost to Baltimore in the playoffs. In 1972, when I first found out I was traded to the Cubs, it didn't bother me that the team I was leaving was on the cusp. I had grown up as National League fan. I was happy to be a member of the Cubs, because the first uniform I ever had as a kid in Santa Monica Little League was the Cubs. Even though I had to pack up and leave California, where I was from, I felt like I had really arrived as a major leaguer to be in the National League.

The first thing I learned when I came here that winter was that even though it was 1972, everything was linked to 1969. I was overwhelmed. I had heard a lot about Chicago being a great sports town, but I had no idea of the level until I arrived that winter. It was 13 degrees and you heard people talking about what the Cubs were going to be doing. I had come from Oakland, where there were days when you wondered if anybody knew there was a game that day or they knew the right start time. It was a cultural shock to hear everyone talking about the Cubs.

As a center fielder, I walked the field and had to learn it. It wasn't the smallest or biggest field, but the big difference was the short power alleys. I had only seen pictures of games at Wrigley with all the ivy, so seeing the bare

Cubs center fielder Rick Monday swings at a pitch against the Philadelphia Phillies during a game at Veterans Stadium on August 2, 1973.

walls was new. There was cold red brick underneath, and if you challenge the wall, especially before the ivy comes in, you are going to lose. I found that out the hard way by spending three days in the hospital after hitting it while going after a fly ball. It's a challenging park, and you have to make adjustments. You have to know how many steps you have once you hit the warning track and know where you are.

I had a great relationship with the Bleacher Bums. My A's teams didn't have any fans in the outfield. The fans were not only here, but they were into the game and hollering at us and each other the whole time. Last year, I met a fan who said, "You don't recognize me." I cut him off and told him I remembered him from when he sat in the third row of the right-center-field bleachers. He introduced me to his son, which was great because it's about tradition in Chicago.

What I enjoyed most about Wrigley was the lack of lights. When you are traveling all over the country and don't know what town you're in unless you grab a newspaper, to play day games gives you a chance to go home and have a normal life. That includes fighting rush hour traffic both ways, too! Chicago is a special place and always will be, especially because both my children were born here.

Don Kessinger was my roommate, and on the road we played a silly game every day called "King of the Room." How we came up with the idea I don't know, but it really meant something to both of us. The "King of the Room" had total control of the TV remote in our room each night. To win, you had to have the best game that day, and it included both offense and defense. I had to hit, because Don didn't make many mistakes with his glove. There was one game I won't forget in Veterans Stadium in Philadelphia when Don went 5-for-5 but was not "King of the Room." I had one of those magical games where, the first time up, I hit a home run to left, second time up hit a homer to center, third time up hit a homer to right, and my fourth time up, got a base hit up the middle. He beat me in the number of hits, but three of my four hits were home runs, so I said, "Roomie, I've got to call you on this one." He gave in and reluctantly handed me the channel changer when we got back to the room that night.

There were times when it was trying to come to the ballpark. We didn't have a whole lot of depth on those clubs. If we were down, there weren't guys who could produce off the bench. The guys we had tried and gave it all they had, but we couldn't compete on a daily basis. It didn't diminish our efforts on the field, and we took the field expecting to win, even if we didn't on a consistent basis.

The incident with the American flag took place at Dodger Stadium in 1976. When I think back to that moment, I was in center field in the middle of the fourth inning and I saw out of the corner of my eye two people coming on the field. When that happens, you really don't know. Are they there on a bet? Are they coming out because they don't like you? I saw that one of them had something under his arm. They ran past Jose Cardenal, who was in left field, and went to shallow left-center. I saw one guy take out what looked to be an American flag and almost spread it out as if it were going to be a picnic blanket. I saw the reflection on the sun off the can and it looked like lighter fluid that they were dousing it with. It was windy at Dodger Stadium, and the wind blew their first match out. The second match was lit and that's when I arrived. To this day, I don't know what was going through my mind, except that what they were doing was wrong. I scooped the flag up, and fortunately it was not on fire. The guy threw the can of lighter fluid at me, but he wasn't a prospect, and he missed.

I gave the flag to Doug Rau, a pitcher who had come out of the Dodgers' dugout. Tommy Lasorda was coaching third base and ran by me and was livid, as well. For an instant, I was thinking if I should bowl those guys over, but I just scooped the flag up. I'm very happy there was no violence involved and no one was hurt. I'm proud of the fact that I was able to stop them, but you don't think about the possible consequences at the time.

It stays fresh in my memory because of the number of pieces of mail I receive when the anniversary rolls around each April. That flag is in my home. I still look at the flag and the pictures, and what has not changed is that I felt then as I do now that what those two people were trying to do was wrong.

I feel honored and proud when I am asked about the flag, not because I stopped two people from burning the flag that afternoon in Los Angeles, but because it represents a lot of rights and freedoms. A lot of years have gone by, but it's important enough that people still discuss it. That flag is still a part of my life, and my wife and I have been blessed to be able to take it around the country and raise a lot of money for charities. It's meant a lot to me. I spent six years in the Marine Corps Reserve, and I met a lot of people who gave a whole lot more than just the time that I spent. That flag represents a lot to be proud of. This is a wonderful country, and it can be better if we want to try.

89

Someone asked me if it was irritating to have been blessed to play 19 years in the majors and still be most recognized for stopping two people from burning a flag. If that's the only thing I'm known for, that's not a bad thing, because it's very important. Baseball has been a wonderful conduit for us to help raise money for military charities.

I had mixed feelings when I was traded to the Dodgers. I was going back home to Southern California, and I had almost signed with the Dodgers out of high school. Tommy Lasorda was the coach of the high school tryout team I was on at that time, then he became my manager when I got to Los Angeles. That being said, I love Chicago, I love what it stands for, and I love the fact that for five years I was part of the Chicago Cubs.

Center fielder Rick Monday was traded to the Cubs from Oakland after the 1971 season for Ken Holtzman. He played five seasons with the Cubs, with his best year coming in 1976 when he posted career highs with 32 homers and 77 RBIs. After rescuing a flag from two men who were attempting to set it on fire between innings at Dodger Stadium, Monday became a national hero. The Dodgers presented him with the flag at a Wrigley Field ceremony a few weeks later. He still has the flag and uses it to help raise money for military charities across the U.S. Monday was part of a trade to the Dodgers that brought Bill Buckner and Ivan DeJesus to the Cubs prior to the 1977 season. Monday played in three World Series for Los Angeles, winning the championship in 1981. After a 19-year major league career, he worked as a radio analyst for the San Diego Padres, then joined the Dodgers broadcast team in 1993, a role he occupies to this day.

JOSE CARDENAL

OUTFIELDER

1972–1977

I WAS WITH THE ST. LOUIS CARDINALS in 1971, and during the season, they traded me to the Milwaukee Brewers. I went from a team in second place to one that was about 40 games behind. I went to the general manager and said I'd play the rest of the season, but after that I wanted to be traded to Chicago so I could play day games in that city. Right after the season was over, I went to Caracas to play winter ball, and in December John Holland called me to say they had traded for me. I told him it was the best Christmas present I ever had.

My first year here was in 1972, and Mr. Wrigley didn't want to spend any money. They wanted to keep the payroll flat. We needed some more pitching, and Mr. Holland went to him, but he didn't want to do it. It was sad, because in the first half of many of those seasons, we would lead the league. If the season had only been 60 games, we would have won the pennant every year, but we didn't have the pitching. That was very disappointing for the fans and players because we knew we were short of being a true contender. We needed more pitching, and they wouldn't do it.

One of my favorite days was a Saturday afternoon on NBC's *Game of the Week* with Tony Kubek and Joe Garagiola. We were playing the Dodgers, and Andy Messersmith was pitching. My first time at bat, I hit a home run to give us a 1–0 lead. I came up and hit another homer off Messersmith in the sixth

As an outfielder for the Cubs for the six seasons from 1972 to 1977, Jose Cardenal was a steady offensive force, hitting .296 with 61 home runs, 343 RBIs, and 129 stolen bases. *Photo courtesy of Warren Wimmer*

to win it 2–1. Everybody was watching the *Game of the Week*, especially some of my family.

I got six hits in a game in 1976 in San Francisco. It was unbelievable. It was the kind of afternoon where you feel so good that every time at the plate you know you are going to get a hit, and that's exactly what happened.

I always tell everybody that when I was playing here, we didn't make big money, but we loved the game. It was fun for the fans, too. Right now, I know the game is different. It's turned into a business. People ask me if I wish I could play today, and I say no. When I played here in my era, I enjoyed the game, and I have so many great memories that I wouldn't trade for anything.

Playing the outfield at Wrigley was great, especially because the fans were right behind you all the time. Heck, they could get in the bleachers for a dollar when I played here. I was friendly with them, because they were all good people. Before the games, I would fool around with them because that was me. I was a showman. I played with six different organizations, and I told my family if they ever let me in the Hall of Fame, I'll wear a Cubs cap. If you play in Chicago, it's the greatest experience, and you will never forget it for the rest of your life.

I owned Tom Seaver, and he knows it. I felt comfortable against him. I was small, and he was a great pitcher who wanted to throw the ball right by me. Well, I was a dead fastball hitter and a high fastball was just what I wanted. He did get me a few times, but I had many more good times than bad. I was working for the Washington Nationals and traveling with the team, and I saw Seaver broadcasting with the Mets, and he told me, "Jose, you owned me." I told him, "Tom, it's because I knew you would never knock me down, so the whole plate belonged to me." He never came in close.

J.R. Richard was just the opposite. I had absolutely no chance against him. Each time when he was pitching, I knew I was good for an 0-for-4. I would try, but he had me so intimidated I couldn't get a hit against him. Number one, he was at least 6'8", and he would call me "midget." He said to me, "I'm not going to fool around with all you midgets." Then to make it worse, he would drop down sidearm, and he knew I didn't like that. When that came in sidearm, I didn't know if it was going to hit me and there was no way I could touch him.

I had a lot of managers. Leo was great. I came in 1972, but then he got fired that year. He was great to me. Then we went through Whitey Lockman, Jim Marshall, and Herman Franks. I didn't have any problems with those guys. I just wanted to be in the lineup and play every day and try to help the team win. As long as you go out there and do your best to win, nobody will give you a problem.

I had a big Afro, no doubt about it. People still ask me at the Cubs Convention, "Jose, why did you cut your hair?" I say, "C'mon guys, time has gone by!" I did it more for the fans than anything. I loved it, though, but it was hard to keep it up, especially when it was June and July here, when you're sweating all day long. People asked me if I put in bobby pins, but it was my normal hair. I looked like Bozo the Clown with my hair coming out the sides of my hat. You had to do it for the fans, you just had to.

I would do anything to entertain our fans. In those days, there would be several thousand Cubs fans coming to Arizona to watch us in spring training. That's the reason I was so popular around here, because I would never turn anyone down. I stayed 30 or 45 minutes after the games to sign autographs, especially for the kids.

Jack Brickhouse was always great to me, and I loved him. I did pull one trick on him, though. When we traded for Ivan DeJesus, Jack pulled me aside and asked me the proper pronunciation of his name. I told him to say it "Dee-Geezus," and that's what he did for about a week. WGN was getting calls and letters, and when he found out I had tricked him, he wouldn't speak to me for about a month!

My teammates were like family. We'd go out and have drinks or dinner together. It was fun to be together talking baseball. After the game, we would stay around and have a beer and talk about what we could do to win the game tomorrow. Who's pitching, what do we know—we'd still be in our uniforms a lot of time talking baseball. If there's one thing that disappoints me today, it's that I wish the ballpayers would stay around a little longer. Fifteen minutes after the game ends, the clubhouse is empty. I know it's a different breed, but that's a big difference and one of the ways we were family.

If you play in Chicago, you're hungry to try and bring a pennant here. Some ballplayers can handle the pressure, and some can't. They know the fans want to win so bad here that I think sometimes they try to do too much.

94

Every year I have to be at the Cubs Convention because I love it in Chicago, even though I know it will be freezing cold. When you see the people ready to go for another year, willing to forget what happened the year before, it is beautiful. I see little kids, and they come up to ask for an autograph, and if I ask them if they saw me play, they always say yes! I love playing with both the young and old fans. The Cubs fans are the best in the world. Anybody who comes from another organization and plays here will tell you the Cubs fans are the best. I played in Philadelphia for two years, and man, those fans weren't too friendly. This is a great organization, great fans, and always a great time.

Jose Cardenal was acquired in a trade with Milwaukee for Jim Colburn, Brock Davis, and Earl Stephenson on December 3, 1971. The Cuban outfielder with the giant Afro quickly became a fan favorite and cult hero at Wrigley Field. In a five-year stretch from 1972 to 1976, Cardenal averaged 12 home runs, 65 RBIs, 25 stolen bases, and a .301 batting average. In 1976 he went 6-for-7 against the Giants, including a double, home run, and four RBIs. He was traded to the Phillies after the 1977 season.

RICK REUSCHEL

PITCHER

1972–1981 ★ 1983–1984

I CAME UP IN JUNE 1972, and my first game I came in as a reliever. I threw to one hitter, Bobby Bonds. I struck him out, and then they took me out for a pinch-hitter. The next day, I came in again in the fourth inning and pitched long enough to get my first win in relief. Those games were against the San Francisco Giants.

It was strange for me as a small-town farm boy being in the big city at Wrigley Field. It really had been my brother Paul's dream. He was the one who listened to the Cubs at night under the covers. To get here and to play and be in the dugout with all the guys I'd heard him listening to for years was incredible.

A few days later, I got my first start and beat the Phillies 11–1. Eleven runs in your first start always helps. I got off to a good start and won my first three decisions. I remember trying to keep my emotions down enough to do what I knew I could do. I had a lot of help. I had some great guys—Randy Hundley was catching, and all those '69 guys were there, including Fergie, who I still look up to, to this day. I tried to watch him and learn from him, not so much from talking to him, but watching what he did on the mound every time out. I give him a lot of credit for helping me pitch as long as I did. I wanted to follow him.

Don't get yourself in trouble, make them beat you every time, and don't beat yourself. If you watched it, it was very apparent, and I had a lot of trouble watching other guys pitch who couldn't figure it out. Fergie kept it very simple, and I tried to do the same thing. Throw a lot of strikes and let your teammates work behind you. Don't let them get bored. You can't score if you're out on the field so get back in the dugout as quick as you can and let your offense have the chance to score some runs.

I was very proud of pitching a lot of innings, but it wasn't that unusual. I grew up watching Fergie, and as many innings as I had, he always had more than I did. I took pride in going nine if I could and always getting into the seventh or eighth innings so that we didn't have to use a lot of people out of the bullpen. Later, when I had Bruce Sutter in the bullpen, he'd say just get me to the ninth and I'll take care of the rest. That's what I tried to do. In fact, when he got hurt and left, I hadn't pitched the ninth inning in so long that I had some troubles. It's different finishing that ninth inning, and you forget what you need to do.

In the first nine or 10 years I was there, I went through at least three rebuilds. I was probably part of the third rebuild when they sent me to the Yankees. For me, it was the best of all possible situations when I came up. I got to play with and against guys like Billy, Fergie, Hank Aaron, and Willie Mays, so I caught the tail end of those great Hall of Famers. They were people who, to me, played the game the way it should be played and put out all the time. Now, when I watch a game, and a pitcher gets through five innings, he's a hero. It's changed a lot, and I'm glad I was able to pitch when I could go a bit longer than that. We pitched in four-man rotations, so for me to go seven innings every fourth day wasn't bad. If I had to wait and pitch in a five-man rotation, I'd go nuts. There's nothing worse for a pitcher than sitting in the dugout watching a ballgame you have no chance of helping your team win.

Nineteen seventy-seven was very exciting. I remember the day we went into first place, the fans wouldn't go home. They stayed out in the bleachers and cheered. Driving home, I heard people cheering, and I thought it was from my radio, but it was people in the streets. It was very exciting. It's just a shame that Bruce Sutter went down when he did. We not only missed what he did, but it made everybody's job more difficult, because he wasn't there to fall back on. It created some pressure that we really hadn't had up until that point.

We came back and beat Cincinnati 16–15 that year. I think I threw one pitch and got a win. That win enabled me to get to 20 wins. I got a hit in the last inning, then someone else got one, and I went from first to third. Dave Rosello got the game-winning hit, and I scored. That was about as

96

Drafted by the Cubs, Rick Reuschel pitched for 19 years in the majors, 12 with Chicago, and won 214 games with a career ERA of 3.37. His best year was with the Cubs in 1977, when he went 20–10 and posted a 2.79 ERA.

exciting as it gets—come in, throw one pitch, get a win, score a run, win the game—perfect!

It was weird and a little bittersweet to play on the same team with my brother Paul. As I said, he was the Cubs fan who would listen to them every night. He was two years ahead of me but had hurt his arm in Double A. That set him back a couple years and gave me the chance to leap past him and take a job that I kept for 10 years. All things considered, if he hadn't gotten hurt, it would have been him doing that instead of me. I probably would have been the guy to come out of the bullpen and mop up after him, instead of the way it turned out. It was fun to play with him, but a little bittersweet for that reason.

Herman Franks would put me in to pinch-run once in a while. When I went to the Pirates, Rick Rhoden would pinch-hit all the time, then I'd come in to run for him. I wasn't that fast, but I knew the game of baseball. I knew how to get a jump and the situations where I could go from first to third and when I needed to stay at second base. It was a way to get off the bench and do something to help the team win that day, instead of sitting there with your thumb somewhere.

When the Cubs traded me in 1981, it was probably the hardest day of my baseball life. It was in the middle of the strike, and I just remember I got traded to the Yankees. As a farm boy growing up and being able to only watch the Yankees, I hated the Yankees. New York was even more intimidating as a city than Chicago. It was the American League, so I didn't get to hit anymore, and it was a totally different situation. After my first two months, I hurt my shoulder and was never able to pitch for them again. From that standpoint, it was disappointing because I wish I could have stayed there and pitched for the team and helped that club.

After my surgery, I rehabbed with the Yankees' farm team in Columbus. They watched me pitch one or two games and decided they didn't want to wait for me, so they released me. The Cubs picked me up, and I went to their Class A club to continue my rehab down there. I got called up in September of '83 and got a win at the end of the season that was big for me. Two years before that, I didn't know if I'd ever pitch again in the major leagues.

98

Nineteen eighty-four was very bittersweet, because early in the year I was pitching a lot. Dick Ruthven was hurt, and Steve Trout was having some problems. It seemed that only Chuck Rainey and I were healthy. We weren't doing great, but we were in first place. Then we got Sutcliffe; we got Eckersley; Ruthven and Trout got healthy; and they had no room for us. Neither Rainey nor I were on the playoff roster at the end of the year. That was the bittersweet part of it, feeling that we had carried the team through some struggles and then were out of there. It hurt me especially, because I spent eight years there in previous bad times and now we had a good team with a chance to go somewhere and I couldn't contribute. I could only sit and watch.

When Ryno hit the two homers off Sutter, right then I think it determined that we were going to win the division, but that just doesn't happen twice in the same game. After that game, we all knew we were going to win it that year.

The Cubs let me go and didn't want me to come to camp. I couldn't find a job in spring training 1985. All the players had been in camp for a week or two when the Pirates called me and offered me a chance to come down to their camp for the chance to win a job. I went down there, and that to me was the worst possible situation because their pitchers had won the team ERA title the year before; they were all back, were younger than I was, and were doing well. I didn't see myself fitting in there at all, but when it's the only job you can get, you take it. I started out in Triple A for them, and I think I pitched six games down there before I got called up. I had, in my mind, the best year of my career that year. I don't think I had a game in the minors or majors where I gave up more than two runs. It was a lot of fun.

These fans are unbelievable. Every time I moved, I was disappointed. I didn't want to leave Chicago. New York I wasn't disappointed to leave. I went to the Pirates, and when they traded me to San Francisco, I was very disappointed because we were right on the edge then with Drabek, Bonds, and those guys they had coming up. They got real close three years in a row, and I just missed that. I went to San Francisco and got to play with Will Clark, Kevin Mitchell, and probably the best ballclub I played on. I got more wins there, but my body gave out there at the end, especially my knee. I couldn't cover first base anymore, at least the last two years I was there. I don't know if anybody found out about it, because my teammates covered for me so well.

I'm not sure I was any part of what this Cubs thing has become. I guess I left just before it happened. Maybe I was the last old piece to get rid of before they could make this happen! It is good to see, and I know that all my family back in Illinois are avid Cubs fans who still die hard deaths every September when things don't work out. It's good to see them up there and having an opportunity to go a little further than they have.

99

Rick "Big Daddy" Reuschel was drafted by the Cubs in 1970 and made it to the big leagues in 1972. Rick's finest season came in 1977, when he won 20 games for the only time in his career, posted a 2.79 ERA, and was named to the National League All-Star team. He was the epitome of a workhorse from 1973 to 1980, averaging almost 37 starts and over 245 innings per season. He was traded to the Yankees on June 12, 1981. After being released by the Yankees in June 1983, Reuschel returned to the Cubs for the next year and a half before leaving as a free agent. He had great success with both the Pirates and Giants before retiring in 1991 at age 42. Reuschel made a total of 343 starts for the Cubs, second on the team's all-time list, and his 2,290 innings ranks sixth. Reuschel's brother Paul also pitched for the Cubs from 1975 to 1978, making 163 appearances, all but two in relief.

BILL MADLOCK
THIRD BASEMAN
1974–1976

I WAS MORE OF A CARDINALS FAN growing up in Decatur, because St. Louis was where I went to my first game with our American Legion team. The Cardinals were playing Cincinnati, and I was a big Pete Rose fan. I started watching the Cubs a lot in '69, and I was planning that my graduation gift to myself would be to go to Chicago and watch the Cubs in the World Series. I guess we all know how that worked out. I definitely used that money for something else!

I had finally made the big leagues with the Texas Rangers in '73, and I went to winter ball knowing that I'd be the starting third baseman for the Rangers the next year. I was playing in the Dominican Republic, and a Spanish reporter came up to me and said in Spanish, "You a Chicago Cub." I had no idea what he was talking about at the time. Finally, somebody came and told me in English.

I was disappointed. At the time, Ron Santo was still there, and I knew it. I thought, *Oh, no, here I go again. I finally made it to the big leagues, and now I'm coming to Chicago, and they will send me back to the minors after having a good month with Texas.* Then they traded Santo to the White Sox.

It was tough, because I had been traded for Fergie and he was a Cubs legend. Once you're a Cubs player, people think you're part of their family, because they see you so much on TV. WGN was a big superstation, and the fans could see the Cubs wherever they went. That's why you still have so

Cubs third baseman Bill Madlock was a standout rookie in 1974 and won batting titles in 1975 and 1976, hitting .354 and .339. *Photo courtesy of Getty Images*

many loyal Cubs fans. They were a little upset with me, but I didn't have anything to do with the trade. The Cubs were getting rid of guys who were part of their family for 10 years in Jenkins and Santo.

My first year, Billy Williams and I always talked. Watching Billy hit was seeing a work of art, because he was the Picasso of hitting. He was such a good, soft-spoken guy and was really open about talking hitting. I was lucky to be around him and guys like Willie McCovey and Willie Stargell that way.

My second year in '75 was fun. Jon Matlack and I were co-MVPs of the All-Star Game that year, and I got the game-winning hit. That's when the National League was winning all the time. In my den, I have the picture of that team with Lou Brock and others. It was a fun time for me, because we didn't have a good team at all with the Cubs, so getting to be around all those great guys was a treat.

I went 6-for-6 one day that year, but Rennie Stennett came in and went 7-for-7 not long afterward, so that didn't last too long at Wrigley Field. Bruce Kison fractured my thumb at the end of the season, and I was out for a few days, but I still won my first batting title pretty easily.

I didn't look at the flags at Wrigley Field every day when I got there like some guys. I was more of a line-drive hitter, so I liked Wrigley, because the gaps were shorter. I wish I had played there longer, because I would have had a lot more hits with my line drives to the gap. The wind didn't really affect me one way or another, though.

My second batting title was harder. I went into the last day a few points behind Ken Griffey, and I went 4-for-4 to win it. I really didn't think I had a chance at all. Pete Rose and some of Griffey's teammates told him to sit out that day. Well, he probably should have sat the day before when I think Phil Niekro one-hit them. That would have been the day to sit and then play the final day. Our game started an hour or so after the Cincinnati game. People in the booth were keeping track of it, but I really didn't know I won until I got home. I know they put him in the game once they heard I was doing well, but he didn't get any hits.

I was talking to Pete Rose one day, and he said, "You're a lot like me. The rest of these guys get to see their batting average on Sunday when the paper shows everybody, but we get to see ours every day up with the leaders, because we're always in the top 10." I always used to talk with him and about being hungry hitters. He'd say, "You get some of these hitters, and if they get a hit in their first at-bat, they're satisfied. When I get one hit, I want two. If I get two hits, I want three. If I get three hits, I want four. If a pitcher gets me out 10 times in a row, I'm going to make him work 10 times as hard to get me out that 11th time." You have to have the mindset that you're always the best any time you step into the box.

I bunted and did everything I had to do. Now, hitters just go up and swing. When we had two strikes, we shortened up our swings. Too many hitters don't know how to hit. Sometimes you have to back off and put the ball in play. I see too many guys who swing the same no matter what the count, and you can't do that. They've got all the money in the world, so why not help your team?

Nobody hits for the situation. It's all about hitting home runs and playing for yourself. Nobody takes a strike anymore, either. When you're down three runs or less going into the last inning, we didn't ever have to be told to take until you saw a strike. We did it anyway. That was a team thing. Everything now is about the individual. I know players do care about their team, but too many seem to forget that when they get into the batter's box.

I got kicked out of a few games in my time. I just did whatever it took to win, and if I thought someone was keeping my team from winning, I got a little upset.

When I was traded, I didn't want to go after having won two batting titles in a row. If the current group had been there at the time, I would still have been a Cub, but the Wrigleys were very conservative. Getting traded from Chicago to San Francisco was going from the best to the worst.

Regardless of where we played or where we went, it always seemed that we had more fans in the stands than the home team. Guys on the home team used to get upset with us. Once you're a Cubs fan, you're always a Cubs fans. It's not like other places where, when you move, you might pick up the team in your new town. Not Cubs fans. They can go anywhere in the world but will always stay Cubs fans. That's pretty great.

Third baseman Bill Madlock was acquired by the Cubs along with Vic Harris from the Texas Rangers in exchange for Ferguson Jenkins on October 25, 1973. Madlock hit .313 as a rookie, then followed with his first National League batting title in 1975 with a .354 average and was co-MVP of the All-Star Game after driving in the winning run for the National League. Madlock hit 15 homers and drove in 84 runs for the Cubs in 1976 and won another batting title with a .339 mark. The Cubs chose not to pay Madlock what he was worth and traded him to the San Francisco Giants for Andy Muhlstock, Bobby Murcer, and Steve Ontiveros on February 11, 1977. Madlock was traded to the Pirates in 1979, where he won a World Series ring and two more batting titles before finishing his career with the Tigers and Dodgers. He retired after the 1987 season.

LARRY BIITTNER
FIRST BASEMAN/OUTFIELDER
1976–1980

I WAS ECSTATIC WHEN I FOUND OUT the Montreal Expos had traded me to the Cubs in 1976. Being from Iowa and having WGN and the Cubs on there all the time, the people at home, my family and friends, got to watch me just about every day. It was great, and I loved it. I'm a Midwestern guy, so I definitely enjoyed coming to Chicago.

When I took the field in my first game at Wrigley after the trade, Yosh Kawano, the clubhouse manager, had given me No. 26. I came out on the field wearing No. 26, and a lot of the fans were booing me. I got, "What are you doing with that number on? You shouldn't be wearing that number. That number should be retired!" I remember saying, "Hey, I didn't ask for it. That's just what they gave me. Why?" They hollered back, "That's Billy Williams' number." Oh. I wore it for a couple years until Billy came back as a coach and then said, "Yes, you can definitely have your number back, Billy." That's what I remember most about my first game as a Cub.

In 1977 we had a good year, and that was really the first team I played with that was a good ballclub. I had been with Washington, then Texas, and those teams weren't very good. Montreal wasn't very good, either. That was the first experience I had being with a contender, and it was by far the best time I ever had in baseball. It was terrific.

For our home opener in 1978, I didn't start the game, and Bill Buckner was playing first base. He hurt his leg, so I came in the game against the Pirates.

We got to the bottom of the ninth inning in a tie game, and I jokingly turned to Herman Franks and said, "I'm just going to hit a home run and get this game over with. I might hit a home run." Jim Bibby was the pitcher, and I had played with him in Texas. He was a big guy, and I knew he was going to throw me a fastball. I just jumped on the first pitch he threw me, which was a fastball, and it went out of the park. That was pretty exciting and a very memorable moment in my career, for sure.

Playing several positions meant that in spring training you had to work a little more. I'd take a lot of ground balls at first base. I'd go out to the outfield and work out there, taking fly balls, whatever I could do. I just basically tried to acclimate myself to those positions and get ready to play. It was a little harder, but not much. It was a fun time, it was really was.

I don't know if there's a way to really prepare for pinch-hitting. My idea of pinch-hitting was to get up there and not get cheated. I never liked to take a first-pitch fastball. I went up there swinging, and that was pretty much my approach. I never liked the pitcher to get ahead of me with a called strike, so I went after the first pitch a lot. "Grip it and rip it" was my philosophy. Fortunately, I was able to do a pretty good job at it.

Randy Hundley has told the story of my pitching debut many times, but this is what really happened. It was the first game of a doubleheader in about the eighth inning, and it was one of the hottest, most humid days ever in Chicago. It was unbearable. I was down in the runway, and I might have had a hot dog in my hand. We were down 11–2, and I was just waiting for the second game because I knew I was playing left field. I was just resting and getting ready for the second game.

Then I heard this call, "Hey Biiiiiiit!" I didn't answer Randy, and after three times, he said, "Hey Bit, I know you're down there dad-bummit, so c'mere!" I said, "What do you want?" He told me he wanted me to get loose, and I said, "Randy, I can't hit a nine-run pinch-hit home run. What are you talking about?" He said, "No, go out and get loose on the mound. You're going to be pitching." I know the color drained from my face, and I said, "What? You've got to be kidding me." Randy said, "Yeah, Herman wants you to go out and warm up."

Jim Todd was the pitcher on the mound getting beat up, heck, all of our pitchers were getting beat up that day. So I went to the bullpen mound to start throwing. Somebody called down to the pen to say that if Todd didn't get the next hitter out, I was going to be in there. I thought, *Oh, no! Jimmy, please get this guy out.* No, he didn't, so in I came, and the rest is history, so they say. It was brutal. After the game, I went up to Herman and said, "Please don't ever do that again. I don't get paid that much money to just be 60 feet away from the hitters. This is not fun!" That was the one and only time I ever went out there to pitch.

The hat play still lives on, too. It was late in the season in 1979. Joey Amalfitano was our manager at the time, and we were playing the Mets. There was a runner on third, and Bruce Boisclair hit a line drive to me in right. I was famous for my hat always falling off or, on the bases, for my helmet falling off. In fact, if it didn't fall off, I'd flip it off. I hated running with a cap on. It slowed me down a lot, not that I was that fast, anyway. Every little bit helps.

He hit a sinking line drive, and I thought I had a chance to catch it, so I dove for the ball. I caught it and didn't realize what happened until I saw it on replays. My hat went forward and flipped upside down. As I hit the ground with my glove, it opened, and the ball just kind of rolled out of my

Larry Biittner slides safely into home after a single by Jerry Morales, as the Pirates' Duffy Dyer waits for the throw in the fourth inning of a game at Wrigley Field on Friday, May 27, 1977.

webbing right into my cap and flipped it upside down. I was looking all over for the ball and had no idea where it was. The fans were yelling, but I wasn't paying attention, I was just trying to figure out where the ball was. I was looking back by the fence, I was looking everywhere, because I thought I had caught it.

Jerry Martin was playing center field, and he came running over, laughing so hard he had to hold his glove over his mouth, and he giggled, "It's under your hat." The guy that hit the ball was stopped and started two or three times at second base, not sure if I was decoying him. Just as I found the ball, he took off for third, and I threw him out at third. It was a weird play, and everybody in the dugout was going nuts. Amalfitano and I are good friends, and he shook his head and said, "Why are you doing this to me?" I said, "Joey, I was diving for the ball and trying to catch it. Things happen. What are you going to do? Sorry, but I got the guy out at third."

I played with several teams, but most people remember me as a Cub. WGN carried all of our games back then, so they know me as a Cub more than anything else. There's no comparison anywhere to the Cubs fans. Of the different places I played, Chicago is totally different. The Cubs fans are the Cubs fans. There is nothing else like them.

I'm very honored to have played for the Cubs, as well as major league baseball of any sort. Playing with the Cubs was just a great feeling, it really was.

Larry Biittner was traded to the Cubs on May 17, 1976, along with Steve Renko in exchange for Andre Thornton and proved to be a valuable outfielder, first baseman, and left-handed pinch-hitter for the team until 1979. Biittner is second on the Cubs' all-time list with 46 pinch-hits. His finest season came in 1977 with the Cubs when he hit .298 with 12 homers, 62 RBIs, and 28 doubles. In his lone pitching appearance against the Montreal Expos in 1977, Biittner gave up six runs in one and one-third innings, plus got a warning for throwing a pitch that went close to Del Unser's head. He was granted free agency after the 1980 season and spent two seasons with the Reds and one with the Rangers before retiring after the 1983 season.

MIKE KRUKOW

PITCHER

1976–1981

IGOT DRAFTED OUT OF HIGH SCHOOL in 1970 by the California Angels, and a buddy of mine was drafted by the Cubs. I thought to myself, *Why couldn't I have gotten drafted by somebody like the Cubs?* I was always a National League fan. I didn't sign then, but I went to college at Cal-Poly San Luis Obispo and was drafted by the Cubs. I was ecstatic. I was staying in the National League and was drafted by an old organization that had 100 years of history. I liked the idea of getting to a ballpark where Babe Ruth played. The history of the game meant something to me, and the Cubs' history was intriguing. It was my hope when I signed that the first big-league field I would ever step on would be Wrigley Field, and that's the way in happened in September 1976.

My first day here, I was out in left field running with Bruce Sutter and Bill Bonham. That was so great I don't think my feet even touched the ground the whole day. I ran out toward center and was walking back to the foul line when a guy in the bleachers yelled out, "Hey, number 40, what's your name, man?" I looked up at him and ignored him. I was kind of embarrassed. We ran down again and were walking back, and the same guy called, "Hey, 40, what's your name, man?" So I was getting embarrassed, and Bonham, who had been here six years, said, "Listen, kid, if he asks you that again, tell him to go buy a program." Now I was waiting for the guy. I was loaded with ammunition. I ran down and came back. I was looking up, and sure enough, the same guy shouted, "Hey, 40, what's your name, man?"

Right-hander Mike Krukow was drafted by the Cubs in 1973 and made his major league debut in 1976. He moved into the starting rotation in 1977 and remained there through 1981. Krukow returns to Wrigley Field each season as a member of the Giants broadcast team. *Photo courtesy of WGN-TV*

109

I said, "Go buy a program, Meat!" He said, "I did, and you're not in it!" Welcome to Wrigley Field.

There was a time here when we were searching for our identity. We had a lot of young pitchers, and our team wasn't made up of home-run hitters. We had to out-pitch and out-defend you. [Sports columnist] Bob Verdi called us the "Rush Street Offense": a lot of singles, but not much scoring.

Well, in '77 I came up here for my rookie year and, you know, I didn't know any better. I thought that was the way it was supposed to be. I couldn't wait to get to the ballpark. Charlie Grimm was one of our minor league instructors, and he always told me if I got to the big leagues to get there early and stay late so my time there would last longer. We did that in 1977 because we did not want to leave each day. I thought it was supposed to be every time you walked out on the field, you got a standing ovation. When I got up here, just the blanket of love they threw over you every day was overwhelming. It also carried out into the community. My wife and I were freshly married. We would go out into the malls and the restaurants, and we really thought we were related to all the fans in Chicago. It was unbelievable how they knew us; it was fantastic.

I think we could have kept it going if Sutter hadn't gotten hurt. It's so fragile going into the month of September, and we were very thin. I was disappointed. We ran out of gas. The day games kind of caught up, and I thought that was the determining factor in our ballclub. We just lost gas. I'll never forget it.

Nineteen seventy-nine had the 23–22 game. We used to come down Irving Park on the way to Wrigley. As soon as we came down Irving Park, we'd take a right, come down Clark, and check out the flags. That day, it was like howling Jack! *Wooooo*! I charted pitches that day. I had to go on the disabled list because I had carpal tunnel syndrome. It was bad: the chart was about four pages; between both teams, there were 50 hits; I went through three pens; and I had ink all over my uniform. It was unbelievable. The 50th hit was a home run that Mike Schmidt hit off Sutter in the tenth. In fact, it was 21–9 them in the fifth, and we got the bases loaded. Tug McGraw threw a 3–2 curveball, whoops, ball four. I turned to Bruce and said, "We're going to win this game." We all felt we were. I'll never forget that game.

We were conditioned in the minor leagues for pitching at Wrigley. Everywhere we played the wind blew out to left, and the home parks were all offensive ballparks. By the time you got there, you realized the wind blowing out could be your friend, but you had to learn how to pitch inside. You couldn't keep trying to shave the outside corner, or you'd get killed. You learned the wind in your face helped your breaking ball. Our lack of power as a team those years took us down a bit, when we needed three hits to score a run, but the power teams we faced could get that run with one swing. I would watch visiting teams come in and take batting practice, and there were teams playing Home Run Derby, dropping their shoulders to lift the ball. That's what you want to see if you're a pitcher. You want to see a guy change his swing for the ballpark. Learning how to deal with the elements was a big part of my education as a pitcher.

My first day in the big leagues I'll never, ever forget. The very first Opening Day was incredible. Little moments like when Bruce Sutter struck out three Montreal Expos on nine pitches. I'll never forget that. That was unbelievable. One year, we beat the Cardinals 15 out of 18, and that was awesome.

We could make more money here in the off-season than during the season with speaking engagements and the Cubs basketball team, so we hung with a bunch of guys. We shared each other's lives and felt like a family. I really think it's too bad that this generation can't have a Cubs basketball team, because those caravans were so much fun, to go into Indiana, Wisconsin, Iowa, and southern Illinois, the response we got was incredible. When I see the movie *Hoosiers*, I say, "Hey, I played in that gym!" The love those people had for the Cubs was so deep-rooted and sincere that you couldn't help but be touched by it. I thought that was a great way to rub elbows with your fan base. You can't do that anymore, because guys are making too much cash to expose themselves to injury. That was one of the most fun things we got to do here.

Bill Buckner and I became very good friends. He was the heart of that club. Buckner was an absolute champion, a winner. It was tough for him to play here in those years when they did the rebuild. He had an ankle that did not move. It was just locked. What he did before the game and after the game to even play was excruciating to watch. He was the heart of the Cubs. He was the darling of Chicago on some pretty bad teams. I'll tell you one thing: you can have champions on bad teams, and he certainly was one of them.

We went through the death of Mr. Wrigley and his wife, and that really set the organization back. I thought I was going to be here forever. I watched my friends leave, like Bruce Sutter and Rick Reuschel. One by one, everybody seemed to be taken out of the organization. We went to the ballpark and didn't expect to win, and what could be worse for an athlete? That's the way it was in 1981.

111

When I got traded in '82, Dallas Green had just come over to the Cubs and told me, "I've got good news and bad news. The bad news is we have to trade you, but the good news is you are going to a class organization in Philadelphia." It was hard for me to leave here.

These fans sign up for history, they sign up for the chance to do something people haven't done in a long time here, and they sign up to sit next to the fan they don't even know, but they've got worlds in common. It's a pretty neat family here that is the Cubs fans. I know I was blessed to be able to play here, and I think that everybody who comes through these doors and the home field clubhouse says the same thing: it's a unique area, it's a unique tradition. I was really disappointed to be traded from here. I always thought I was going to wind up staying here my whole career. I always felt that I wanted to be on the team that finally won it, because when that happens it's going to be like the Pope coming to Chicago, it's going to be unbelievable. All those guys on that team, they'll all be canonized that same day. Saint Theriot, it will be St. Everybody.

The one thing you play for is to be remembered. To play in a city like Chicago that remembers you is special. No matter what the dysfunctional gene the Cubs fan has, he only remembers the good days. That, my friend is magic. That's why players love to play here.

Right-hander Mike Krukow was taken by the Cubs in the eighth round of the 1973 amateur draft. He made his big-league debut in September 1976 and moved into the starting rotation the next year, going 8–14. He remained a starter for four seasons but after the 1981 season was traded to the Phillies for Keith Moreland and two other players. He pitched one year for the Phils, then played in San Francisco for seven more seasons, including a 20–9 All-Star campaign in 1986. For the past 18 seasons, Krukow has been a member of the Giants' broadcast team and is one of the most entertaining announcers in the game with his baseball acumen and unique sense of humor.

IVAN DeJESUS
SHORTSTOP
1977–1981

IT WAS NICE FOR ME when I was traded from the Dodgers to the Cubs. I remember when L.A. had called me up in September and I got to play at Wrigley Field. I loved it, and I loved the tradition. It was good. To come here as a visiting player was nice, but to be here as a home player was really nice. The feeling of this ballpark and all the fans was great. With cable and WGN, they had a chance to see the games back home in Puerto Rico. It was a nice feeling, my family had a chance to see me play, all of my friends back home.

I didn't know what to expect in my first year in 1977, but I was able to adjust right away. We had a lot of Latin players—Jerry Morales, Manny Trillo, Jose Cardenal—a bunch of guys who helped me a lot. I was really excited and didn't care about the cold weather. It was the best thing in my life at that time. I was happy and came out with a purpose to play hard every day.

All the day games hurt us a bit, I think. We lost one of our key players when Bruce Sutter got hurt. We were good all the way through August, but we ended up finishing fourth. It was a good year, but we needed a few more players. We had a few big comebacks that year. We beat Cincinnati 16–15, and I remember Rick Reuschel got on base and scored when Dave Rosello got a hit. I left that game early, and Dave replaced me. It was almost like a blowout, but we made a nice comeback. You never know what to expect at Wrigley Field when the wind is blowing out. That whole year was a good experience for me.

Cubs shortstop Ivan DeJesus tags out the Padres' Gene Richards on an attempted steal in the third inning of a game at Wrigley Field on July 13, 1978.

The next year we were close again. We had all the day games, and every time we came back from a trip after a night game, we had to play the next afternoon. The team was there, but we just couldn't put it together. We had some real great players.

I played in the game where we lost to Philadelphia 23–22. It was a long game. The Phillies scored early, but we came back and finally tied the game until Mike Schmidt hit a homer to beat us.

Herman Franks was a manager almost like Lou Piniella. He expected you to play the game the right way all the time and do things the way you were supposed to. He let you play, was good at building your confidence, and you could talk to him anytime. Herman couldn't speak Spanish like Lou, but he tried to help out the Latin players.

Playing shortstop at Wrigley, you really had to know the playing field. Also, I always knew my pitching staff. The grass was really high here, and it helped me as an infielder to have more range. I liked it because it helped my defense. Of course, as a hitter, you hit some hard balls that didn't get through. You got used to it, though, and the long grass definitely helped me.

The wind at Wrigley affected everything. As a hitter, you had to know how to hit with the wind blowing out and with the wind blowing in. If you were strictly a fly-ball hitter, you were in trouble here. You could help yourself by hitting the ball on the ground or concentrating on hitting line drives. As a fielder, you had to concentrate on every pop-up. You also had to worry about the sun. It was important to learn how to play those elements.

Manny Trillo and I were a good combination. We each knew how the other liked to play, and we were smooth in the field. A good combo needs to work well together, and we did. The first day in our first spring training, I told him where I wanted the ball, and he told me the same thing. We just clicked. From then on, we got along really well.

I hit for the cycle in 1980, and it was one of the highlights of my career. You never forget something like that, because it is really hard to do. It was just one of those days. I got up and came to the park, and it was fun. The best days were when you would play like a little kid and have fun. That day was so unexpected, but I did it, and it was great for everybody.

Nobody wants to leave when you have fun, you know lots of people, and you know the fans. Everything is a business, and the Cubs needed to make some moves. I was professional about it. It was sad, yes, but I knew I had to go through with it. Bowa and Sandberg came here, and I went to Philadelphia.

When I was hired on Lou's staff, they needed somebody to help deal with the Latin players, to help with the infielders, and help Larry teach the pitchers how to bunt. I do a little bit of everything, and it's nice to be back as a coach. I love Chicago, and this is one of my favorite cities. It was a great opportunity to come back here.

The fans have been great. People still remember me. The fans follow your career and remember you, no matter how long you've been away or how old you are. They remember what you did for the Cubs, and that's nice.

Shortstop Ivan DeJesus came to Chicago on January 11, 1977, when he was traded to the Cubs with Bill Buckner and Jeff Albert for Rick Monday and Mike Garman. He quickly earned the starting job in the Cubs' infield and scored 91 runs. In 1978 he led the National League with 104 runs scored. DeJesus stole 41 bases that year and 44 in 1980. In 1982 he was traded to the Phillies for Larry Bowa and Ryne Sandberg. DeJesus returned to the Cubs in 2006 and is now the team's first-base coach on Lou Piniella's staff.

BILL BUCKNER

FIRST BASEMAN

1977–1984

To be honest, it was pretty disappointing when I found out I had been traded to Chicago. I was playing with the Dodgers, and they were considered the top organization in baseball, while the Cubs at that time were known for finishing in last place, so it was a tough day when I found out about the trade to the Cubs. I soon found out it was a great place to play. When I came into town that winter before spring training, I'd walk down the street, and people would yell, "Welcome to Chicago!" That never happened to me in L.A. I found out the people here were great fans and great people.

My first year in 1977, nobody really knew what to expect because we had so many new players. We had Bobby Murcer, Steve Ontiveros, Ivan DeJesus, and me with a couple holdovers in Trillo, Cardenal, and Morales, but those guys came out of the chute and were having career years and meshing with the new guys. All of a sudden, we were seven games in first place, and the city was going nuts.

They had me at first base with the Cubs. I was a first baseman/outfielder growing up and had played first base for Tommy Lasorda in the minors, before they moved me to the outfield in Double A ball. I was an above-average fielder at both positions, but I had a below-average arm, and that didn't help me in the outfield.

Cubs first baseman Bill Buckner connects on a long drive against the Pirates at Three Rivers Stadium in Pittsburgh during a game in 1979. *Photo courtesy of Getty Images*

The Phillies were tough in our division, but we had a good foundation with some young arms in Sutter, Krukow, Reuschel, and Bill Bonham. There was some potential there. That's always the key, to have some pitching. I would say in '77 and '78 we overachieved a bit. Things seemed to be starting to change a little bit.

Then it got tough. Chicago's a great place because there is always optimism every year, but it's a team sport. You don't want to be out there playing for yourself. You don't want to be thinking, *I have to do this if I want to make this salary*, you want to be thinking about winning. That puts the focus where it should be and what sports are all about. We had a tough time there for a few years.

I expected a lot of myself, I expected a lot of my teammates, and if they didn't have that kind of attitude, I didn't like it. You know what? When you show up at spring training, you have your warriors, and then it's time to go out and win. It doesn't matter who's here, we can do it. You go fight it out, and by the end of July it's pretty hot at Wrigley Field, and if you're 25 games out, it's makes it tough. It's a unique city, and the fans will support you either way, but they still like to see that white *W* go up more often than not.

118

Nineteen eighty-four was tough, because I knew where they were coming from when they wanted to trade me, but it was more the way Dallas treated me. I needed a bit of respect. I knew I needed to move on, which is part of the game, but I had a no-trade contract, and he traded me without asking me first. That was a lack of respect, and even though there was no way I wasn't going to go, it got kind of ugly sitting around and wasting a few months there. It's part of the game, and I understood Dallas's situation, because everyone was trying to win, but it was the lack of respect that bothered me.

It was tough to get ready to play every day. People say, "You had a great career, you hit this, you won a batting title, you drove in 1,300 runs," and you know all that is good, but deep in my heart, I don't think anybody could have done what I did under the circumstances. My ankle was so bad, I don't think too many people could have walked on it, much less have played 162 games. That's the thing I am most proud of—what I was able to do under those conditions. I went to the park, and the first thing I'd do was stick my foot in an ice bucket for 30 minutes to get the blood going. Then I'd be in the whirlpool, get taped, put on the hot balm, put the sleeves over my legs with Capsolin on them underneath so my legs were sweating bullets, all just to get through the game. I loved to play. It didn't matter. It was worth it to be able to play, and I'd do it all again.

I didn't have a big stride at the plate. When I came up, there weren't many guys who struck out 100 times a season, except for maybe a few 30-home-run guys, and that was a lot of homers then. The game has changed, especially seeing guys strike out with a man on third and less than two outs. In my day, managers hated seeing that because it was all about getting that run in, even if you just hit a ground ball, but guys today don't make adjustments. They're bigger and faster athletes and put up real big numbers, but sometimes the big numbers don't help you win games as much as doing the small things. Being able to put the ball in play is one of those things. Guys may be better hitters and put up bigger numbers, but for what? My style was to hit line drives and put the ball in play.

I hated to strike out ever since I was in Little League. It may have hurt me at times, but I could always put the ball in play. If I had a borderline pitch a couple of inches off the plate, I tried to put that in play. If I was going to go back and change anything in my career, I might have struck out some more. Not intentionally, but I could have been a little bit more aggressive with two strikes in certain situations. Now, there's a time when you can't afford to strike out, like a runner at third with less than two outs and you have to put the ball in play. Instead of lunging at a pitch two inches off the plate to put it in play, maybe I could have been a bit more patient and hit for a bit more power. I just hated to strike out. I didn't want to deal with it. I probably had 10 hits in my career where I literally threw the bat at the ball with two strikes. I can remember a few times where I hit it on the bounce.

I never struck out three times in one game. I came close once when we were playing the Pirates. I had struck out the first two times up, and the next time up, I popped the ball up behind home plate. It was the only time in my life I ever hoped the catcher would get my pop-up.

I played in the 23–22 game in 1979, but I can't say it's my favorite because we lost. Keith Moreland told me later he was on the Phillies, and he was the only guy who didn't get into the game! I had four hits, a grand slam, and seven RBIs, and I wasn't even the best hitter on our team that day because Dave Kingman hit three home runs and had six RBIs. There was a group of games in 1977 when we were starting to build a lead, and the place was going absolutely nuts. That really turned me on to Chicago baseball.

119

When I won the batting title in 1980, I came on at the end of the season. I got hot, and some of the other guys slipped down. I really didn't come into the picture until there was about a week left in the season. All of a sudden, I jumped in front, and we had the last game of the year. I could have sat out, and there was no way I could have lost, but the only way I was going to lose was if I went 0-for-4. Joey Amalfitano was our manager, and he kind of wanted me to sit out. I decided to play because I thought if the shoe was on the other foot, I would want the leader to play. We were in Pittsburgh, and all I had to do was get one hit, but I went 0-for-4 and even tried to bunt for a hit. Meanwhile Keith Hernandez of the Cards got hits his first two times up, but then didn't get another one. I had to sweat it out a bit, but at least I didn't back into it. What was fun was to have your teammates and coaches pulling for you. They were pretty excited about it, which made me feel better.

I lived in a nice condo down on Belden in what used to be an old Lutheran church. They left the steeple part of it, which was about five or six stories high, and then they built around it. It was pretty interesting. It had the big arch windows in it and stained glass. It had great acoustics, and Mike Krukow would go up there and play his guitar. It was convenient, and some days I'd ride my bike to the ballpark. I think maybe it helped me out living there—I didn't have to go too far to pray for the wind to be blowing out! It was funny, because the first thing I would do in the morning is climb up to the top floor and see how the flags were blowing down at the ballpark. If the wind was blowing out, I was in a hurry to get to the park. If it was blowing in, I fiddled around and wasn't exactly racing to the park.

Wrigley Field always varied depending what time of year it was. Early in the year, it could be a tough place to hit if the wind was blowing in. In July and August with the wind blowing out, it was great to hit the ball in the air. But if they let the grass grow high, that slowed balls that might have gotten through. There were always a lot of variables about Wrigley that made it interesting and fun every day. The downer was when we weren't winning and school started, there was nobody in the stands. It was disappointing going out in the cold some days and playing in front a few thousand people.

There was a pitcher named Tom Bradley whom I owned. He had a good arm, but it seemed like he made bad pitches to me, and I didn't miss them. I also hit Doug Rau of the Dodgers—really, any of the Dodgers pitchers, maybe because I had been traded from there and wanted to take some vengeance on them. I wore them out.

It's awesome now. I'd love to have the opportunity to play there now with a full house every day and the team being very competitive. It would have been great to play 15 night games a year to help out when the travel was tough and you got back late from the road the night before like they can now.

When I get asked where my favorite place to play was, I always say Chicago. L.A. was a great place, and I got to play with a lot of great players in Boston, but overall, when you evaluate the whole experience, Chicago is right there at the top. It's a great place to play.

Bill Buckner came to the Cubs from the Dodgers along with Ivan DeJesus and Jeff Albert in exchange for Rick Monday and Mike Garman on January 11, 1977. "Billy Buck" immediately became a fan favorite at Wrigley Field for his competitiveness and was respected for his ability to play through pain. Buckner won the National League batting title in 1980 with a .324 average and was chosen for his only NL All-Star team the following season. He had his best season in 1982, when he hit .306 with 15 homers, 105 RBIs, and 15 stolen bases. Buckner never struck out more than 30 times in a season while in a Cubs uniform. On May 25, 1984, he was traded to the Boston Red Sox for Dennis Eckersley and Mike Brumley.

STEVE GOODMAN

SINGER/SONGWRITER/CUBS FAN
1948–1984

CUBS FANS KNOW THE MEANING of pain at an early age. We suffer through with them, with the White Sox, too. Being a Chicago sports fan teaches you all the humbling lessons you need to know.

I used to come out to Wrigley Field as a boy. I had a great-uncle, my grandmother's brother, who worked for the *Chicago American*, and he took me to the press gate and introduced me to a guy named Tates Johnson, the Andy Frain usher in charge of letting people in for free. From the time I was nine until the time I was 20, I used to come out to Wrigley 50 to 60 times a summer.

I'm not real sure that you can put your finger on it. You know they are going to field a team, you just never really know how. It's only depressing if you expect success like everybody else. If you like baseball and you love the town you were born in, then it's okay to be a fan.

I like the Cubs and the White Sox. I like the Chicago teams. They've managed to let us down as much as any other sports franchises. When I moved to Los Angeles, I wasn't able to give them up. I think I love baseball more than I love the Cubs, but the reason I love baseball is the Cubs. The Cubs are a team that need parents or something. They need someone to help them. Kids see that I think at an early age. There are all kinds of excuses— no lights, but the big excuse is no pitching.

Folk singer and composer Steve Goodman was a lifelong Cubs fan who penned the classic "City of New Orleans," as well as "A Dying Cub Fan's Last Request" and "Go Cubs Go," which is now played after every Cubs home victory.

123

Chicago is blessed. It has two of the three great ballparks—[Fenway] is the other one. These are playing fields from another era, from another time, and they still work.

It doesn't pay to boo. They'll be back to screw up some more tomorrow. There hasn't been a summer when I didn't get a Cubs game in. When they get to the West Coast, I see them out there, too. There's nothing like coming to Wrigley, even with the changes. They've changed some of the food, stuff like that. These things happen. They changed the net so when foul balls go behind the home plate now, thousands of people go, "Wooooooooooppp!" as the ball slides down the net. These are little things we have to adjust to.

There's something about how it feels to come out here in the afternoon and see these grown men do this for a living, actually play baseball. You remember it's a game.

The fan forgets sometimes baseball is a business to these guys. It's a game and it's a pastime to us. To the Chicago Tribune, it's a business. The Chicago Tribune hates to lose. Maybe they should go to their wallets and get some pitchers if they don't like to lose. I can see how they take it personally that they haven't won since 1945.

The Cubs are fugitives from the law of averages. It's bound to catch up with them sooner or later, and they are liable to win in spite of themselves. Maybe when the sun comes up in the west—I don't know when they are going to win.

This interview was done by Mike Leonard of NBC in 1983 and is used with his permission. Singer/songwriter Steve Goodman was a lifelong Cubs fan who immortalized his team in songs such as "A Dying Cub Fan's Last Request," "When the Cubs Go Marching In," and "Go Cubs Go." In the early '70s Goodman introduced a fellow musician to life in the bleachers, and Jimmy Buffett has been a huge Cubs fan ever since. Goodman wrote "Go Cubs Go" in March 1984 for WGN Radio, which used the song for promotion and the theme for their Cubs broadcasts. Later that summer several players, including Jody Davis, Gary Matthews, and Jay Johnstone went to a studio and added their voices to the song. Steve Goodman died of leukemia on September 20, 1984, just four days before his beloved Cubs snapped a 39-year postseason drought by clinching the National League East title. In 2007 Cubs management decided to begin playing Goodman's "Go Cubs Go" on the Wrigley Field sound system after each home win. The song immediately enjoyed a rebirth, and a new Cubs ritual was born.

The
EIGHTIES

LEE SMITH

PITCHER

1980–1987

IT WAS RANDY HUNDLEY who put me in the bullpen the first time when I was in the minors pitching for Midland. I was in the pen in Little Rock, Arkansas, screwing around and pretending to be Al Hrabosky. I was turning my back in the windup, the whole thing, and having a good time because it was my day to throw on the side. Randy said to me, "Lee, don't throw anymore. I'm going to use you tonight." I protested that I had a start in two days, but he insisted and told me not to throw anymore. That night, he brought me in and told me to throw everything sidearm. I said okay, and I think I struck out the side on 10 pitches. After that, he told me I was done starting.

I wasn't happy, because at that time, it was like a slap in the face to be sent to the bullpen. If a guy wasn't good enough to start, you put him in the bullpen to come in after the game was out of hand most of the time. I ended up doing it, and they started me in the pen the next year in spring training. Our first road trip that year was to Shreveport, and one of my teammates asked me why I was packing so many clothes for the trip. I told him, "You guys are going on a two-week road trip. I'm going on one for the rest of my days." When the team got to Shreveport, I got off the bus and went home.

I sat at home for three or four days, and the Cubbies sent Billy Williams to talk to me about being a relief pitcher. I can't tell you in print what Billy said to me, but in so many words, it was that I hadn't done a thing in my career yet and I should give being a reliever a chance. He told me to give it a

126

Cubs closer Lee Smith strikes out the Mets' Keith Hernandez with the winning run on base to save a 6–5 Cubs win on September 18, 1983, at Shea Stadium.

try and see if I liked it. I told him no way, that I was a starting pitcher. I idolized Fergie Jenkins, Jim Bibby, and Bob Gibson—all starting pitchers. Finally, I told Billy to go back and tell the Cubs if they doubled my salary, I'd come back. I never thought they'd do it, but they did, and afterward I wished I would have asked for triple! It wasn't really about the money. I just didn't want to go back and play baseball at that point.

I came back and went into the bullpen, where Randy used me all the time. The next year, I went to Triple A and got called up to the Cubs not long after that. The rest is history. I was a sidearmer when I first came up.

I got called up in September 1980, and they told me I wasn't going to pitch. Some of us had been promoted to see how things worked, et cetera. Well, I got there, and Doug Capilla and Willie Hernandez both got hurt. I was sitting down in the bullpen all by myself because everybody in the pen had already pitched. Whoever was pitching took a liner off the leg, and before I knew it, Herman Franks was out there signaling for a right-hander. I was looking around, wondering who he wanted, when it dawned on me that I was the only dude down there! I didn't even have my cleats on! I had to run into the clubhouse, change my shoes, and go back to the bullpen mound to take my warmup pitches. But the umpire told me I had to go right to the mound for my eight pitches. I was scared to death. Before I walked out there, a fan was yelling at me and looking in the media guide at a left-handed dude with glasses wearing No. 46, whose name was Dave Geisel, and he was confused because now I had on 46. He hollered, "Hey, 46! I thought you were left-handed, you bum!" That was my initiation to the big leagues. I got out of the inning, and I was thinking to myself, *Yeah! I pitched in the big leagues!* That's when Herman came over and told me, "Son, your day isn't over. We don't have any more players so you have to hit." Well, I was the leadoff hitter, and of course, I went up and punched out on three pitches. Talk about being thrown into the fire! I ended up pitching in 18 games in September that year.

Fergie Jenkins was a big help to me. He took me under his wing, and I was trying to get him to let me room with him, but I think he wanted some peace and quiet because I was always picking his brain about pitching. He taught me my slider grip and really became my pitching coach after Fred Martin died. I idolized him, and he was great to teach me the slider. To this day, I know hitters who swear at Fergie for helping me with that pitch. He taught me the curveball, as well, but they told me to only use two pitches in the pen, so I canned the curveball.

I was a basketball player and played all the time after games with our fans. I'd go to the courts on Foster Avenue and play basketball with some of those guys until 10:00 or 11:00 at night. The Cubs would have had a fit if they ever found that out. That was my love and a great way to release some of the tension. It was a great escape.

Yes, I liked the shadows at Wrigley. Oh, man, it was beautiful. I wish we could have played all our games at 3:05, but some of the games went too long, and they had to pick them up the next day, I guess. The main reason [we played those 3:05 games] is when we got in late coming from the West Coast. I don't know how the guys who played every day did it. It was crazy.

I did take my time getting to the mound. I had an agreement with the grounds crew—they got time and a half after 4:30, so that's where my slow walk started. It was for my buddies.

The stories about my naps are mostly true. There was nothing better than waking up with a three-run lead. It was refreshing! If nobody saw me in the dugout, they said, "Smitty's asleep." But you don't last 18 years in the big leagues sleeping. I'd watch the umpires, and occasionally I'd take a nap, but the clubhouse now is so plush, I'd never wake up. I'd have to hire a guy to wake me up.

The '84 team was amazing because it wasn't only on the field. Off the field all the guys stuck together like a family. You never saw one guy go out by himself. It was always at least two or three guys together. We'd always be talking about the next series and things like that. The guy who taught me so much about winning was Gary Matthews. I used to listen to him all the time. I said, "We need to put together an eight- or 10-game winning streak." And he said, "No, that's not how you win. Look, you can win 10 in a row, then drop six or eight, and you're back where you started. What you have to do is win series." That hit home with me and made a lot of sense. Win two of three, three of four, sweep the bad teams, and over a six-month period good things will happen. That really struck me, and he gave me a lot of advice that sticks with me to this day.

We had a great bench on that team with Thad Bosley and Tom Veryzer, whom I never heard anything of again. They all had good seasons but never get recognized because we had that great starting lineup. To me, Richie Hebner was one of the key guys, because he played a little third base, some at first, and he could pinch-hit. Those guys really gave our regulars key days off so they could stay fresh.

There were so many great moments that year. We were playing Cincinnati, and a young kid named Barry Larkin came up for them. I was feeling pretty good about myself, and he was a young guy, so I thought I'd see what he could hit and started him off with a slider. He hit a bullet right back up the middle and nailed me in the ribs. I caught the ball wedged against my side and didn't want to let him know it hurt, so I let it fall and watched him run to first base before I threw him out. I'm sure he thought I was crazy because I was staring at him. I had to have about five cortisone shots after that, and it really stopped me from being able to throw my breaking ball.

I wasn't going to admit I was hurt. I was a young player, so I wanted to make sure I stayed up. There is no way I was going to let that '84 team down. I'd go to Sandberg's room, and he would have a swollen ankle. There were lots of guys playing in the M*A*S*H unit, but we stuck together.

Ryno really impressed me, because he had this air cast he would take off and he kept going out there every single day. That showed me a lot. I got to

129

play with Cal Ripken Jr. later on in my career, and I'd put Ryno in the same class with Cal.

At the end of the year, I was in bandages from my armpits to my ankles, but I had to go out there. That was my chance, and I might never get back there again. You can't say I can't play or pitch. That made me tough. If the manager asked me if I could go, I would always say yes because it might be my best day.

I don't make excuses because a pretty good guy in [Steve] Garvey got me with the home run in San Diego. I'm pretty sure I'm not the only guy he got. I felt that I gave it my best. I can lay my head on the pillow at night and know I gave it my all. He just got the best of me that day.

We were playing the St. Louis Cardinals once. I was protecting a two-run lead, and Jack Clark was the first hitter. Jody Davis was my catcher and came out to give me some pitching tips. He told me to go right after him, and I thought it was a good idea because I was feeling good that day. He went back and gave the sign for the fastball, and I threw. Jack must have been standing between us when we were talking because he hit a bullet into the family section for a home run that stuck in the fence out there. There were three kids trying to pry that ball out of the fence! After Jody got the new ball, he wanted to come out and talk again, but I said, "Stay the hell away from me. I don't tell you how to catch. Stay away from me forever!" So I always said every time Jody Davis called a pitch and they hit it out, it was his fault. But when I got 'em, the credit went to me.

When they traded me after 1987, it didn't bother me, because I didn't think we were trying to win. I just didn't feel at the time the team had an idea of winning. They had a profit made before the season even started because everyone loved the Cubs and wanted to come see Wrigley Field. It didn't bother me at that time, but now when I think back on it, if we had stayed together a little longer, something could have come of it.

If there was a guy I knew I could get, it was John Kruk. I faced him a bunch of times, and I don't think he got a hit off me. He hit some good balls, but most of the time I made good pitches, and he'd make outs, either way. Howard Johnson was another guy I did well against. One time I was working on my splitter, and we were way ahead, so I thought I'd go out and throw it in the game. HoJo was up and got a dribbler up the middle for a hit. After the game, he sent the ball over to the clubhouse to get my autograph.

I thought maybe it was his 2,000th hit, but he told me it was the first hit he ever got off me.

The guy that really hit me wasn't much of a player, but his name was Mike Schmidt! I'll never forget going to the Vet in Philly with [Rick] Sutcliffe, and we were bopping in there and happened to see our names on the wall. We were psyched until we saw it was a list of guys Schmidt had hit the most home runs off. Sut was near the top at about eight, and I wasn't far behind with five. I told Sut that wasn't the wall we wanted to be on, a Wall of Shame. Man, he pounded all the Cubs in his day.

The fans here and in Boston are very much alike. When I was with the Red Sox, they were very hungry for a championship, too. If the Cubs ever win a World Series, I don't even want to be close to the state. It will be crazy. The Red Sox fans were like that. The Cubs-Cardinals rivalry is great, but the fans downstate don't know how to take me sometimes since I pitched with both teams. I can walk in those places that have a Cubs jersey on one side and a Cardinals one on the other, no problem.

My teammates and I are still family. We did more than play together, we started our day with breakfast together and went from there. There's something amazing about being so close as teammates that guys know what you are going to do before you do it. [Larry] Bowa, Bobby D, Ryno, they all knew what I was going to throw before I threw it. We were together and understood each other.

To be associated with the city of Chicago is wonderful. I still see my drinking buddies on the grounds crew, try to see the guys at the fire station, and as many of these great Cubs fans as I can. I went on a trip one time to Alaska and was amazed how many Cubs fans were up there. It's something.

Lee Arthur Smith was drafted by the Cubs in the second round of the 1975 amateur draft and went on to become the Cubs' all-time leader with 180 saves. From 1983 to 1987, Smith had 29, 33, 33, 31, and 36 saves as the Cubs' closer. He was traded to the Red Sox after the 1987 season for Calvin Schiraldi and Al Nipper. He pitched until 1997 with the Red Sox, Cardinals, Yankees, Orioles, Angels, Reds, and Expos. At the time he retired, Smith held the major league record with 478 saves (since broken by Trevor Hoffman).

LEON DURHAM

FIRST BASEMAN/OUTFIELDER

1981–1988

WHEN THE CARDINALS TRADED ME to the Cubs in 1980, I looked at it as a chance to be an everyday ballplayer. After leaving a first-class organization in St. Louis and coming over to Chicago, it was the chance to play and get to know some of the guys I had been playing against. Leaving St. Louis was a tremendous opportunity.

I really didn't feel any pressure. I had been playing baseball all my life, and it was something I loved to do. Going about it with fear wasn't me, because that type of situation didn't faze me at all. I was doing something that I loved to do since I was a child, and being able to make a living doing it was all a pleasure.

The Cubs weren't the Cubs we know now, but I was with a major league team, even if there were only 8,000–9,000 people there every day. The team was finishing way below .500 every year, but I looked at it as a chance to put them back on the market. I wanted to come in, along with a lot of other ballplayers, put some more names in the lineup, and find some guys who wanted to play the game. There were all day games, and you just had to alter your schedule to get used to that. When Dallas Green got here, he did a great job of bringing in players who wanted to play hard every day.

I wanted to be a first baseman, but in order to stay in the major leagues, I had to be flexible as far as being able to play more than one position. I did some center field and also played games in right and left. When you have

132

Keith Hernandez at first base in St. Louis and Bill Buckner at first in Chicago—plus I was left-handed, so I wasn't go to play anywhere else in the infield—I had to head out to the pasture. It was either that or go back to the minor leagues. I was just glad I had some good instructors to work with me, and that gave me the chance to stay in the major leagues. Basically, I learned how to play the outfield while I was in the majors. Gene Clines and Billy Williams helped me, and when I got to the majors, Steve Henderson was an outfielder who took me under his wing and showed me the ropes of what to do. Jerry Morales and Scot Thompson were outfielders I watched playing the wind and the sun. Somehow I got through it all and even made the All-Star team my second season.

I was introduced to the ivy and the brick wall several times, so it was a learning experience, and I loved the Friendly Confines. If I had my choice, right field was where I wanted to go, even though it was a sun field. Out of the three positions out there, I preferred to play in right.

I made two All-Star teams in '82 and '83, and it was a dream to see guys like Johnny Bench and Pete Rose, guys I grew up watching. Some of our guys were there, and it was a great time. It was an honor to feel like you were one of the best at that time, and that experience will always be with me. I introduced myself to some of the guys in the American League, because we didn't play them except for a few times in spring training. In the '83 game Fred Lynn hit the only grand slam in All-Star history, and I was proud to be on the field for that. I had my family at Comiskey Park, and that was outstanding.

In 1984 I tried contact lenses. I had soft lenses, and they were fine, but my field of vision just wasn't right and upset me a little bit. I went to the hard lenses, and I could see, but they were uncomfortable. I went back to my glasses, where I was comfortable. I did hit a few home runs with the contacts in, but I was better with my glasses, and I still wear them.

I don't really recall the bad spring-training start everybody talks about that year. We got off to slow start, but we knew we had some good ballplayers on that team. Things started to come together right away in the regular season, and that's why you can't count too much on spring training. You're down there to prepare for the upcoming season and get ready. Spring training is for the young guys who are trying to open the eyes of the major league coaches and front office people to say, "If something happens, I'll be down here in Iowa, so come and get me. I'm ready for the major leagues." We got off to a good start and rolled. It was an unbelievable year for me, of all the years I

133

Cubs first baseman Leon "Bull" Durham hits a grand slam against the St. Louis Cardinals in the third inning of a game at Wrigley Field on August 11, 1983.

played, to have a year like that in baseball. I had some good minor league years as a coach with our teams winning, but in the majors, that was by far the best year.

One play I still talk about with Lee Smith happened in St. Louis in June. Lee was the hitter, and Joaquin Andujar was on the mound using a windup because we had the bases loaded. He was using a couple of different deliveries to mess up the hitters where he would swing his arm around a few times and then deliver the ball. Zimmer was coaching third, and I turned to him and said, "Hey, I can take this." He told me to go ahead and gave the sign. I took off from third and was running down the line hollering, "Smitty, don't swing!" I slid in, lost my glasses and everything, but I was safe. Smitty looked down and said, "Man, what are you doing?" I told him, "I knew you were up and weren't going to make contact, so I had to find a way to get this run in for us." That was the only time I ever stole home, and it was a great moment.

Every day it was an honor to walk into the locker room and see my jersey hanging up with my name facing me as I came in. That was always memorable for me to walk into a major league locker room every day, see that, and know that this was my job. To have guys like Bobby Dernier, Jody Davis, Keith Moreland, Gary Matthews, Ryne Sandberg, and everyone as your workmates was great. We all got along well, no matter what your race or nationality. You could have been purple, and that would have been fine. We just got along like a family.

One day I told Rick Sutcliffe that I wasn't swinging the bat very well and wasn't feeling it. He was pitching that day, and the wind was blowing in about 500 miles an hour. I said there's no chance and that we'd have one of those short, quick games. The grass was high, and we were playing Houston, so it looked to be a low-scoring game. My first time up, I hit a long home run to straightaway center field against the wind. I came back in the dugout, and Sut said, "I thought you didn't have it." Then he turned around and sang the Tina Turner song to me, "What's Love Got to Do With It?" I laughed and said that love has nothing to do with it, I just got my confidence back. Sut was the kind of guy you could talk to about anything, from country-western music to pitching or hitting, and he always had some answers for you. He's still the same.

I can't sing and never could. They put together a foundation for charity, and Keith Moreland had somebody write "Men in Blue" for us. A bunch of us went to a studio and recorded it. It worked out great, and they raised a lot of money with that song. Matthews, Davis, none of us could sing, but we were representing the Cubs, and it was special. We took pride in everything we did, from when we took the field to things like this, we always took pride. I think that's one of the reasons we stay together to this day.

When we clinched in Pittsburgh, we had a nice time in that stadium. I wished it could have happened in Chicago. There wasn't much of a crowd there, but the front office people came, and some of our wives were there. I remember pouring champagne on Dallas Green's wife, but I asked her first if I could do it! That was a funny moment that night. It was a great moment for us, because we had been waiting for it all season. Everything about that year was outstanding.

Then the Padres series rolled around, and it was best-of-five. Now they play seven games. Baseball is a game, and we enjoyed it. Whatever happens, happens, and as long as you give 100 percent while you're doing it, that's what counts. You don't know if you are going to strike out four times, if you will make an error, if you will get drilled, you don't know. As long as you feel like you give it all, that on a ground ball back to the pitcher you bust your behind down the line, that's what you have to do, win or lose. Then you can accept the consequences while the game is going on and afterward, as long as you give everything. I can look at myself in the mirror and walk with my head proud, because there is no shame. We did our best out there, and you don't ever know which way the ball will go, in the park or out of the park, you don't know. All that matters is we gave our best.

The Gatorade thing [in Game 5 of 1984 NLCS against the Padres] is just something that happened. Whoever thought my glove would be right there when the Gatorade got knocked over? We were at the major league level, so I had a couple of backups. In the minor leagues, we only had one pair of shoes, one glove, one batting glove. I had someone run into the clubhouse and get my backup glove, which was a glove I used until the game started, then I would go to my regular glove. I had a feel for both gloves, but I couldn't take a wet glove out there.

Injuries hurt us after that, starting in spring training the next year. It was hard to get back on track again, and the next thing you know, that team broke up as a unit. That '84 team, I really thought we could win or be in it for at least three or four years. We were a young ballclub that jelled, but couldn't do it again and stay together. Injuries came in, and it destroyed what we were trying to carry on for a few years.

When I was traded in 1988, I was going home to Cincinnati. That was fine. It was hard to leave, but at the same time, when you get the chance to go home and play for the team you grew up watching, I thought that was going to be a treat for me. It worked out, and it didn't work out. At the time, the Reds were struggling. I got there and was trying to do too much for a team that was known for winning. It was the old Big Red Machine. I knew all along I couldn't carry a team and wasn't the guy who was going to do it by myself. It's not tennis or golf. It just didn't work out, but I had a chance to play in my hometown in front of my mom and kids. That worked out well.

The '84 team was fun, and right to this day it's the same. I can see Jody or Moreland or the Sarge [Matthews] and pick right up. Ryne Sandberg was the big practical-joke guy. He was the guy who would do things, and you'd think, *Was that Ryno doing this?* He got comfortable the longer he stayed in the league. We cared about one another—we ate together, worked together, and were a unit. Even our families did things together off the field. After the game, we would go to each other's houses. That team was special, and most of us still stay in touch to this day.

We all meet up at Randy Hundley's fantasy camp each year. To be together for seven days is great. We just sit back and talk about the days, and there's not enough time for that. We don't even repeat ourselves! There's something new that comes up all the time when we talk about our careers. Everything back then was all good for us. That's why we're together to this day, always loving one another.

Coming from St. Louis and then going to the Cubs was going from bleeding red to bleeding blue. I had the honor of playing for both teams. Whitey Herzog was a great manager to me. My time in Chicago was unbelievable and hard to put into words. It's an honor to come to the Cubs Convention every year and see some of the old Bleacher Bums and my teammates. People come up to you with things like, "I grew up watching you and loved you so much we named our dog after you." You take that the right way, and they tell you that you were one of their special Cubs. That is special.

Leon "Bull" Durham was acquired by the Cubs along with Ken Reitz and Tye Waller for Bruce Sutter after the 1980 season. He blossomed in 1982, when he hit 22 homers, drove in 90 runs, and hit .312. He was selected as a National League All-Star that year and followed up by being named to the 1983 team. Durham hit 23 homers and drove in 96 runs for the 1984 Cubs. He followed with 21, 20, and 27 home-run seasons, but after getting off to a slow start in 1988, he was traded to Cincinnati on May 19 for Pat Perry and cash. Durham is currently the hitting coach for the Toledo Mud Hens, Triple A affiliate of the Detroit Tigers.

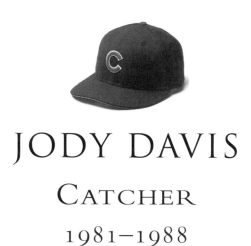

JODY DAVIS
CATCHER
1981–1988

WHEN THE CUBS DRAFTED ME from the Cardinals, it was exciting to me because I knew I was going to get a chance to play. I was in Triple A with the Cardinals, and they had Ted Simmons, Steve Swisher, Terry Kennedy, and then signed Darrell Porter as a free agent. I knew I was the odd man out or the low man on the totem pole. It was exciting to know I was going to get a shot at playing in the big leagues. During my minor league career, we watched the Cubs every afternoon on WGN, so coming here was a blast for me.

I give Johnny Oates all the credit in the world as our catching instructor. In the minor leagues, I was always the guy hitting fourth and pretty much played because of my bat. I was just learning how to catch in the minor leagues, because I had never caught before I signed. It pretty much took me five years to learn how to catch, and when I got here Johnny taught me a lot.

Nineteen eighty-one was my rookie year, and toward the end of the year, I had established myself as the starting catcher. In 1982 Keith Moreland came over from Philly with Dallas Green and got the starting job. Through it all, we were both just country boys who liked to hunt and fish, and that's where we hit it off. We knew we were fighting for the same job, but Keith realized sooner or later they were going to keep his bat in the lineup somewhere and get me in there defensively to catch. He's the one who really kept telling me

Cubs catcher Jody Davis is about to connect on a solo home run in the second inning of Game 5 of the NLCS against the San Diego Padres on October 7, 1984.

to keep my head up and keep battling, because they would move things around. He was right, and they did.

They used to chant "Jo-dee." It still gives me goosebumps. I think it started in '83 when the Cardinals were here. They were always chanting, "Oz-zie, Oz-zie," so I think the Cubs fans started with "Jo-dee, Jo-dee" because of that. Any time I heard it, it really meant a lot. My friends in Georgia would call up and laugh if Harry started singing when I came to the plate. That was a lot of fun.

It had been so long since the Cubs had been in the playoffs, and all of a sudden that team seemed to come out of nowhere. You could see early that Dallas was building a team that was competitive. The guys were winners everywhere they played. To me it kind of set the table for what is still going on today. I know 1981, '82, '83, there were big weekends where Wrigley Field sold out, but ever since the '84 season, it's been hard to get a ticket. It's almost like that team kind of made a new generation believe that we could win it. I take pride in being part of that.

140

I don't think we won but six games in spring training. We knew we were getting better. You could see Ryno growing and getting better, but we didn't have a leadoff guy, and we didn't have anybody at that point to take charge. The trade [that brought Bob Dernier and Gary Matthews over from the Phillies] was huge, because Bobby D came over, and now we had a legitimate leadoff guy and stolen-base threat to hit in front of Ryno. When Sarge walked in that clubhouse after that trade, it was almost like throwing the switch of confidence for everybody. All of a sudden, Sarge wasn't going to take any crap from anybody. We had somebody to lead us, and that was huge. It's hard to explain how a couple of guys can turn the whole clubhouse attitude around, but that's what Sarge and Bobby D did. We got Sutcliffe a couple months later, and all the pieces of the puzzle seemed to fit. We started to believe we could play with anybody—confidence is a powerful thing.

I had a big weekend when St. Louis was in town and Ryno hit the homers off Bruce Sutter. It seemed that I always hit well against the Cardinals, whether it was because I was there before or just the tremendous rivalry between the teams. I don't know what it was, but you knew it was going to be a sellout no matter which ballpark you were in. There was always tremendous excitement.

The highlight of my career was the grand slam against the Mets at Wrigley in September. All the talk leading up to that series was that the Mets had to sweep us to get back in the race. The first game of the series was on Friday, and to go out and hit a grand slam against them to guarantee they wouldn't get that sweep was great. We won the series and really put the nail in the coffin. I have that video at home, and every time I see it, I still get chills. It's a great moment.

We clinched in Pittsburgh. Sutcliffe still gives me heck about the last out. I went out to the mound with two outs—we felt like we had the game and were going to win it, so I told him I wanted to catch a strike three to end it. He was riding me, "Hey, don't be afraid to give me a little more pressure. Win this game, pitch a complete game, and now you want me to strike the last guy out too so you can hold the ball!" But that's what happened—he struck out Joe Orsulak to end it. I still have the ball, and I can't believe I got away with it as easily as I did. Most of the time if a guy came in and got a save, I always gave the pitcher the ball. But that last-out ball went in my glove and stayed there.

I still look back at the Padres series, and at the time, yes, it really hurt, especially after winning those first two games. We thought we were going to the World Series. San Diego played a little bit better. They got the big hit when they needed it and got the breaks. That ball to Ryno took a bad hop, and things just happened, but we were all young and were all coming back. We thought we'd get it next year, but we had so many injuries that it didn't happen. In 1985 we thought we would pick it up and do it again. The pitchers got hurt, and I ended up in the hospital in June.

141

The day games did take a toll, but at the time, I didn't care. When I woke up in the morning, I wanted to play because I thought our best chance to win was if I played. Looking back, I could have had a longer career with more rest, but my mentality was that I wanted to go play, and that's just the way it worked out.

I was in two All-Star Games, and it was a lot of fun. My first one was at the ballpark I hated the most—Candlestick Park in 1984. I couldn't stand to play in that ballpark, but I made the All-Star team, and there we were going to Candlestick. It was a blast being around the guys you competed against and being able to joke around with them in the locker room.

It was tough to leave the Cubs. I still felt like I had some good years left and wanted to be one of those guys who played his whole career with one team. It didn't work out, because they had Damon Berryhill, who had been a No. 1 pick. He worked his way up and deserved his chance. They felt like it was time. I didn't have a problem with that, but I didn't want to leave the greatest baseball fans in the world.

Now when my teammates sit around and have a cocktail, we like to take credit for all those sellouts they have now. We were there when it turned around. Nineteen eighty-four was a magical year with that bunch. Our goal was to win each game, and we ended up winning the division and coming up one game short of the World Series. The closeness of that bunch was magical.

I want every bit as much now as I did back then for this organization to win it. It's good to be a part of it, working with the young players and getting them to Chicago so they can make a difference. We were close and wanted to win for the Cubs and now, we still have that goal in our hearts of being a part of a championship in Chicago.

The fans make this organization. It's hard to describe how you can take the oldest ballpark in the National League, no parking, play mostly day games, and still sell out every day with a team that hasn't won a World Series in more than 100 years. It's the hunger of those fans that keeps pushing us all.

In 1980 the Cubs selected Jody Davis from the Cardinals in the Rule 5 draft. After splitting time behind the plate in 1981, he emerged as the team's everyday catcher in 1982 and became an offensive force with 24 homers and 84 RBIs in 1983. He hit 19 homers and drove in 94 runs in 1984 and was named to the NL All-Star team that year. In 1986 Davis returned to the All-Star Game and won a Gold Glove that year, as well. Davis was a workhorse behind the plate—from 1983 to 1986 he appeared in 151, 150, 148, and 142 games. He was traded to the Atlanta Braves at the end of the 1988 season. Davis rejoined the Cubs in 2006 and has served as a minor league manager and catching coordinator.

LARRY BOWA

SHORTSTOP
1982–1985

I PLAYED IN THE 23–22 GAME here for the Phillies. The thing I remember is that everybody was hitting home runs, but I got five hits that day! It was a big game for me. I remember going out that day, and the wind was howling. It was howling. Any time you go to Wrigley Field, the first thing you do is look up at the flags. If it's blowing in, it's gonna be real quick—3–2, 2–1—but if it's blowing out, you've got a chance of missing your dinner reservations downtown. I remember the flag was at attention just blowing out, and I said, "This could be a long game." Not only was it long, it was high-scoring. That's what makes that park so unique. You can go in there one day, and it will be a 2–1 game, and the next day you're playing the same team, and it's 13–12 or 22–21. It's a special ballpark. The only thing I've got to say is, the players in the American League who didn't get to play in Wrigley didn't know what they were missing.

I was excited to be traded to the Cubs because I knew what Dallas Green was all about, and Chicago was always a nice place to come and play. It's a great, clean city with great fans. When I played with the Phillies, we had a lot of people come out just to root against us. I thought it would be a good challenge, because the Cubs hadn't had that many winning seasons.

We were used to winning in Philly, and it was an attitude. They always had some talent here, but it's all about attitude. Dallas came here and didn't gradually change it, he just said, "Okay, this is the way we're going to do it,

Cubs shortstop Larry Bowa gets ready to apply the tag to the Pittsburgh Pirates' Omar Moreno, foiling his steal attempt during the fourth inning of a game at Wrigley Field on April 25, 1982.

and if you don't like it, get out." He had a plan and he executed it. From '84 on, the way the city and fans have supported the Cubs has been unbelievable.

When I got traded with Ryne Sandberg, they weren't sure where he was going to play. Once it was decided he was going to play second, I made it a point to be at spring training early. I called him and told him I was going to Arizona early and wanted him to come out and work with me every day. We talked a lot about work ethic and the need to do the same thing every day whether you were a veteran or a rookie, an All-Star or a bench player. Get into a routine and do it every day. Take your ground balls and trust yourself on your work ethic. Ryno grabbed onto that from day one, and from what I understand, he passed it along to the kids who came up when he was a veteran. I don't think anybody thought he would be a Hall of Fame player at first, but he had a great attitude.

People don't know that he was a real instigator in the clubhouse. He'd do something, then walk away, and if you looked at him, you could tell he was smiling. They will never forget a guy like Ryne Sandberg here. I got to teach him some things about being a big-league ballplayer, but the one thing he never learned was how to pick up a cab fare! No matter where we were, he'd always jump out of the cab, and I still kid him about it whenever I see him.

I loved playing here and loved day games. We didn't have the lights when I was here, and people told me I'd find a big change when we came back from the West Coast and had to play a day game. It did wear on you a little bit, but I thought it was great to play here because it was like a regular job. You could get home to your family and barbecue at night. I liked the day games, then hitting the road for night games. For me, it was a great change. I loved playing and ending my career here.

In 1984 we had a lot of come-from-behind wins. When Ryno had the Sutter game, from that point on, we had a mentally tough team, and you have to have that to win a division. There are peaks and valleys, and you have to be able to overcome the down days. We had enough veterans on that team like Ron Cey, Gary Matthews, and myself, and then a mix of the younger guys. We believed in ourselves and started playing well. It was a great feeling to come out here on a Wednesday afternoon and see the place filled up. There was no questions the fans motivated us to the nth degree. If you come out here, you'd better have your game on, because they'll let you know if you're playing well or if you're playing badly.

We had guys like Dernier and myself who could do the little things and steal a base, but then we also had the thumpers in the middle. It was a team that had versatility. We could win 2–1 or 11–10 if we had to. With Sutcliffe, you knew that every fifth day, we had a great chance to win, even if we only score one run. We could catch the ball, had great pitching, and were never a one-dimensional team.

In 1984, whenever you went out to dinner, you never had to pay a thing, because people were always picking up the tab. To see the city come together and watch the bleachers fill up every day was something that I'll never forget. The city was talking about the Cubs nonstop. When we clinched in Pittsburgh, I remember looking over at Ryno before the game and saying, "This is what we play for. This is why we play the game." In the ninth we had two outs, and he said, "This is it. This is it." The biggest part of that celebration to me was being able to see the celebration in Chicago on the Pittsburgh scoreboard, and that was a scene I'll never forget.

The last home game that year, we went back on the field. Jim Frey and Dallas thought that it would be a great tribute to the fans, to let them know

145

how much we appreciated them, to walk around the ballpark. It was a special moment. There's not a lot of times you get to mingle with the fans; spring training you do, but during the season it's tough. That special moment stands out because it was our way of saying thank you, and they really appreciated that. They were going crazy. Everybody was walking around, and there were standing ovations. Nobody wanted to go home, they wanted to enjoy the moment. Those are moments, as a baseball player, when you're in it a long time—and I've been in a major league uniform since 1970—that always stick with you. When you're going through bad times, you sit down and reflect a little bit and say, "You know what? There were some good times," and those are the moments you look back on.

I was able to be part of the World Series team in Philadelphia in 1980 and ride in that parade. I wish they could have had one here. Winning the first two games against San Diego and then coming up short hurt. I really believe we were the best team in baseball that year, but you have to win it on the field, and we didn't do it.

It was tough not winning the next year. Once you've had that taste of it, and it's unfinished business, it was tough. We had so many injuries, but baseball is all about being able to overcome that. Nineteen eighty-four really jump-started Chicago into being a big-time baseball city. It's a great satisfaction to see what we started. These people don't forget. When I come in here, I know they want to see the Cubs win, and I might get a boo when I go out there, but they also remember. I hear thank-yous for 1984 all the time. You're playing in front of avid fans who live and die with their team.

146

After 12 years in Philadelphia, shortstop Larry Bowa was traded to the Cubs along with Ryne Sandberg for Ivan DeJesus on January 27, 1982. Bowa immediately supplied the team with a steady presence in the field and veteran leadership in the locker room, while mentoring his infield partner, Sandberg. Bowa hit .246, .267, and .223 in his three full years with the Cubs, but made his mark with defense and an ability to bunt and move runners along from the eighth spot in the lineup. He was released by the Cubs on August 13, 1985. Bowa managed the Padres and the Phillies and was honored as National League Manager of the Year while with Philadelphia in 2001. He has also held a variety of coaching jobs and currently is the third-base coach for the Los Angeles Dodgers.

KEITH MORELAND
RIGHT FIELDER/
THIRD BASEMAN/CATCHER
1982–1987

To BE HONEST, when I was traded to the Cubs, I was quite disappointed. With the Phillies, I had been in three playoffs and won a World Series. I felt like I had earned a job as an everyday player in Philadelphia, and then I got traded. After going back and looking at it, I wouldn't change a thing. A lot of people say that, but I really mean it. To be a part of the transition was great.

When I first came to Chicago, there were 38,000 people in the stands for Opening Day 1982. It had snowed the night before, and they were shoveling snow off everywhere. The next day was an off-day, and when we played the following afternoon, there were 1,500 people in the stands. To be a part of the transition that made Cubs tickets some of the toughest tickets to get in the world is something I will cherish for the rest of my life. We were a group of guys Dallas Green brought in from a lot of different directions, and you see what it has become now. It was quite a transition. Just ask the players who came before, and they will tell you there were a lot of empty seats at Wrigley. It's not that way anymore.

Not having a regular position might have cost me a few All-Star Games, but I didn't care. I came to the ballpark every day of my career with what was instilled in me when I was young—I was there to win. I just wanted to win games. I'd have done anything they asked me to do. It might have cost me some individual honors. There were five or six years in a row where I was playing a different position than where I was listed on the All-Star ballot. It didn't matter. My job was to come to the ballpark, swing the bat, drive in runs, and win.

When I first came to Chicago, we didn't have a lot of fans, and I thought that was unfair, because Wrigley Field plays so different every day. With the wind factor and other things, it played so different that I thought it was going to be a big disadvantage. I came to find out after being here a few years that it was a big advantage because opponents would come in here and have no clue how the wind was going to play. It's still the strangest ballpark in the world, and things still happen today. For example, when there is a southerly breeze blowing out and a fly ball is hit down the right-field line, it will look like it's going to end up 50 rows in the stands, but that ball is going to come back into play. As a right fielder or first baseman, you knew that and would see opponents panic when it came back into play and they didn't make the play. As the home team, you knew it was a huge advantage, knowing things like that. The ballpark became a much bigger advantage to us than I would have ever thought when I first got here.

I had a pretty good year in 1983, and then we made a lot of good trades. I was being platooned and not playing every day. I didn't understand that. I had finished something like fifth in the league in hitting the year before and then wasn't playing. I was upset at that point and thought my Chicago career was going to end quickly. Instead it went another direction when they made a trade with Cleveland and brought Rick Sutcliffe in, and I then got on the field every day.

The month of August in 1984 was a great memory for me. I was the National League Player of the Month. We came to the ballpark every day and expected to win. I don't think any of us, especially the fans in Chicago had ever been part of that experience. You always hoped that the Cubs could win, but nobody ever believed they would. In 1984 I think everybody knew we were going to win when they came to the ballpark every day.

As for games that stood out that year, nobody will ever forget the Sandberg game. He hit those two home runs off Bruce Sutter, and you can't forget that. We had the big series with the Mets at Wrigley in early August. I wasn't an older guy at that point, but I was a veteran because I had been through the playoff wars a bit. Ron Cey, Larry Bowa, Gary Matthews, and

Keith Moreland slides in safely at home to score on Ron Cey's double to left during the third inning of the Cubs' 4–2 victory in Game 2 of the NLCS versus the Padres at Wrigley Field, October 3, 1984.

I had been in those types of situations. I remember having a conversation with Jody Davis. We lockered next to each other and are great friends to this day. I looked at him before that series and said, "You know, this is our chance for a knockout blow. We've got a chance to separate ourselves right here." Usually being fired up in baseball doesn't work very well. I played football at a high level, and emotion can play a big part in that sport, but for baseball, emotion can get you into trouble.

Well, we were focused. The Mets came in, and we got after them in the first game and beat Ron Darling, who was one of their best pitchers, and that set the tone for the rest of the series. They were frustrated, and in the second game of the doubleheader, Ed Lynch hit me with a pitch, I went out and tackled him, and the benches emptied. Now, Ed and I don't have any problems. There were some guys who threw at me that I had problems with and still do today. Eddie was doing what he thought he needed to do, and I was doing what I had to do.

Another game that stands out is when we were in St. Louis at the end of the year and beat them. We clinched a tie and knew no matter what happened, at least we'd be in a playoff. Those games were special because the Cardinals were always good and our huge rival. Great things happened that day, and we came away with a doubleheader win. You're tired after playing 18 innings on a sunny day, and even though it was late September, it was hot in St. Louis, especially on that turf. I remember looking around and saying, "Can you believe this?" We knew we'd win at least one more game in that last week, and even if we couldn't, if the Mets lost one, we were going to win it. That was a great day.

The "Men in Blue" happened because Jimmy Ritz was a friend of mine who was a writer for *Happy Days*. He was a big Phillies fan, and I met him when I played there. We wanted to give something back, so we talked to the Spina Bifida Foundation, and they were very interested. I sat down with Jimmy and asked him if he'd ever written any music, and he said he had written some songs. I told him to write me a song, and we'd publish it and give all the money to charity and have some fun doing it. We put it together and had fun with it. That's how it came about. We had a great night putting it together in the studio, and, yes, there were some adult beverages consumed while we were doing it. Obviously, I'm not a singer, and you can tell that from all our voices, but boy, did we have fun doing that!

The only thing that bothers me about losing to the Padres is when you hear Cubs fans say, "Leon did this," or, "So and so did this." We won and lost as a team, and we did not get the job done in that series. We took the two games here, but out there we didn't get it done for whatever reason. It wasn't any individual's fault. You can't blame just one person, because we all had our opportunities. We had a chance on Saturday night to come from behind and win that Game 4, and we didn't get it done. We had a lead on Sunday and didn't get that done. There are a lot of things that can happen. I will be in Chicago when they get to the World Series, and I sure hope it gets done before the Lord takes me.

Nineteen eighty-five was tough. I remember a stretch in May when Sutcliffe tore a hamstring running to first base in Atlanta, Dick Ruthven got hit with a line drive that broke his toe, then Eckersley got injured. If you look at Sut, Eck, and Ruthven, those were guys who were 200-inning guys. They were guys who went out and did their jobs and weren't injured much. Trout went down, too, and it was all in the span of a few days. We went from being in contention to playing with people you had never seen before. There were pitchers going for us we hadn't even seen in spring training. Who is this guy? Not to take anything from them, but emotionally it drained us. We never did recover that year. When you lose your starters, you put too much pressure on your bullpen. The pen was really good at the start of the year, but at the end of the year they had thrown so many innings and been out there so long they just couldn't be effective.

I was disappointed to be traded to San Diego in 1988. I call it the blackest day in baseball for me. You know, you're still playing in the big leagues, but I had played in two great cities in Philadelphia and Chicago. I fell in love with Chicago, and I really thought I was going to end my career here. I had signed a three-year contract and thought, *Well, this may end it, but if I play after that, hopefully I can get another one here.* To be moved is the nature of the game, but it was hard. It was a black night.

I'd have loved to come back here at some point and play just one more game at Wrigley in a Cubs uniform. That would have been fun.

I get asked about being named in the song "A Dying Cub Fan's Last Request." Steve Goodman was ill, and I was in the clubhouse one day and the phone rang. Usually, there are no phone calls in the clubhouse. Yosh Kawano, our longtime clubhouse man, called me and said, "Keith, there's a call for you." I said we didn't take calls there, but he told me it was Steve Goodman. Yosh knew who Steve was. I did, too, because I'm a country music fan, and I had listened to a lot of music he had written.

Steve said, "Hello, Keith. I'm Steve Goodman and I'm a songwriter." I told him, "Steve, I know who you are." He said that was great and told me he had written a song that mentioned my name and wanted to know if he could play it for me. I said sure, and he strummed it, and there was the line, "Have the Cubbies run right out onto the middle of the field / Have Keith Moreland drop a routine fly…" He said, "Would that be all right?" I told him absolutely yes, that it wouldn't bother me, because I had dropped my share of fly balls, the same as any player who goes out there, and I always tried my hardest to catch everything. It's a great song, Steve was a great guy, and it doesn't bother me in the least.

151

My team has gotten to know the '69 guys without playing together. That bond has developed because we have so much in common. We all played in Wrigley and were all on the cusp but didn't get it done. It is fun to see them, and believe me, Ron Santo should be in the Hall of Fame. That whole group is a great bunch of guys, and that would have been a great team to be on.

Relationships with teammates are special. You get to know so much about a person you play with because you're together competing and going for the same goal. You get to know the soul of a man then. You know what's going on in their personal lives and their wives, kids, family. Emotionally, you are in the same boat. We all live in different parts of the country, but when I see them, we can always pick right up. Those relationships will be forever.

Being a Cub is something I cherish, and I am proud to be a part of the group that changed this team. The 1969 team came alive and made it a tough ticket, then in the '70s there weren't a lot of people in the stands. It wasn't this, the happening that it is now. To be part of that transition and see what a tough ticket a Cubs game is, to see how the Cubs Convention has grown, and to see how it's even a tough ticket at Hohokam Park in spring training, and know that our 1984 group was a major part of making that transition happen is something I am proud of.

152

Keith Moreland came to the Cubs with Dickie Noles and Dan Larson on December 8, 1981, and the Phillies received Mike Krukow and cash. The catcher/third baseman/outfielder quickly became one of the Cubs' most consistent hitters, posting a .302 average in 1983. After platooning in the outfield early in 1984, Moreland still hit 16 home runs while driving in 80. He followed with his finest all-around season in 1985, hitting 16 homers with 106 RBIs and a career-high .307 average. He hit 100 home runs and had a .281 average in his six seasons with the Cubs. Moreland and Mike Brumley were traded to the San Diego Padres on February 12, 1988, in exchange for Rich Gossage and Ray Hayward. He does radio work for the University of Texas football and baseball broadcasts and has done fill-in work in the Cubs' booth for both WGN-TV and WGN Radio.

RYNE SANDBERG
SECOND BASEMAN
1982–1994 ★ 1996–1997

M Y FIRST MAJOR LEAGUE HIT came at Wrigley Field. I was a September call-up for the Phillies in 1981 and came in a game to play shortstop. I got a base hit to right field off Mike Krukow. I still have the bat I used for that hit, and I still have the ball.

I was initially a bit shocked when the Phillies traded me to the Cubs. The trade was strange because it involved three shortstops—Ivan DeJesus for Larry Bowa and me. I was the throw-in to the trade that Dallas wanted. After I looked at it and thought about the situation, I thought this really was an opportunity for me to go and break into the major leagues. The Philadelphia Phillies were stacked at that time and had just won the World Series in 1980. Here at the Cubs, there was a big contingent of Phillies with Dallas Green, Lee Elia, and some of the players they had brought over. I looked at it as a big opportunity.

When I was 1-for-32 to start out, I had all kinds of doubts. The whole atmosphere was different. I was in a different city, in cold weather, and I wasn't used to that. It became almost a standard for me to struggle in April. Not only did I have doubts that year, but I had them other years because I got off to a lot of slow starts. That became the norm for me and a lot of players. Guys would come in here at the start of the season and ask, "How do you do it?" I'd say, "I don't. That's just how it goes."

Cubs second baseman Ryne Sandberg slugs a triple during a game against the
Cincinnati Reds on August 29, 1984, at Wrigley Field, on his way to winning the NL
MVP award, during the breakout season in his Hall of Fame career.

Jim Frey came over from the American League, where the mentality then was to hit the ball out of the ballpark. It was a more offensive league with the DH. Jim was just over from Kansas City, and he watched me play for about 10 games in spring training. He told me I had some size and questioned me on why I tried to stay on top of the baseball and hit the ball on the ground all the time. I told him that was what I'd been taught to do to that point.

He said, "I'd like to see you hit the ball out of the ballpark every now and again," and I said I sure would. He worked with me for three or four days in a row in the morning on how to get the head of the bat on the ball on the inside pitch and use more of a power-pull swing. He told me, "Now that you have that move down, what I want you to do in these next spring training games is if you hear a whistle from the dugout, that means swing like that on this pitch." He was anticipating a fastball in, and he trained me for that situation. I started driving the ball, and in 1984, we opened on the West Coast for the only time in my career, which was nice because of the warm weather as we came out of Arizona. I hit a home run off a pretty good pitcher in Greg Minton of the Giants. We won the game, so there was that instant success that Frey was talking about.

Nineteen eighty-four changed everything. I really saw a big change that year. I was there, and Harry Caray was a big part of that. We had a bunch of guys that fans could relate to, and Harry had a great time with us, giving out nicknames. The way the season went, the fans came out in droves. Since that year, it's been pretty consistent year-in and year-out, because I was here in '82 and '83, and it was nothing like it was after '84.

My big game against the Cardinals was June 23 and my number was 23, so there was some magic there that day. It was one of those wild games, wind blowing out a little bit—it was going to be an offensive game from the get-go. One of the things I remember is we ended up being the national game of the week, which was a big deal then, as you didn't have all the ESPN games. Those Saturday games were what everybody watched. We were the backup game, but there was a rainout, so Bob Costas and Tony Kubek were here, and everybody ended up seeing our game. The crowd was a typical Cubs-Cardinals group, so the atmosphere was there, plus it was a high-scoring game.

Willie McGee was announced as the player of the game because he had hit for the cycle, but moments later, I hit the first home run off Bruce Sutter in the ninth to tie the game. That was totally unexpected. Here's the best reliever and sinkerball pitcher in the game, and I was able to get underneath one of his pitches and lift it out for a home run. While I hit that, they were showing the credits, then they had to stop that in a hurry! We went to extra innings, and I ended up doing it again in the tenth, hitting another home run to tie the game again. At that point, they took the player of the game away from Willie McGee and gave it to me. We were able to win the game on a big hit by Dave Owen. A lot of the players said that was a big game for us that year and kind of put us on the road to winning that year.

No question about it, from that game on, life was different. After that game, [Cardinals manager] Whitey Herzog said I was the best player he had ever seen. He was caught in the moment and exaggerated, but that's how it came out. Well, I read that the next day and was thinking I had to play really well the rest of the year so I didn't let him down or make a guy like that eat his words when he had built me up. I took that compliment personally and really took off after that. That game had a lot to do with the rest of my career.

There were so many big series that year. It felt like all odds were against us. We heard all the horror stories about past Cubs teams and what had happened and how they would fall apart down the stretch, especially the '69 team. It was kind of a history lesson for me along the way. It was only my third year in the big leagues and I hadn't heard about a lot of those things. For the last half of the season, all we heard was that we were up against the odds and probably wouldn't win. We beat the Mets in a doubleheader in Wrigley Field, and they were the big rivals that year. Those were exciting games. We went to St. Louis and swept a doubleheader late in the season, too.

The night we clinched was in Pittsburgh. They were out of it, and I bet there were a couple thousand Cubs fans there, and they were all sitting above our dugout, thinking that this might be the clincher. Here we were in Pittsburgh, right at home, Sutcliffe on the mound—it couldn't have been more perfect. Leading up to that, believe it or not, I had to learn what a magic number was, because I didn't have any experience with what a magic number was. I knew that there were about 10 games left, and I wondered, *What's the magic number, what do they mean by that?* So I went to Ron Cey or Larry Bowa, and they had to explain that. "Oh, okay, so if we win tonight, that clinches it." That's how naïve I was at 24 years old. We clinched that night, and that was one of the biggest thrills in my career.

One thing I'll never forget was our last home game that year against the Cardinals. We won and were all in the locker room about 20 minutes after the game taking off our uniforms when someone came in and told us we had to go back out because no one had left the ballpark. We went out and paraded around the field, and the fans sent us out in style.

As far as the loss to the Padres, I don't accept it. I don't say it wasn't our year or things didn't go our way. It still doesn't sit very well. I still have that inner drive or inner feeling to do more than we did that year. That's what keeps me in the game—looking for that chance again. That team was built to go to the World Series, and we proved it all year long and in the first two games of the playoffs. Then we went out to San Diego, and if we were complacent or loose, some of that is understandable. For me, as a 24-year-old, I didn't know any better. I thought, *Wow, this is great. We just beat them at our place and now we'll go out there and win one.* Now, being older and much wiser, I might have handled my mentality differently.

We went out to San Diego and played three very good baseball games with a lot of dramatics, including Steve Garvey's home run off Lee Smith to win Game 4. We had a late lead in Game 5, then they scored three runs to put them ahead with Sutcliffe on the mound. Everything was there for us to win one of those games. We just didn't do it.

We had a good group of guys, we really did. We enjoyed ourselves on the field, which was very evident with our enthusiasm and how we played the game. We also enjoyed our time off the field. Many times on a road trip, we'd have three or four foursomes go play golf together. We'd rent clubs and spend the day having fun with each other. We went to movies a lot. We were big fans of the country group Alabama that year because of Rick Sutcliffe. I think there were three or four concerts we went to after day games. We really had a lot of fun together. The plane rides were fun with card games, guys sitting together and talking a lot about what we did in baseball. Guys like Gary Matthews and Ron Cey were influential in talking about what we would have to do in the upcoming series. We'd talk about who we were facing, what we had to do to win, and a lot of baseball talk, which was very healthy, especially for me as a young player. That was great, and it was a special group of guys. Now when we hook up, it's almost like we haven't been apart.

The process going into the Hall of Fame was that I heard more about it from everybody around me. I'd be walking down the street, and the fans would mention it or I'd hear during interviews that I should be in the Hall of Fame. To hear that for a couple of years, the attention about that came from the fans.

When I got elected in my third year of eligibility, it was a big relief to me and to be done with all the attention that I was getting for not being in yet. I enjoyed seeing those fans, hearing the congratulations, and having that behind me. I can't imagine how some of the guys who have to wait 10 to 15 years to go in or worse yet, the guys who never get in. When there's talk about it, it gets on your mind, and it can be agonizing. With that feeling, when I did get the call, it was that much more special.

The Hall of Fame to me is about all the players who are there. You're talking about the best players who ever played the game. I remember all the days when I was struggling in the minor leagues, a time when all I could hope for was to be on a major league roster and have a chance to play in the big leagues.

It was a lucky situation for me that all our games were on WGN-TV. Most of my family was up in Washington, but because of WGN they were able to watch almost all of my games. That was ideal. I knew that every game was going around the nation, and with all those people watching, I wanted to make sure I was prepared for each one. There was the chance to do something special, knowing that not only was the park full, but there were viewers everywhere. I think it helped my career that so many people saw me play, and it was great that so many people who knew me could watch my games.

I remember in '84 we were in the dugout, looked out, and saw one guy on a rooftop the first time. "Wow! Look at that guy on the rooftop!" Then it was two guys and then three and more. They were standing there, because nothing was built yet, so I saw all that happen.

We got a taste of winning in '84, and it was unbelievable. Everywhere I went, it was, "Let's go, Ryno!" or, "Keep it going!" Cubs fans are everywhere in the United States, and it seems like all of them I've met have been to Wrigley Field at least once. The Cubs fans pack every ballpark on the road. I think that year it became fashionable to become a Cubs fan. I witnessed in '82 and '83, it was not. I saw that change, and it was all for the better. To this day, it's still a big snowball that keeps rolling.

The challenge I have now as a minor league manager is to try and get the most out of my players. At my level, it's about teaching and helping the players move up the ladder to one day hopefully play in the major leagues. It's a day-to-day thought process about what we need to work on today and what does each guy need to do to move up. I enjoy it because it's about the roots of baseball and is a good learning experience for me.

There's nothing like Wrigley Field; it's the place to be in Chicago. The place isn't big enough for all the people that want to be there every day, and you can't say that about too many other places.

Ryne Sandberg was acquired along with Larry Bowa from the Phillies on January 27, 1982, and spent his rookie season as the Cubs' regular third baseman. He switched to second base in 1983 and won his first Gold Glove that year. His breakout year came in 1984, when he hit .314 with 19 homers, 19 triples, 84 RBIs, and 114 runs; led the Cubs to the NL East title; and was named the National League's Most Valuable Player. He would remain the premiere second baseman in baseball for a decade, and his 30 homers helped the Cubs to another division title in 1989. Sandberg led the National League with 40 homers in 1990, and his 277 career home runs was a major league record at the time for a second baseman. He retired midway through the 1994 season, but returned in 1996 to play two more years. Sandberg was selected to 10 straight All-Star Games and won nine straight Gold Gloves. He set fielding records for second basemen with a .989 career percentage and a then-record 123-game errorless streak. He was elected to the Hall of Fame in 2005, and his No. 23 was retired by the Cubs on August 28 of that year. Since 2007, Sandberg has been a manager in the Cubs' minor league system.

HARRY CARAY

BROADCASTER

1982–1997

THE ONLY YEAR I WORKED for the new owners of the White Sox, they were going into pay TV. The first year I worked for them, they wanted me to sign a five-year contract. When they knew I wouldn't go for that, they tried to make it a three-year contract. I said, "I don't know you fellas, and you don't know me. Why don't we make it one year and go from year to year? What's wrong with that?" When they saw I was serious, we went on a one-year deal.

The next year, they started talking to me about pay TV, and I didn't know anything about it. I told them, "Last year, you wanted security. This year, I want security if I'm going to go into this. In our business, out of sight, out of mind. If you're going to sell the television rights to pay TV, how do I know it's going to go over?" They assured me we would all make a lot of money if we sold something like 50,000 homes. They made me a heck of an offer, really a tremendous offer. Don Drysdale, who replaced me, later gave me credit for getting him the biggest raise he ever got, because when they found out I was going to the Cubs, they needed a name, and they got Drysdale and paid him what they offered me.

We set up a final day the following Tuesday when I had to tell them yes or no. I was thinking as I was driving home, *Why are these guys suddenly down to one year, when a year ago they wanted me for five or three years?* I came to the conclusion they only wanted me for one reason: to sell the 50,000 homes. They

160

Cubs broadcaster Harry Caray leads the crowd at Wrigley Field in singing "Take Me Out to the Ballgame" during the seventh-inning stretch.

only had to pay my salary one year and then they could release me. I would have to start all over again.

I picked up the phone and called Andy McKenna, who had been president of the Cubs and was responsible for a group Bill Veeck headed when he bought the White Sox. I said, "Andy, I'm really surprised at you and disappointed." He said, "What are you talking about?" I told him, "Here I am available, and you know the kind of job I could do for you at the Cubs, and you haven't even called me." He said, "You're tied up with the White Sox." I said, "No, I'm a free agent right now." He asked if I had a commitment, and I said no. He said, "Don't move. I'll either call you, or a guy named Jim Dowdle will call you."

Jim Dowdle [Tribune Broadcasting president] called me, and we had to meet secretly on a Thursday night. The next night, it was like CIA stuff. We were supposed to meet at the Union League Club, and they told me to come in through the side door, go right on the elevator, and get off at the third floor. They wanted to make sure nobody saw me. Well, I walked in the door, and in the lobby I saw a whole bunch of guys who wanted to say hello and talk! Once I got upstairs, we did a two-year deal, shook hands, and that was that.

I had to call Jerry Reinsdorf and Eddie Einhorn to tell them. We had a conference call, and Reinsdorf wanted to make sure I told everyone they had made me a good offer, that I wasn't fired, and I was quitting the Sox. I said, "That's right, that's the way it is." And that was that.

I don't think about who's listening. I don't know whether they listen in the millions or they listen in the hundreds. When the game starts, your job is to make it as interesting and exciting as you know how to make it. That's how you do your job. You hope a lot of people listen. I'll bet some of the greatest broadcasts I ever did not too many people were listening, but I was great. Other days, maybe I was terrible.

The '84 season was great. Here was a team that went through a terrible preseason, but Dallas Green made a couple of deals, and the next thing you know, you had Dernier and Matthews in the outfield, you had Sutcliffe coming over winning 16 and losing only one, and they won the division title. The '89 team won their division title, too, and that was special. It's not the World Series, but having the team win those years wasn't bad.

The playoffs in '84 were extremely disappointing. Nobody could have figured that the Cubs would lose three straight in San Diego. If it hadn't been for a guy named Steve Garvey, they never would have lost three straight, but Garvey was Superman. That's what makes this such a great game. There's no form sheet in baseball. Nothing ever happens that is supposed to happen. That's baseball, it happens every day. This is why the game is the great game it is. The impossible is possible. The unbelievable is believable.

My stroke in 1987 was the greatest despondency a man can go through. When all of a sudden, he finds he can't move his right leg, when he finds he can't move his right hand, and he finds he can't talk coherently. If they had told me I was going to die in the next 15 minutes, I'd have been very happy. But I didn't die, and my wife Dutchie began bringing in box after box after box of letters, and I had nothing to do but read this mail. We stopped counting at 75,000 pieces of mail, and we must have had 50 more boxes from all

162

over the country. People I didn't realize ever even heard me wrote. I began to realize that I did mean something to people and that people did get enjoyment from what I did, that people did love what I stood for. I don't know if that led to my recovery, but who knows how the mental aspect of anything helps? I know that it made me think that I wanted to get well, and I wanted to get back to work, and I did.

When I got back, I knew President Reagan was going to call. Arne Harris had tipped me off. We were just going in the bottom of the first, and we had the great "Daily Double" in Dernier and Sandberg. Dernier would get on, Sandberg would get a hit, and we'd have runners on first and third and nobody out. So Bob Dernier is at the plate and I'm talking to the president, reminding him of St. Louis days, and then Dernier bunted, and I said, "Dernier bunts for a base hit, and Mr. President, I'm going to have to go," and I did.

I broadcast the St. Louis Cardinals and St. Louis Browns, because in two-team cities, you had to do the home teams' games. I was saying "Holy Cow" way back then. I never took any credit for it, because a lot of people said "Holy Cow." A guy named Halsey Hall wrote a column with that title, but he wasn't writing about major league baseball until years later when he did things with the Minnesota Twins. I never took any special distinction for using "Holy Cow." I was just the first guy to use it on the air. The reason I used it is, in the neighborhood I grew up in, profanity was very common. I needed to develop something to say without using profanity, so I came up with "Holy Cow." I would say something stronger ordinarily, but I had to train myself to say "Holy Cow" so I wouldn't use profanity.

When a ball is hit, you know it "might be." You see the left fielder moving back, and you know it "could be." Then it lands in the bleachers, and "it is." It seems to me it's the only call, and I always tried to let the play finish and then call it, which is the easy way to do it because then you never make a mistake. Many is the time I thought it was a home run, and I'd say, "It might be, it could be…oh, he caught the ball."

When the game's over, you win or lose, and you don't like to say, "Cubs lost." Everybody knows you got beat. When you win, it's an ecstatic moment. You develop things, you don't want to contrive. "Holy Cow" I developed because I didn't want to use profanity. "That wouldn't be a home run in a phone booth"—I used that all my life. We're all creatures of habit.

Anything you contrive in our business is bad. You have to be your natural self. What you see is what you get with me. You may like it, you may

163

dislike it, you may think it's corny, whatever. I say it the way I'm accustomed to saying it. I say it as simply as I can put it. A ballplayer might be a little angry when he finds out I talked about his error, but the score said it was an error. What are you going to do about it?

There was a long, long Polish name, and I said, "I wonder what that would look like backward?" I wrote it out, and you couldn't pronounce it either way, frontward or backward. I started doing that. When you come up with an idea and the people like it, you know about it through the mail. If there are enough letters saying they like it, I jot it down and use it at times.

I think baseball is a radio game. It is because the ability of the announcer can be used much better in radio than on TV. We talk too much on TV. The technological job done by the cameras is so outstanding we can get by without much conversation. The picture tells the story. In radio, it's the imagination and excitement of the announcer. The announcer's vocabulary and ability to be an artist who paints a picture are what you do on radio. If you try to do it on TV, right away they say you talk too much, and they're right!

I always thought it was a shame that Bill Veeck didn't wind up with the perfect story, which would have been him owning the Chicago Cubs. He started as a kid with the new scoreboard and planting the ivy, and his father was the general manager. He went on to own other ballclubs, but never the Cubs. What a perfect story it would have been in the great life of a great baseball man in Bill Veeck.

164

The best change I've seen is that we don't have to worry about holding a tag day now for a ballplayer. They are making so much money now, their futures are secure. They can hardly spend the money they are making. The education of the players has improved so much they know the importance of getting good money managers who make sure their money is in good hands.

The game is great. How can you affect the game? The bases are still 90 feet apart and the pitching mound is still 60'6" away. If they ever build a new ballpark for the Cubs, I'm sure they will copy Wrigley Field along with the modern refinements. You can't beat this ballpark for familiarity. The fans can see the expressions on the faces of the players, can read their lips, and can hear what they say to each other. It's great.

I worry about the ownership of ballclubs. Whatever you want to say about the old-time owners, most of them were really sportsmen who spent most of their lives in the baseball business. Maybe they were more frugal than they should have been and not as understanding of the ballplayers' rights as they should have been, but all of that has corrected itself. I think the idea of owners losing money when they buy a club for $20 million and sell it a few years later for more, then how can they be losing money? I like the old days where Sam Breadon of the Cardinals was thought to be cheap, but he took care of an awful lot of people. Gussie Busch was a sportsman. He wanted St. Louis to be the greatest city in the world, and one way to do that was have a great ballclub.

The fan is the guy that the owners and the players should cater to. The players should look to the fans and encourage them to ask for an autograph. These people make it all possible. I don't care what the contract is, I don't care what they hit, I don't care how much money they get paid, if that fan isn't sitting in the seat, the game won't be around very long.

I think if fans like me, it's because they can envision themselves doing the game exactly as I do it. When the big hitter hits a home run, you're ecstatic. When the big hitter strikes out with the bases loaded and you lose the ballgame, you're despondent. When it's a boring game, you let them know it's boring. There's a sense of integrity and honesty there in telling people what you actually see and feel.

Style is personality and whatever your personality might be. I'm a people guy. Everywhere I go, I look for people to talk to. Not only do I go to bars because I like to drink, and I do like to drink, but I go because, who do you see there? Baseball fans, and you see firsthand what they like and what they don't like. You can't learn that any other way unless you have occasion to talk to the true fan.

165

I have a feeling somewhere along the line somebody will remember me and say, "Gee, the Cubs just won the world championship. Isn't it a shame Harry's not here to see it?" I imagine a lot of people will say that. It's a funny thing, I was with the Cardinals 25 years, Oakland one year, the White Sox 11 years, but you would think I've been doing Cubs games all my life. Before me was a great man and wonderful announcer, Jack Brickhouse. He was here many more years than I was, but people still seem to think of me as being the Cubs. That makes me feel good, but I know it really isn't true. I don't know why that is, but for some reason that feeling exists.

Having the fans reach out and want autographs is a small price to pay for something you like. I like the fact that people like me. They make it very clear. I'm not being immodest, it's quite obvious people like me. Whatever the reason, they just do. I go out out of my way to shake hands with people in the handicapped sections, because there but for the grace of God go I. For a little orphan boy, from a very humble origin, I'm kind of proud of my life, and I'm proud of my relationship with these fans who I think the world of. There's no fan more loyal than the Chicago Cubs fans. Believe it.

After 36 seasons with the St. Louis Cardinals, Oakland A's, and Chicago White Sox, Harry Caray became the voice of the Cubs for the 1982 season. For the next 16 years, he entertained Cubs fans across the nation with his enthusiasm, frankness, and unparalled love of the game. Whether leading the crowd in singing "Take Me Out to the Ballgame" for the seventh-inning stretch, giving out nicknames, or moaning "he paaahped it up" after a bad at-bat, there was no doubt that Harry was a key reason the Cubs soared in popularity during that time. He was honored by the National Baseball Hall of Fame with the Ford Frick Award in 1989 and was inducted into the Radio Hall of Fame in 1990. Caray suffered a fatal stroke on Valentine's Day 1998 and died shortly afterward. His funeral was one of the largest in the city's history. In 1999 the Cubs unveiled a statue honoring him that stands outside Wrigley Field near the corner of Clark and Sheffield. To further honor his memory, guest conductors lead the crowd in singing "Take Me Out to the Ballgame" for each Cubs home game. This interview was conducted at Wrigley Field in May 1994 by Bob Costas as part of the WGN-TV special *When Harry Met Baseball*, celebrating Harry's 50th anniversary in broadcasting.

STEVE TROUT

PITCHER

1983–1987

MY FATHER PITCHED IN THE major leagues, so I grew up with Ted Williams coming to our house to shoot pool or join us for a barbecue. Maybe it would be Walt "No-Neck" Williams, Gary Peters, or Tommy John. My dad brought Billy Pierce over to give me pitching tips because, "He's a lefty, and I want a lefty to show him how to throw the ball." Pretty nice, huh?

Since Dad worked for the Chicago White Sox, Comiskey Park was my playground. I would run around the field when the team wasn't there. Dad would go down and sit in the sauna, and I would raid food from the Bard's Room and go down the ramps on a skateboard. I was lucky to be raised in baseball with all these wonderful people who were part of my dad's era. It was pretty neat.

I went on to pitch for the White Sox and I didn't know know much about the North Side. I think Roland Hemond did me a favor when he traded me to the Cubs. In all sincerity, I think he made sure I stayed in Chicago, because I was a mommy's boy! I have a big family on the South Side of Chicago, and I think they didn't want to see me leave. The Cubs saw some potential in me, and the key was Billy Connors.

Dallas Green became my second father. Maybe he doesn't know that, but he really did. There were many times on the mound I would look up for Dallas sitting in his booth, and I did feel a good connection to him. I call pitching coach Billy Connors my "avatar," because he was like my baseball

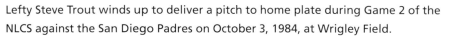

Lefty Steve Trout winds up to deliver a pitch to home plate during Game 2 of the NLCS against the San Diego Padres on October 3, 1984, at Wrigley Field.

god. He was my teacher, my leader in that way, and he and Dallas helped me when I came over from the South Side. The big question was how many of my friends and family were going to change sides? We were White Sox–raised, and now they had to become Cubs fans. It was kind of cool.

Billy and I connected. When I went to his house the first time, my wife was eight months pregnant. I said, "I'm going to see Billy Connors for a few days to talk about pitching." I got to Tampa, and Billy's neighbors made dinner for us. Their names were Bob and Jan Tatum, and I told them, "Isn't that ironic? If I have a baby girl, we're going to name her Tatum." As soon as dinner was served, I got a call from the hospital that my wife was in labor. I got up and flew right back, and our baby girl, Tatum, was born the next day. There was something about Billy and me.

I went back to see him after Tatum was home with my wife. Billy and I were going to play some golf. I didn't know much about golf, and I was about 15 feet off the green. Billy was telling me to keep my arms locked, and sure enough, I chipped it in the hole. It was one of those things; we had a great relationship.

He really wanted my best. In all due respect to Ron Schueler, who I think was a good pitching coach, we never really clicked. Maybe I wasn't a good listener at the time. Billy helped me so much. So did Dallas. That combination got the best out of me, and I enjoyed being around them. I think it's important for an athlete who's got God-given talent that when you put it all together, it is because of all the things around you. I loved all the coaching staff with John Vukovich and Johnny Oates. What a great coaching staff! It just worked for me big-time.

I really liked Lee Elia and that staff and in 1983, I was learning the sinker Billy Connors was teaching me and revamping my mechanics from what I had done at the White Sox. I trusted Billy and went full-bore into what he was teaching me. I had some success, and it wasn't too bad. We had Tatum, and I was holding her all the time, and I did some things to change my life. I took yoga and martial arts. Everything was about concentration and making my body more flexible. Things were working in my private life along with the things I was doing to improve my physical and mental self.

Spring training came in 1984, and Jody Davis came out to the mound and told me the umpire wanted to know if it was the same guy out there on the mound as it was last year. I said, "Tell him it's a totally different guy." He laughed and told me how good I was throwing. Everything just started working.

I think I had 31 starts that year, and they were all special to me, even if I wasn't always great. We swept doubleheaders in New York and St. Louis, and I started and got the win in the first game both times. Maybe those stand out because we played two big games in one day and won both times. It was hot that day in St. Louis, and our lead was shrinking a bit at the end, but that win gave us a boost.

When we clinched in Pittsburgh, it still is a great memory. I have great home movies of that locker room. It doesn't feel like that many years have gone by. I have great memories of the fans and everybody. There was the book *The Year the Ivy Smiled*, and that was just so appropriate.

They called me in before the playoffs and said, "You're going to pitch the second game at home." I knew Sut was going to be No. 1, and rightfully so. The question was whether it was going to be me or Dennis Eckersley next. They said they would give me the ball. I think they wondered if being at home was too much pressure. I was so relaxed on the mound, and we beat them 4–2. We didn't have a regular umpiring crew because of an umpires' strike, but we had a Big Ten crew calling the game. I might have gotten a pitch or two, but there was never an issue of fairness. I had a lot of ground-ball outs that day. I got a base hit, so when they wanted to talk to me afterward about the game, I said, "Let's talk about my base hit." I got on base, Bobby Dernier hit the ball to short, and I slid pretty well into second base to break up the double play. Bobby was safe at first, then scored on a Sandberg hit, so it felt really great to be able to contribute, especially since my hitting was never that much to talk about!

170

We got a little bit loose at the fringes in San Diego. I think we lost a little bit of the edge we had in Chicago. Some of it I blame on the late Mike Royko. He wrote an article that was not too positive to the people in Southern California, and when I went to get my rental car, that article was posted on the bulletin board there. When I went to a restaurant, there it was on their bulletin board! Those people came out in droves after that. The fans got together and stood behind their team as they never had before. We were just a little bit off. Getting on the bus and leaving San Diego that Sunday was a horrible day.

In 1985 Bobby Dernier had a foot problem, and Sutcliffe was the first pitcher to go down when he pulled a hammy running to first base. I hurt my ulnar nerve, then Dennis and Scotty Sanderson went down. We started out to a good season, I think we were 35–17 or something, but it happened where there was a chain reaction of injuries, and that's all it takes. When 100 percent of your starting rotation and 50 percent of your regular players go down, it's tough. It gave some other players opportunities, but that was all. We thought we were going to come out and do it all again, but injuries hurt us. That's part of the game.

When I was traded to the Yankees in 1987, I had just pitched a couple great games, both of them shutouts, and there was talk of me going to the All-Star Game. The trade occurred on the Sunday before the All-Star break. Yosh said that he'd pack my uniform just in case. My ERA was right at 3.00, I was 6–3 and was pitching good ball with a couple of shutouts, so the trade was unexpected to me. When I got there, I didn't pitch well. I guess there was too much heartbreak for me, and I never really did recover baseball-wise. The most gratification I got was when Andre Dawson came out and said, "I guess we're giving up on the season." We were only six or seven games out, I can't remember exactly, but I do remember Andre saying that we got rid of our best pitcher, and I was at the time.

I was going to be the best pitcher for the rest of the year. I wanted to be that good. I competed every day, it was all coming together, and then they traded me, which was unfortunate. The Yankees had good intentions, but I just got there and became stiff and had vertigo. I was heartbroken. I never saw baseball as a business. I only saw it as a fun thing, and then the fun was taken out for me when I left Chicago.

Nineteen eighty-four changed things, no question, because a lot of people became fans then. There's a lot to say about the year the ivy smiled, and it certainly has been smiling ever since from a business standpoint. We had something to do with that, but to me, it's important just to have been part of the Chicago Cubs. I love the people who work for the Cubs. I love the ushers and all of them. I love when you walk in and see something like Ollie and Judith, who are married and work sections side by side in the lower boxes. It's just great, and I'm proud to be a part of all of that. Our success in 1984 was just icing on the cake.

My team always talks about one guy—Gary Matthews. He was the key guy to the team. He taught us all about leadership and the things you have to have to get to the next level. Remember when Willie Stargell with the Pirates started the "Family" and handed out the stars? We had it somewhat similar with the blood, sweat, and tears, the happiness, the high-fives, the low-fives, and all those things that take place during the season and even during the off-season. It's like a strong chain that is tough to break.

I was raised with my dad in baseball in a big family of nine brothers and sisters on the South Side of Chicago, and I've always cared about the people. To me, that's what makes everything work in life. To me, there's a sense of connection that comes out with me and the fans. I don't know if you can ever give our fans enough. Maybe you could give them a refund for all the years of waiting! They are respected, and there is a love affair. Players feel that about them, too.

These fans always treat the players with the same kind of awe and respect and admiration as they hold the team. They still come out, now especially that the Cubs are putting a good product on the field and doing their best to play winning baseball. These fans come out no matter what. They come out because there is a loyalty and perhaps a spirituality to the Chicago Cubs and that ballpark. All the history and mythology is hard to take away.

It becomes part of your family and part of you. The ballpark is definitely a sacred place. Everybody realizes that the game is bigger than any player and that fans make the game. They are there through thick and thin. I think players have done a good job of reciprocation with this love affair they have with the Cubs.

It's like a church. People don't leave their church. It's a temple, Wrigley Field is, and people will never leave that temple because all their love and experiences are from there. With WGN, a lot of kids watch, and when they go to that first ballgame, they stay with the Cubs. A lot of people saw that 1984 team and said that was the year. They have stayed with the Cubs because that was the year they fell in love with baseball and had so much fun watching it. They know the players and the nicknames and everything else.

It's something kind of powerful, isn't it?

Steve Trout, the son of former major league pitcher Dizzy Trout, came to the Cubs before the 1983 season in a trade with White Sox. He posted his best season in 1984 with a 13–7 record and 3.41 ERA. Trout was brilliant in his Game 2 win over the San Diego Padres in the NLCS that year, giving up only five hits and two runs in 8⅓ innings. Trout stays active in baseball by tutoring young pitchers and is the author of *Home Plate: The Journal of the Most Flamboyant Father and Son Pitching Combination in Major League History.*

JIM FREY

MANAGER

1984–1986

GENERAL MANAGER

1988–1991

THE LAST WEEKEND OF THE '83 season I was in Chicago coaching with the Mets. The Cubs had replaced Lee Elia with Charlie Fox, who was the temporary manager. After the Saturday game, Billy Connors told me Dallas Green wanted to talk to me. Dallas invited me to dinner, and we went to his home. After dinner, we went down to his office and sat and talked for quite a while. He asked me a bunch of questions, and we reminisced a bit since we had played and managed against each other. Whatever happened, he ended up hiring me. I asked him later why he wanted me, and he told me I was the only guy who said if we got a couple pitchers we could win now, while the other guys were talking about long-term rebuilding programs.

When I got there, Connors told me the joke in Chicago was that after Labor Day, if you were late to the game, you had to sit in the second row! I didn't really have a history with the Cubs, but I was familiar with a few of the old players. I thought if we could field a competitive team and make it fun for people to come and bring their kids, that we could draw some big crowds. I hear accounts of the Cubs, and they make it sound like the Cubs' attendance has been sold out forever, and that's not what happened. Nineteen eighty-four started all that.

The other thing that ticked me off is that I thought the Cubs had a bunch of excuses, and the writers seemed to enjoy helping. It was day baseball, too hot, too windy, all kinds of built-in excuses, and it ticked me off. I wanted to change that, and we did.

I thought we needed two starting pitchers and a center fielder who could catch the ball. Watching the spring-training games in 1984, when we lost 11 or 13 in a row, Mel Hall was playing center field, Leon Durham was in left, and Bill Buckner was on first. I said to Zimmer one day, "Every time a ball goes into the gap, it's a triple here. I'm tired of this. We've got to get a center fielder who can run and catch the ball." So I said that to Dallas, and he ended up getting Dernier and Matthews. I loved Billy Buckner as a player when he was young, but by the time I got to Chicago, he couldn't run, he didn't have any range, and he really didn't have much power. I thought we were going to be a lot better with Durham at first and put Matthews in left. Dallas traded Buckner for Eckersley, then he got Sutcliffe. I'd said, "If we could get a center fielder who could run and catch the ball and a couple starting pitchers, we can compete." Well, he went and got 'em. All of a sudden we had a pitching staff.

174

Turning it on in the summer of '84 was the result of having about six guys who could loft the ball up in the air. We didn't have a speed team. We had Dernier and Sandberg. Bowa and Durham could run some, but our real speed guys were Dernier and Sandberg. The rest of them were big guys like Cey and Davis and Moreland and Matthews. We had a power team. If we could control the other team by throwing strikes and keeping the ball down, we were going to score, there was no question about it. I can remember managing against some people that came in there, and they were bunting for one run or two runs early on, and I used to love it because I knew our big guys were going to get it up in the air with the wind blowing out. We were going to score runs and did. We had a bunch of our guys who had real good years in '84. Six of them hit 14 or more home runs and had 80 or more RBIs. I lived in an apartment over the center-field fence. The first thing I did in the morning when I woke up was to run to the window, look out, and see which way the wind was blowing. When the wind was blowing out, I put those big fat guys in there, and they just lofted the ball, and it was wonderful. We were just a slam-bang team in '84, with pretty good pitching. We had pretty good starting pitching.

Manager Jim Frey took over the Cubs in 1984 and led them to a 96–65 record, an NL East title, and a postseason berth for the first time in 39 years. After being fired in 1986, he came back as general manager in 1988 and oversaw another division title in 1989.

In anything you do and especially in sports, there seems to be something that clicks at a point where it turns the players on. There seems to be a team coming together, a team excitement, spirit. I think that Sandberg game was the thing that turned our season around. We were a pretty good team, and when we won that game, especially against the Cardinals, I mean, that was a big series for the Cubs. When we won that game against the Cardinals on national television, it seemed to give everybody in the organization a lift. I think it gave our players a sense of confidence that maybe we could carry this through. For me, the most exciting thing that happened to me as a manager was when we went to New York in the second half for a four-game series. Gooden beat us 2–1 on Friday night, and we took the next three. Then we took four in a row in Chicago. When we took those four in Chicago, I thought, *You know what, maybe we can do this.*

As time passes, you put things in perspective about a season rather than just a game. They talk about the last game in 1984 and a ball through Durham's legs or other things, but you have to remember, we put in a lot of effort and work to get there. There were many great memories from that season. Our players played hard, and when you are managing a team, there is a feeling that you get when you realize a team has come together. When you achieve that, it is pretty special, and that's what we did.

In 1985 I thought we had a better team, because of our bench. That is one of my sad memories. People forget that we were in first place, then we lost three or four of our starting pitchers; Dernier went down for a while; Davis went down for a while; and all of a sudden we started losing and couldn't win a game. We ended up fourth. We won 77 games, 19 less than in 1984, but I managed my butt off that year trying to win. Every manager goes through the same thing in those periods, when you work even harder and even though you didn't win, you are proud of what you did. Take four starters off any major league team, and see how good you play. We did the best we could.

When things are going well, a lot of times the manager just sits and watches. Heck, you can sit in the second row and eat peanuts. When Sutcliffe is throwing a three-hitter, my wife could run the team, but try managing when you have a Triple A pitching staff. That's when you work.

After I was replaced in 1986, I didn't know what I was going to do. I didn't want to coach anymore. I thought I might end up as an advance scout or assistant to a general manager. Stanton Cook offered me a job on the radio. I asked if Dallas was okay with it, but I was assured he was. Carl Pohlad offered me a job with the Twins as a manager or general manager, but wouldn't give me more than two years. He wouldn't budge, and I wouldn't budge, so that's how I ended up on WGN Radio. I wasn't intimidated by working with Harry Caray. I knew him long before the people in Chicago knew him.

176

The Cubs had a terrible year in 1987. I had promised my wife I would take her to Switzerland, and after that season we went. On the last day we were there, a friend showed me an English paper, and I read the Cubs had fired Dallas Green. We came home, and my daughter told me there were a bunch of calls from Chicago. John Madigan asked me about becoming manager or general manager. I thought about doing both and having a coach succeed me as manager in two or three years, but he didn't think I could do both. I took the GM's job and said, "I've had two ballclubs that played really well for me, and I got fired both times. I've had enough of that crap. I'll go to the front office, and if the team plays badly, maybe *I'll* get to fire somebody!"

When I was general manager, I can tell you this honestly, there were a lot more games where I was nervous sitting upstairs than I was in the dugout. In the dugout, I was doing what I thought I should do. When you're up there, it's like you are helpless. It's like watching one of your little grandchildren play T-ball. You get nervous, you know? You don't get nervous when you're playing. When you're watching somebody else, you get nervous. I had a lot of anxiety watching those teams. It wasn't that I didn't have confidence, it's like you have a helpless feeling. When things are going well, you feel bad because you are helpless.

I took some heat for having Don Zimmer as my manager. People always look for an ulterior motive. I was accused of hiring a friend because I grew up with him. I said, "Do you know how many guys I grew up with? They've got no chance of coaching third or managing the Cubs. I brought Zimmer in because I respect him. We've both had professional careers as players and have had lots of experience." We had similar ideas about how to play and put together a team. I had better friends than Zimmer, but they weren't going to be in a Cubs uniform!

I didn't leave because I didn't like it. I thought it was time to go home. When they made me fire Zimmer, that kind of took the heart out of me a little bit. I didn't appreciate that. From that point on, things weren't quite the same. I told the Cubs I was going to retire after the '92 season when my contract was up, and they tried to get me to stay. Stanton Cook offered me a new three-year contract, but somebody got in there and said if I wanted to leave a year away, I should go now. They wanted Larry Himes to be GM, so I left a year early, and they paid me for the season. I induced my own departure.

The Tribune Company always treated me great. It was a lot of fun. It seemed like the whole city and state of Illinois got the monkey off their back. When you say the Cubs and Wrigley Field, you can't talk about that without understanding what a great place Chicago is. It was such a wonderful place for us to be. I'd been in Baltimore, Kansas City, and New York, but Chicago is just a better place to be. We loved every minute of it. We still do.

177

Longtime Orioles coach Jim Frey was hired to manage the Kansas City Royals in 1980 and promptly led them to the franchise's first World Series, where they were defeated by Philadelphia. Frey was fired during the 1981 season and spent the next two seasons as a New York Mets coach. He was hired by Dallas Green to manage the Cubs, and in his first season, the Cubs went 96–65 to win the National League East and play in the postseason for the first time since 1945. The Cubs lost the NLCS 3–2 to San Diego and slumped to 77–84 the next season. Frey was fired in 1986 but hired as the Cubs' general manager before the 1988 season. The Cubs won the NL East again in 1989, but lost in the NLCS to the San Francisco Giants 4–1. He left the club after the 1991 season.

BOB DERNIER
CENTER FIELDER
1984–1987

IN 1984, RIGHT AT THE END of spring training, I was traded with Gary Matthews to the Cubs for Bill Campbell and Mike Diaz. At first, there was a little bit of confusion and uncertainty for me. I felt like I had a greater opportunity to play every day in Chicago, so I really looked forward to it, even though I had great friends in Philadelphia and ended up finishing my career there. I wanted to play there, everybody wants to play for their first team, but that wasn't going to happen. I knew the opportunity was awaiting in Chicago with Dallas Green. Ryno was already here and so was Keith Moreland. I really felt like I was where I belonged. For Gary Matthews, I'm not sure about him at the time, but I was fortunate he was traded with me. When we got on the plane, he said to me, "Look here, we're not playing that lovable loser thing. We're going over there to win." We had just played in the World Series the year before in 1983, so we expected to win, and we did.

The word that I received—and Gary made me aware of it—was that Mel Hall said I couldn't fill his shoes playing center. I tried to think of some way to respond to that, and all I could think of when I got to the Cubs in spring training and met Mel, was to ask him what size shoe he wore. The way I looked at it was that we could all play together, but I was going to start in center field. Part of that was ego and having a certain amount of arrogance, I guess. I wasn't afraid. To me, it was healthy competition, and I really didn't have a problem with Mel. I like him, but I looked at it as he was going

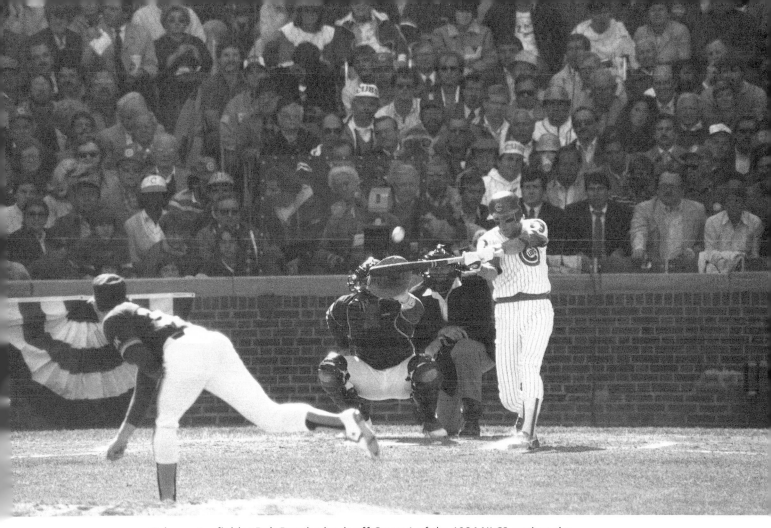

Cubs center fielder Bob Dernier leads off Game 1 of the 1984 NLCS against the San Diego Padres with a home run to left-center field off of pitcher Eric Show.

to have to play right field. Matthews was playing left, and I knew Keith Moreland would have something to say about what happened in right. As fate would have it, Mel went to the Indians along with Joe Carter, and we got Sutcliffe. Eckersley came in May for Buckner, and our team changed.

I was a leadoff hitter from the time I was seven or eight years old. The one great thing about baseball is that it's friendly to little guys. You don't have to be 6'6" and 280. I was short, and I was always one of the smaller guys on any team, slight of build, but with good speed. It was a natural marriage for me to be in the leadoff hole, so I did it from the time I started little league. That was my role, and I always took pride in being the guy who got on base so the big guys could then do some damage. That's part of the personality of winning, and we had those monsters in Cey, Sarge, Keith, Durham, and Jody.

I always felt that it was my good fortune to play three years with Ryno in the minor leagues and for four more here, so I knew him when I came here as a teammate and a leadoff hitter. He always hit second behind me in the minor leagues. We developed a natural relationship on the field as far as our games went. He knew what I would do in certain situations and vice versa. That's where the "Daily Double" that Harry talked about came from. Ryno and I had created that years before and then were reunited. Anytime I got on, he sure seemed to take advantage of it, and I still like to remind him how much he liked to hit with the pitcher in the stretch!

In the Sandberg game, I remember being on base all day. I think Ryno and I were on base nine times between us. He hit those two homers and drove in all those runs and was just incredible. Anything Ryne Sandberg did never surprised me, though. He was just built to win. In the tenth, he got the chance to hit the second one because I walked with two out. I fought off a few tough pitches and drew the walk, which wasn't my forte as a hitter. I usually tried to get ahead in the count, then get a pitch I could drive because they don't want to walk a leadoff guy like me. That game stood out because not only was Bruce Sutter a lights-out closer, but he threw that splitter that fell off the table and was hard to lift. How Ryno managed to get it over the wall twice was something, and it added to the legend of that day.

180

At the end of the year, we were in St. Louis for a Sunday doubleheader, and we clinched a tie for the division. It was hot, I was on base all day, and it seemed like Sarge was scoring me with a double or homer all the time. We were beating Joaquin Andujar, and I think I lost 11 pounds that day, which for me was a big portion of my body weight. Beating the Cardinals was special, because you knew every year they were going to be a good club and battle us.

We were in Pittsburgh the next day with the chance to clinch, but I was completely cooked and had no energy at all. I think I went 0-for-5 that night, but I never had a better oh-fer than that one. It was such a wonderful day and stayed wonderful right into the morning hours! Ryno and I were supposed to be on *Good Morning America*, but there was no way we made that after, let's say, a little too much champagne.

The loss to the Padres in the playoffs happened so suddenly, because we never lost faith that we were going to win in each of those games in San

Diego. In Game 4 we came back and felt like we could have won that one. In Game 5 we were ahead 3–0 in the middle of the game, but it didn't quite pan out. I have a lot of resentment for Jack Murphy Stadium, and any time I go to San Diego or see a Padres uniform, I can't help but cringe a little. It's a tough pill to swallow, but I guess it's part of the journey.

That was a tremendous defensive team up the middle with Bowa and Ryno in the infield and Jody behind the plate. There's a deception about Wrigley and how it plays, but we handled it. Our club was acknowledged in many ways that year, and I was fortunate enough to be one of them by winning a Gold Glove. Dallas Green was the Executive of the Year, Jim Frey was the Manager of the Year, and of course, Ryno was the MVP. Sut won the Cy Young Award, and we were proud because those things come with winning. I am proud of it, and I can tell you every time I see that Gold Glove with a Chicago Cubs C on the front, I think of that team and how it's really a team award.

That year, I had really reached a great confidence level. I was 27, and that's the time you peak as a player. We got off to a great start in 1985, and I think we were 15 or 16 games over .500 and felt like we were right on schedule. I broke my foot and then got an infection in it, so it blew up, and I ended up in the hospital. Sut, Eck, and our pitching went down, and at one point I was in a hospital bed watching us lose 13 games in a row. That doesn't do much for your recovery mode—talk about frustrating!

I never really got back after that, and neither did our team. Baseball is built on rejection at some point, and the general managers have to break up and rebuild clubs on a yearly basis. I understand that a lot better now than I did then. I was really frustrated because I played for a few more years, but I was never the same.

Randy Hundley has his fantasy camp, and I started going about five years after I retired. Once I went the first time, I knew I had to keep going. It was a great chance to be with my teammates, and Randy was smart enough to add some of the younger retirees to keep it fresh. It's truly a reunion for my teammates and for the great people that come to play every year.

The older '69 guys like Randy, Beck, Billy, Fergie, and all of them have formed great friendships with my teammates. It's almost like a big brother relationship. They have taken us under their wing and made us feel welcome. It's truly a joy to be around them. When we're with them at the camp, it's also a great way to keep the 10-year-old in you alive and the competitve juices flowing. And, believe me, at that camp, it goes. When we play the final game against the campers, we want to win. They did beat us once, but I think the former Cubs are something like 51–1, and we want to keep it that way!

It's a great reunion with that '84 team any time we can get together at any opportunity. It's a lifelong love affair. We all have a very unique relationship with the Cubs, with the great fans, and it's one we're fortunate to be a part of. I hope the good Lord lets me continue to be part of it as long as I'm around.

Bob Dernier joined the Cubs with Gary Matthews and Porfi Amalfitano on March 26, 1984, in a trade with the Phillies for Mike Diaz and Bill Campbell. He had an outstanding season for the Cubs in the leadoff spot, hitting .278 with 45 stolen bases, and scoring 94 runs while setting the table for MVP Ryne Sandberg as part of the "Daily Double." Following the season, Dernier won a Gold Glove for his outstanding play in center field. Injuries hampered the rest of his Cubs career, and he returned to the Phillies as a free agent after the 1987 season. Dernier currently works in the Cubs organization as an outfield/base-running coordinator for the minor league system.

GARY MATTHEWS

LEFT FIELDER

1984–1987

THERE'S NO DOUBT BEING TRADED to the Cubs worked out well for me. It was bitter at the time only because I wanted to remain in Philadelphia, and I had some unfinished business. Coming from Philly to here was bitter, but after getting here, you couldn't have asked for a better place, because again, they had never won. You've got to remember, Chicago was always a place that if you were in a slump, you could come in and build your average up, then go on from there and be able to take the rest of the season on. To be able think about that and know that you're losing all those hits, it wasn't going to be good for me. But to come in and all of a sudden win, the way that we won, with the characters that we had, I didn't mind the sacrifice and giving up the personal stats for the common goal of winning.

Basically, when I got here, I just instilled the idea that we could win. For example, in batting practice, we would play a game where you have to get a guy over and then get him in. Then, during the game, those situations come up, and you were prepared to do just that. As a No. 3 hitter, if I have a guy on second base, yes, you want to drive him in. But if I sacrificed or hit the ball to the right side in an unselfish way, that stuff really rubbed off. A team that plays the hardest, a team that plays for each other can overcome a team with more talent. That type of team usually comes out on top. Here in Chicago, it's really pretty easy. When I came over, the fans as a whole were really hungry for a winner. I knew that if I went out and gave my best, they would

Gary Matthews, nicknamed "Sarge" for his leadership on and off the field, helped spur the 1984 Cubs to a division title as their starting left fielder. He rejoined the team in 2003 as a coach on manager Dusty Baker's staff.

Photo courtesy of Getty Images

184

get behind me. That's exactly what happened in 1984. Plus, none of the other pro teams in town had had any recent success, so the fans were extra hungry.

When I got there in spring training, I said, "Guys, let's get ready to win this." Most of them felt since I hadn't seen them in spring training when they were so terrible, I was a bit out of my mind to say the Cubs could win in '84. Well, we got off to a good start, but the thing was, we were sacrificing for each other, and when we won three or four in a row, guys started to believe that maybe I wasn't crazy. I had been to the World Series and lost the year before with the Philllies, and there were a lot of guys on our Cubs team I knew from the Phillies organization. We went out fast and put pressure on the other teams in the East, and the rest is history. We ended up one game from the World Series.

There were so many great moments that year, it's hard to pick out one. Seems like most of my teammates can quickly identify one game when they knew it was going to be our year. I do know we were in a bit of a tailspin in September, and I was talking to Garry Maddox, and he reminded me that we always got it done in Philadelphia. I think I got three game-winning hits in a row on the way to the clinch.

Game 1 of the playoffs was a piece of cake. We went out and kicked butt and handled them in Game 2. Once we got to San Diego, there was a big turnaround in the way the games were played, and they were the better team. We needed one game out of three to get to the World Series, but we didn't get the job done.

I didn't feel overconfident. I felt Steve Trout should have pitched in San Diego, given the way he pitched during the season and how he won Game 2 of the series. He was a sinkerball pitcher, and they were a fastball-hitting team. We put all of our eggs in one basket with Rick Sutcliffe in the last game and spotted him a lead. But San Diego had a good-hitting ballclub and got it done.

I've never forgotten about losing to the Padres to this day. There are days when I will actually wake up in a cold sweat, hoping that I could have had just one more good game. I know that it is a team sport, but if you hit the way that you can, you can overcome a lot of things. I think that for the first time, we really tried to force it, maybe, instead of just letting the game come to us.

A superstar isn't always the guy who has the most home runs or RBIs, it's the guy who can make everyone around him better. I got that gift from God early on: no matter what team I was on, last place or first place. I didn't have to score the most runs or get the most hits to be a leader, and I feel good about that.

The players on the '84 team were willing to sacrifice to manufacture a win. I would say it was the most fun I ever had with a team. The camaraderie was great. Nineteen eighty-three was great because we actually got to the World Series with the Phillies. Coming here in '84 after the way they had played in Arizona, then kind of taking the city by storm was really most gratifying.

In '85 we were in first place, but we ended up losing our whole pitching staff. I think after that particular year, it was more about breaking up. Guys were getting ready to, if not wanting to, leave. I think they were getting rid of them. When you look back on it, they might have left a few crumbs on the table.

I was happy to come back with Dusty Baker. In 2003 we should have been actually able to win that one game. Whether that club got enough credit remains to be seen. I thought they did. Funny things happen in this ballpark. I talk with Santo about it all the time. Freak injuries, [Ryan] Dempster jumping up and coming over a railing and breaking a toe, somebody with a bad back, going back to the Bartman days, and so on. Things happen here that you just can't explain.

Having played and been a part of this team as a coach and not being able to get it done is very bittersweet. There's no doubt that thirst for winning here becomes greater and greater as the years go on. I'm sure that Sandberg, Williams, and so on would agree that, "Man, I wish I could have done a little bit more to get our team to the World Series." We haven't been able to get across the finish line—it's like we've pulled a hamstring right at the line the few times we've gotten close. It's unfinished business.

We take pride in realizing that up until the '84 Cubs, you could get a seat at the Friendly Confines just about anywhere. After the '84 season, it wasn't to be, and I think the winning started after that. If you look back before that, they hadn't won before or since '69. I've always felt the 1984 ballclub was responsible for the fact that tickets are hard to come by at Wrigley Field now. If you look at the attendance in the years before '84, it was nothing like it was after.

I love coming here, and I love the fans here. It's gratifying that they feel strongly about your ability to play, but more so about the effort going in as opposed to the final cake. The ingredients going into the cake, that's what blue-collar people want to see.

I was not afraid to be out in front. Teammates have a lot to do with that, with the respect they give to you and the way they talk about you. You've got to have somebody who is out there and will take the heat whether it is good or bad.

Chicago is unbelievable. It's a great city, and more so now, not so much the Friendly Confines, because the people are finally tired of the lovable Cubs and the losing. They want a winner here, and they show it in displeasure with boos when they don't win. So be it. You should be able to come to big cities and play well. Certain things are expected of you, and if you're hitting in the third or fourth spot, if it's too hot in that kitchen, get out.

The Cubs Convention is incredible. Anyone who comes here for the first time, whether you are a fan or a player, it's something you never forget.

There are all ages, and sometimes I think I see some newborns there whose parents want them to be exposed to crowds and noise so they'll be ready to go to Wrigley Field. That's the best playground there is, with all the beauty and sunshine. Wrigley is special because kids can get there without a car via the El train, and that gives kids a chance to come to the ballpark on their own at a younger age than other places. I meet adults all the time who tell me how they skipped out of school to be at games in 1984. The weather here also makes an urgency to get to the ballpark on a nice day. It is a love affair with the fans here, without a doubt.

The Cubs acquired left fielder Gary Matthews, along with Bob Dernier and Porfi Amalfitano, from the Phillies on March 26, 1984, in exchange for Mike Diaz and Bill Campbell. "The Sarge" immediately took over the Cubs clubhouse and informed his teammates he was there to win. He led the Cubs to the Eastern Division title that season with 14 homers, 82 RBIs, 101 runs, and a league-leading 103 walks. Matthews played 97 and 123 games for the Cubs the next two years and was traded to Seattle midway through the 1987 season. He returned to the Cubs in 2003 as a coach under Dusty Baker and stayed with the team until 2006. He is currently a broadcaster with the Philadelphia Phillies.

RICK SUTCLIFFE

PITCHER

1984–1991

I WAS WITH CLEVELAND IN 1983, and I don't know if a lot of people know this, but I demanded to be traded. It was a bad team, and I just wanted to get out. They said to me that I would be giving up my right to free agency, but I didn't care. They said to pick six teams that I wouldn't go to. I told my agent take the six worst teams in baseball, and that's where I don't want to go. One of them was the Cubs in 1983. The Indians talked me out of that. They said, "Don't give up your free agency. You need to hang on to that. Come back. We're going to trade you at some point, anyway." I decided to do that, and it truly is amazing how quickly things changed with the Cubs. Things had changed before I even got here. The very first game my wife saw at Wrigley Field with me in a Cubs uniform was when Ryno just went absolutely crazy on that Saturday against the Cardinals.

That was the day where Ryno basically became known to the nation. He won the MVP, I think, that day, not that he didn't continue to do a lot of things the whole year. I'll never forget after the game when I walked out, my wife was just crying with excitement. She goes, "Are all the games like that here?" We had come from Cleveland, and there were more people at the park that day than we would normally see in a month. It was just amazing, the whole town and what was going on. Nobody could believe that it would actually happen, that we could get into the playoffs. All the things you read,

Rick Sutcliffe winds up in the first inning of Game 1 of the 1984 NLCS against the Padres at Wrigley Field. Traded to the Cubs in June, he went 16–1 the rest of the year, leading the team to a division title and earning the NL Cy Young Award.

all the things you heard about, the ups and downs during that last month of the season, it was really exciting to finally get to the postseason.

When you look back on the memories, obviously the thing that jumps out at me is that we never played a game on the road. I remember going to Dodger Stadium—and I was there, I started with the Dodgers, and the big Red Machine would come to town, but nothing ever happened like what happened in '84 when the Cubs went there. In the seventh inning, Jody Davis came up to hit, and the crowd, everywhere in the stadium, started chanting, "Jo-dee!" All of a sudden in the eighth when Ryno came to the plate: "M-V-P!" We may not have hit in the bottom of the ninth, but that year we never played on the road. We always had more fans in the ballpark than the home team did.

When we clinched in Pittsburgh, I remember walking to the bullpen that night, and there was a huge sign that read, "39 Years of Suffering Are Enough." I went up to the guy—and I'm not one of those guys who is cocky or whatever—and I said, "Is that your sign?" He said, "Yeah." I handed him the ball I'd warmed up with and said, "We're going to end it tonight." We all had so much confidence.

190

The fans made such an impact on me. I'll never forget all of the letters that I got at the end of '84 when I became a free agent. One in particular was from an older couple basically with tears on the paper, and she apologized for that, saying, "You have to come back to the Cubs. You don't understand, you're not just a player. You've become part of our family. Every fifth day when you pitch, we set a plate for you at either the lunch table or the dinner table the night before." I've got goosebumps on me right now remembering the impact that had on me.

I was a free agent after that season. As a kid growing up in Kansas City, Missouri, my dream was to play for the Kansas City Royals. That was the plan all along. In 1985 I was going to do that, but something happened that magical summer of '84 after the trade. Harry Caray gave me a nickname of the "Red Baron." It was just so much more than being a pitcher on a base-ball team. You truly felt that you were part of a family, and it was an honor to go back there for seven more years.

The first night game in '88 was by far the biggest event I was ever involved in. Everybody from Bill Murray to Mark Harmon to Brooks & Dunn to Alabama, all my buddies, everybody wanted tickets to that game. When I came over in June of '84 and I pitched the first game of the playoffs that year, Dallas Green told me I could have all the tickets I wanted as long as I won that game. Well, I got all the tickets I wanted. It was a different story for the Opening Night. I had 10 Opening Days, there was always going to be another Opening Day, but we didn't think there was going to be another Opening Night. I'll never forget, I think Harry Caray and I were the only ones who were on the same wavelength. As I was warming up in the bullpen, I was thinking, *Fine, everybody's got their tickets, I'm in*. I went out on the mound, and I'll never forget, the Hall of Fame said, "Hey, whatever you do, don't let them put the first ball in play." So I was told to just miss the outside corner because they wanted to take the ball to the Hall of Fame. So I did that, but as I turned to go to home, I thought the stadium exploded. I thought, *What in the world was that?* Nobody had ever taken pictures of me not like that. Everybody in the ballpark took a picture. I was kind of blinded, my vision was blurred, and I said to myself, "C'mon, you've pitched in big games before. What's the problem with this one?" The next thing you know, I'm trying to settle down and figure out what just happened. It was special, I'm sure it was a great night for the people at Kodak. I'm sure they sold a lot of film that night.

In 1989 I remember everybody getting hurt the first month of the season, and right after the All-Star Game, Don Zimmer brought Mike Bielecki, Greg Maddux, and myself into his office. He said, "With you guys on the mound, we got a chance. With anybody else, we lose every game. I'm going to run you out there every third day when I can." I remember saying right then, "You can do it to Bielecki and me, but not Maddux. His career is just getting going." Maddux goes, "What do you mean? With my arm I can do it. It's not a problem for me." I knew right then that, you know what, this truly was a team.

I'll never forget when we lost in the playoffs to the Giants. Don Zimmer came in and held a meeting. He said, "Let me tell you something, boys. Most of you don't know my history. When I was in Boston, my family couldn't even come to the game and watch because I was the dumbest manager on the face of the earth. Because of you guys, I'm probably going to be the Manager of the Year. I didn't do anything different. You guys just played harder than any other team in baseball this year." He was bawling. "I just want to thank you guys for what happened." When you look back on that year, Don

Zimmer, where usually a manager might make the difference in 10 or 15 games in a year, he might have made the difference in 25 or 30 that year, with the way he motivated people, the moves he made late during the course of the ballgame, and just bringing people together.

I really don't look at '84 and '89 as a curse. I think about the fans, and now being in the broadcast booth from this angle, we had great summers those two years. It had been a long time since anything really happened here in the month of October. Yeah, granted, no question about it, we wanted to go further and felt that we should have, especially in '84. I've never been a part of anything that overachieved like that '89 team did. I'll take the best Cubs fan out there, and I want you to sit down and tell me what our outfield was the first week of May after Dawson and everybody else went down. We pieced together a rotation, and it seemed like Maddux pitched every third day. We had to—it was our only chance to win. That was a lot of fun.

Eighty-four was a cast of characters. To me, '84 should be a movie, and it could go in a lot of different directions. I don't know if there was a leading character, but there were a lot of people who were supporting actors who did a great job that year. I look at both of those years as a lot of success.

I never wanted to go anywhere else. Everybody knows that. It's kind of interesting. When Andre Dawson wanted to play here, I offered part of my salary to sign him. I got a handwritten letter from Dallas Green telling me that I needed to shut up. He would be the manager/president, you just go pitch. It was the same kind of thing. At the end of the '91 season, I'd had surgery and felt bad that I wasn't able to do more, but I knew that I was healthy. I told Larry Himes and the Cubs that I would come back for minimum salary, just throw in some incentives. They had no interest in me even at that level. It hurt me to go to Baltimore.

These fans were great to me when I got sick. I was sitting around all year with colon cancer, not knowing what was going to happen—chemo, radiation, three different surgeries. I have reread every letter that I got then, and 90 percent of them are from Cubs fans. A lot of them are people I never met, they're just people saying they enjoyed the effort, and if you can overcome these things on the field, we have no doubt you can overcome cancer. A big, big part of that is staying positive and living strong!

It all started for me when I was able to come back for Game 1 of the 2008 Division Series and throw out the first pitch. As I walked to the mound, I was in tears, and when I got the ovation, after going through radiation, chemotherapy, and three surgeries, that felt great. I had an iliostomy bag on when I did it. You set goals and you want to do things, so to get to the booth, have Ron Santo give me a thumbs up, see Vin Scully put his hands together and bow, that was the first day when I was able to say that it was all worth it. I'd like to remind everybody to get a colonoscopy if you're 50, because it gives you a chance. I was 51 and didn't think I needed it. I had no signs of illness, but my wife forced me to go, and thank the Good Lord, that's how they found my cancer.

I truly found out why they call Wrigley Field the "Friendly Confines." When I look back on it now, coming over here in 1984, I met a lot of people I had never met before. When you talk about Dallas Green, Harry Caray, John McDonough, Ryno, Jody, Sarge, Zonk, you're talking about some of my best friends on earth. I'm sure that's where the name originated. You walk into this place, and you're gonna fall in love with the people here, and they're going to end up being your best friends.

It's always like coming home here. You don't know how bad I want to grab a sleeping bag at night, go out on that little bump in the middle of the infield, and spend the night.

The Cubs were just beginning to make noise in 1984 when Dallas Green made one of the boldest trades in franchise history on June 13 by obtaining Rick Sutcliffe in exchange for Joe Carter, among others, in a seven-player deal. Sutcliffe was magnificent, leading the Cubs to the postseason for the first time in 39 years. He went 16–1 and won the National League Cy Young Award. Sutcliffe won Game 1 of the NLCS over San Diego that year but faltered in the deciding Game 5. The "Red Baron" was dogged by injuries for the remainder of his Cubs career, but he posted a mark of 18–10 for a last-place team in 1987 and went 16–11 for a surprising NL East championship team in 1989. The right-hander was selected to the National League All-Star team both years. Sutcliffe remains one of the most popular Cubs in history and can be found at the Cubs Convention, Randy Hundley's Fantasy Camp, and as a volunteer coach during spring training. He is currently a television analyst for ESPN.

SHAWON DUNSTON

SHORTSTOP

1985–1995 ★ 1997

I DIDN'T REALLY UNDERSTAND about being the No. 1 draft pick until I got to the minor leagues and saw guys with just as much talent as I had. I think I always worked a little bit harder. When they called me up in '85, I was ready physically but not mentally. I had just turned 22 and was the only rookie on the team. I watched when other guys came up, and they were always with other guys they had played with in the minor leagues. It's a little easier for those guys.

Playing with Ryne Sandberg was nice. He didn't say much, though. All he ever said was, "Good morning," and, "You have everything." I did lots of talking for everybody in the clubhouse, but on the field I really didn't talk much.

I don't know any shortstop who could throw harder than I did. I'll give you three who are up there with me—Garry Templeton, Rafael Furcal, and Troy Tulowitzki. I think I've got 'em, though. I always threw like that and still do now when I'm throwing batting practice. They don't want me to throw too hard, because I'm breaking bats, but I'm learning to take something off, even though that's hard. I just have always thrown it hard and couldn't throw the ball soft.

To be honest, I was always going to make 15 or 20 errors, but Gracie would save me about 10 a year. I'm really grateful for that and not complaining. I tell him thanks, because he got my house paid for, and I got him four Gold Gloves!

194

Andre Dawson had the most influence on me of any player I played with. He taught me to just go out and play. I'd say, "Andre, I just want to do it so bad." He said, "I know, but the pitcher knows that, and everyone knows that. You have to slow down and let the game come to you." He was always positive with me, whether I had a good game or a bad game.

When I was the veteran, I remember trying to help Dwight Smith. I'd didn't like it, because I was only 26 at the time. I had five years in the big league when guys started coming to talk to me. Andre was babying Dwight and Jerome Walton, and Mark Grace and I got jealous, I guess, so I took Dwight. He was my good friend and still is. I told him to play hard, do the best he could, and we'd see what happened.

Cubs shortstop Shawon Dunston raps a ball to left field against the Astros at Wrigley Field in a May 1990 game. *Photo courtesy of Getty Images*

I like playing day baseball. I didn't know when I came up with the Cubs they only played day games. I was 22, didn't need any rest, and was fine. As I got older, I was fine with some night games!

The "Shawon-O-Meter" started in 1989. I remember coming to the stadium when my average was .172, so I didn't think it was too funny. I was in the parking lot, and the guy who had it told me if I signed it, it would bring me some good luck. At that point, you try and do anything. Everyone was teasing me when I took the field saying, "Shawon, look. They're showing your average!" I didn't think it was funny, but then my average started going up. Harry Caray got to it, and when Harry started saying, "Where's the meter, Shawon? Feed the meter, feed the meter," it really got big. Everyone knew my name. They knew Andre, Ryno, and Mark, then I came in. I was wild Shawon, throwing the ball all over the place and making plays, then my average started going up, too. I was getting noticed, and that helped me in arbitration, too!

It always seemed like it was the older fans who liked me. I think they appreciated the way I played. I wasn't a guy who thought about his stats—I just went out there and played for the name on the front of the uniform instead of the back.

196

In '89 I remember we were losing 9–0 to the Astros and came back and won that game 10–9. That was the moment when I knew we had a pretty good team. The clincher in Montreal was very nice. I had a little cold, but after we won, I didn't. I really enjoyed myself. They put mashed potatoes in my face and all over me. That was a nice feeling and one of the best feelings of my entire career.

We lost to the Giants in the playoffs. I'm with them now, and we always talk about it. Guys say they whupped us, but I tell them, "Whatever. You just had an older team. If we'd have played you again, we'd have whupped you."

When I hurt my back in '92, it was difficult because I was just coming into my own. I had just signed a four-year contract, and the game was starting to come slower to me. I was starting to get it, then I hurt my back picking up my daughter. I always tell her I'd do it again, though. There were times I've thought about what kind of player I might have been if I hadn't gotten hurt, but that's how it goes. I still teach my son, you have to go out and play hard no matter what. I did come back from my back surgery. A lot of guys don't, but I played another seven or eight years.

I was lucky to be an All-Star twice. I didn't play in Cincinnati in 1988 when my wife was pregnant with my daughter, Whitney. In 1990 my wife was pregnant again, and we had Jasmine. So the two years I made the All-Star team I had my daughters. I played with Ryno at Wrigley in '90, and when they introduced me, I got a standing ovation. Andre was in right field, and that was a beautiful feeling. I felt like I had made it when I made the All-Star team with Andre and Ryno.

When I left, it hurt. I couldn't sleep for a few days. I left and went to the Giants, then came back to the Cubs, and they let me go in the middle of the night to the Pirates.

I don't care what anybody says, I'm still a Cub. They still holler "Shawon-O-Meter" at me. I'm proud to be a member of the Cubs. They say the Cubs are losers, but I don't think so. I appreciated playing for them. There were times when we were 30 games out of first and when we came to the ballpark, it was a sellout. If you hadn't told me about the standings, I'd have thought we were in first. Those fans, sometimes I don't know why they root for us, but they really love us. That's why I always gave it my best; I really appreciate them. They are the best fans. I appreciate the Cubs for taking care of me and my family.

The Cubs made Shawon Dunston and his bazooka throwing arm the first overall pick in the 1982 amateur draft. Dunston joined the club in 1985 and became the regular shortstop in 1986. He hit .278 with nine homers and 60 RBIs in 1989 as the Cubs won the National League East. That season saw the birth of the "Shawon-O-Meter," a Wrigley Field bleachers sign by Cubs fan Dave Cihla that tracked Dunston's batting average. Dunston was named to the National League All-Star team in 1988 and 1990. A back injury in 1992 caused him to miss most of the next two seasons, but he turned in his finest offensive season in 1995 with a .296 average, 14 homers, and 69 RBIs. Dunston signed with San Francisco in 1996 and played there one year. He rejoined the Cubs in 1997 and hit .284 in 114 games before being traded to the Pirates. Dunston retired in 2002 after stints with the Indians, Cardinals, Mets, Cardinals, and Giants. He currently works as a coach in the San Francisco Giants system.

ANDRE DAWSON
RIGHT FIELDER
1987–1992

NINETEEN EIGHTY-SEVEN was the best year of my career, but it didn't really start out good. I lost my grandmother that year. I was a free agent without a team. I was being hassled about a contract after 10 years of service. It wasn't really looking up, but I guess I prayed a lot, which is what my grandmother always told me to do. I didn't set any goals that year. I dedicated the year to her. I said I'm just going to go out and have fun, and what happens, happens. I came to Chicago with a blank contract, and that was a huge burden lifted because I knew that, well, now there's somewhere I'm going to play. I wasn't concerned about numbers or anything like that. If I was healthy, all that was going to even out. It just turned out to be a dream-type year. Every time something would happen from a positive standpoint, I would look up to the heavens and think of my grandmother. The fact that things turned out the way they did, the MVP and all that, just made it that much more rewarding. At the end of the season, I said I knew that I could honestly let her go now, because I knew all along that she was with me.

I had reached a stalemate with Montreal ownership over my contract negotiations. I felt after being there for 10 years, that kind of treatment was a slap in the face to me. It really wasn't about monetary issues, it was about being fair. It was about sitting down for negotiations for an extension so I would retire with the Expos. It didn't work out that way, and there were a couple places I envisioned playing. Chicago was my first alternative, and

Atlanta was my second choice because it was closer to my home. Collusion played a huge role in my free agency, and when I wasn't signed, I felt I had to come up with something that was really an eye-opener for an organization but not be too embarrassing and go from there. My agent and I thought about a blank contract, because I still felt I had my best years ahead of me if I got off the Astroturf. We came up with a scenario where, if we let an organization fill in the blank contract, I could go somewhere and play where I wanted to play.

I realized I was sticking my neck out, but I was going to be man enough to live up to it. It wasn't about monetary issues when it came to changing uniforms. It was about finding a natural playing surface and letting the game be fun and enjoyable for me again. When I agreed to the $500,000 the Cubs wrote in, Dallas Green paused for a second and asked if he could get back to me in a half hour. I guess he had to think about my offer, and I told him to take his time. I just wanted to get that behind me, get into spring training somewhere, and get on with the season.

I got off to a slow start and struggled. I didn't really get going until I hit a grand slam in St. Louis off Todd Worrell. I was pressing a little bit because I wanted to make a huge impact right away. I had to look at myself in the mirror and tell myself, "You've been in the game for 10 years. Just relax and have the fun that you set out to have."

In Chicago I can understand how a player will struggle from the outset, but the one thing I always try to reiterate to players who go there for the first time is to get their rest. That's a given. Day games for me played to my advantage for some reason. I always had better numbers during the day than the night. I just felt it was like spring training. In the morning, you eat breakfast and go to the ballpark. In the evening, I always took a nap, even before I ate dinner, then I'd get up and eat, and it made the night a little longer.

By summer, I was swinging the bat really well. We were playing San Diego, and I think I had six home runs against the Padres, and it wasn't even the All-Star break yet. Larry Bowa was managing the Padres at the time, and he made a comment in the paper that morning that his pitching staff needed to back me off the plate. I didn't read too much into it, but I hit a home run off Eric Show to knock him out of a game in San Diego a few weeks before they got to Chicago. Then I hit a home run off him in the first inning that day. The next at-bat, he beaned me in the face, and I was fine until Leon Durham was standing over me and said, "It's a shame. We're supposed to be

199

Andre Dawson made himself at home in right field for the Cubs in 1987, hitting 49 homers with 137 RBIs, and earning league MVP honors. *Photo courtesy of Getty Images*

professionals and not enjoying ourselves, but look at that guy's face." All I could think of was getting up and trying to find Show. It was a rare occurrence for me.

Of course, your teammates are going to stand up for you. Greg Maddux was in his rookie season, and he retaliated by hitting Benito Santiago. That said a lot for a kid who didn't have his feet underneath him to understand that part of the game.

These fans embraced me from day one. As a visitor, I always thought Wrigley Field was special and enjoyed my games here. To have the chance to play here on an everyday basis, that was something that was extra special. I had always heard a lot about Cubs fans and how they build relationships with certain players, but it's only when you play here on a daily basis that you see what people are talking about. For me, it was extremely special. I said one of these days I'm going to stop and salaam back just to show my gratitude for what they have instilled in me over the years. It was a wonderful feeling. It made you feel accepted and know that you did something that was pleasing to the crowd. You don't want to be a crowd-pleaser, but you want to make sure that when they go home, you leave them with the impression they came out saw something exciting.

The first night game was something everyone was looking forward to, especially to be a part of history. We had the rain on the first night and had Sutcliffe going for us. I was excited to be a part of it. The park was a little bit dark to me at the outset, and it took some getting used to. The lights were only so high, and in the outfield, I didn't feel you found the brightness you had at the other ballparks. Around home plate it was fine. A lot of hype surrounded that game, and I enjoyed it for a short time, but from there, you started to add night games here and there over the years.

In 1989 Don Zimmer was magical. He did a lot of things and had these hunches. He'd say, "I've got a gut feeling." That was his favorite expression. He would hit and run with the bases loaded with less than two outs. With Zim, you never knew, so you had to stay on your toes. He was one of the managers whom I had the best time playing for. He turned out to be a good friend after he left the manager's job. All he demanded was that you come to the ballpark every day, play the game, and don't embarrass the organization or the fans. To me, that wasn't asking a lot. That's probably why I felt the way I did about him.

I was struggling with my health by the time we got to the playoffs that year, but there was no way I was going to miss that stage for a team that was trying to get back to the playoffs after what had happened in 1984. I was facing knee surgery, which became a yearly occurrence for me once I got to Chicago, but I knew if I wasn't in the lineup, it would be a huge setback for our young ballclub at the time. Being in the lineup might have been a hindrance to the club, but I was willing to bite the bullet and go out there and give it my best. It was a dismal playoff series for me personally, but I enjoyed

201

the excitement of everything during the season leading up to that point. I didn't do what I would have liked during the playoffs against San Francisco, and obviously our team suffered as a result.

My favorite moment had to be when we clinched it in Montreal in 1989. There was a three-home-run day when we beat the Phillies in '87. I was exhausted after the game. It was almost 100 degrees, and it was very tough running on and off the field for nine innings soaking wet. I could barely swing the bat up at the plate. I found the energy to deliver three home runs, which was a first for me. We won the ballgame, but only scored five runs.

Playing in pain was part of my makeup, part of my upbringing, and I was told that I would probably last all of four years because of my history of knee problems. I won't say it motivated me, but it made me aware of just how fast things can end. I took the attitude that my work ethic had to be impeccable. If I was going to go down, I was going to go down leaving everything on the playing field. My attitude every day was to give it all I had and not worry about the outcome.

It was special for me that all our games were on WGN. I made sure I got my mom a satellite so that she could watch back home in Miami. She never wanted to watch me play live. She wouldn't come to a ballgame, because she feared I'd get hurt. I'd gotten hurt in a high school football game when she was there, so she wouldn't go watch me play again. I purchased a dish for her so she could watch all the games on WGN, and that was special. Harry Caray was a Pied Piper, and the attention that came with him on WGN made us a commodity all across the country.

What stands out for me is that I was able to play on a natural playing surface in front of the greatest fans of my whole tenure. When I look back on my career, those six years for me turned out to be a new beginning. The fact that I won an MVP award on a last-place team in Chicago in my first year there after coming close twice in Montreal kind of sticks out. I was very excited my first year to have the chance to play there on an everyday basis. I played there for six years but wish I would have had the opportunity to play in Chicago longer. I look back at those six years, and they were golden.

I get invited to the Cubs Convention every year, and I look forward to it because it just gets bigger and bigger. The only drawback is if the weather will let you get in or out. It's an opportunity to mingle with these great fans, and I enjoy it. To be among all these fans is really something.

I've sung the seventh-inning stretch a few times now. It was really scary the first time. It's a lot different up in the booth than it is when you look up there from the field. Looking down is a different view, and you can see that every single seat is taken. I was nervous the first time, but I was able to enjoy it more each time after that. You try to mimic Harry, but you can't do him justice. If you can get the fans involved, that's exciting for everyone.

I follow the Cubs every day. I check the box score to see where they are in the standings. Of course, I have loyalty to the Marlins, whom I work for now, but Chicago and the Cubs fans were great to me. Every day I'm anxious to look at the paper and see what the Cubs did the day before.

Anything that has to do with Cubs baseball, Ernie is going to be there, and Billy isn't far behind. It's wonderful to be mentioned in the same breath with those guys. To have the opportunity to play with this organization and this city is overwhelming. Until you do it, you can't understand. Every player should experience being a Chicago Cub. It was golden for me, and I always tell players, if you ever have the opportunity to play in Wrigley Field on an everyday basis, don't pass it up. There's nothing like it. It's not about winning or losing, it's the excitement, the electricity, and the adrenaline that goes through you when you are playing for the Cubs organization in that ballpark. It can't be matched.

203

After being left out in the cold after the 1986 season, Andre Dawson presented the Cubs with an offer they couldn't refuse—to play one year for a blank contract to be filled in by the team. Dallas Green bit, and for a $500,000 bargain, got an MVP season from Dawson. Andre led the league with career highs in homers (49) and RBIs (137), but the Cubs still finished last in the division. Dawson averaged 25 homers and 90 RBIs over his next five seasons with the team, while earning two Gold Gloves for his play in right field and becoming one of the most popular players to ever wear a Cubs uniform. The Cubs let him leave after the 1992 season, and he finished his career with the Boston Red Sox and his hometown Florida Marlins. He ended his career with 438 homers, 1,591 RBIs, eight All Star appearances, and eight Gold Gloves. In 1999 he was named to the Cubs All-Century Team. Dawson currently works with the Marlins as a special assistant to the president. On January 6, 2010, Dawson was elected to the Baseball Hall of Fame, the only player selected in his class.

GARY PRESSY
WRIGLEY FIELD ORGANIST
1987–Present

MY GRANDFATHER PLAYED the violin by ear. He had a cousin in the New York Philharmonic Orchestra, so music is in my family. I would hum music when I was two years old. When I watched baseball, I would listen to the organ in the background. I would go into my backyard and do the national anthem, be the PA announcer and the organist, everything. Sports and music got in my blood. I always wanted to mix them together, and this has worked out pretty well.

I used to play the organ for the Chicago Sting soccer team at Wrigley Field. John McDonough and Connie Kowal were both working for the Sting and when they moved over to the Cubs, I let them know I'd be interested in playing for the Cubs. In 1986 Connie called me, and I filled in on the organ for three games. In 1987 they had auditions, and I got the job on April 1—April Fool's Day.

The first game I ever did at Wrigley was on Mother's Day, which was really cool because my mom is my biggest fan. We played San Diego. I had gotten the call two days before and was all excited. That was my life's dream. My first game as a full-timer was in 1987, and the Cubs lost to St. Louis 9–3.

My favorite game as a fan was June 22, 1969, when Jim Hickman hit a ninth-inning homer to beat Montreal in Game 1 of a doubleheader. That was the first time Ron Santo clicked his heels running down the left-field line.

Wrigley Field organist Gary Pressy also entertains fans each year at the Cubs Convention. *Photo courtesy of Bob Vorwald*

My favorite as an organist was September 9, 1989: we were playing St. Louis and were a half game in first place. Luis Salazar hit a double down the right-field line to drive in Andre Dawson. The Cubs held onto first, and that was my first really memorable game as an organist. I got to play at the 1990 All-Star Game at Wrigley Field, and that was a wonderful highlight.

For a 1:20 game, I get to the ballpark around 10:30 and arrange the CDs the marketing department gives me to play for batting practice. Around 11:45 or so, I'll take over on the organ and play until around 12:20. Then we have public address announcements, which gets us to 1:00. Sometimes I'll play songs to go along with the announcements, like "Steal Away" when they are doing a stolen-base total. When the starting lineups are announced, I will do a song for each Cubs player, such as "You're Sixteen" for Aramis Ramirez or "Happy Days" for Alfonso Soriano.

When Wayne Messmer sings the national anthem, I will accompany him on the organ. Most of the time, the other singers sing a cappella. When the game starts, I play to keep the crowd going, which isn't hard since we're packed almost every day. I play hand-clapping music and other things for that. Between innings, I play some CD music and also a few songs on the organ. Then it's time for the seventh-inning stretch.

I played "Take Me Out to the Ballgame" for Harry Caray all those years. As he got older, he couldn't hear very well. One day, he came in and said, "Gary, what the hell happened? I couldn't hear you." I told him the sound system was having a problem, and he said, "Well then fix it, dammit!" I guess he thought I was an electrician, too!

Playing for Harry was a highlight of my career. He would say, "All right, Gary, let me hear ya!" and at the Cubs Convention, fans would come up to me and say, "Oh, you're Gary!"

When Harry passed away in 1998, we started having celebrity guests sing the stretch, which we are still doing. I meet people from all walks of life—politicians, athletes, actors, all kinds of people.

Some of them get really nervous. I remember the day Kerry Wood struck out 20 guys, because Joe Mantegna sang that day, and he was totally nervous. I remember that day because Joe almost froze when he sang. The day Bill Murray sang for the wild-card playoff game, he threw $20 bills out the window. Unfortunately, none of them flew my way!

The singer usually comes into my booth in the top of the sixth inning to rehearse. It's just awesome. I was a big Boston Celtics fan, and the day Dave Cowens sang, we talked for 15 or 20 minutes about basketball. I love getting to talk to all of them, but they do take it seriously and they do get nervous.

With 40,000 people screaming, it can be hard to hear the organ, but as long as they start off good, they usually do okay. Harry always sang in the key of D, and the song was written in that key. Some of the professional singers don't mess around and want me to play in a specific key. The non-singers do it in the key of D.

206

July 5, 1998, was Mike Ditka's day to sing. Obviously, he didn't stop by the booth for practice, because he was so late and ended up running, or hopping really, into the broadcast booth to sing. When he started into it, I went into the polka tempo. We scored two runs in the bottom of the inning and five the next, and I told John McDonough that he put the stretch on the map with his hurry-up version. It was really funny. Ozzie Osbourne wasn't too shabby. Personally, I think he may have sung the song backward! I don't know if his version was an act or not.

I get to push the button and play "Go Cubs Go" at the end of the game when we win. We put the words on the scoreboard, so I sync up with Andie Giafaglione, who runs the message board. Everybody sings along, and it's a great atmosphere. I keep dreaming that my last song of the year I get to play on the organ will be "We Are the Champions."

When I pick a player's song, I try to coordinate with his number or his name. For Carlos Zambrano, I play the bull chant. For Mark DeRosa, I used to play the "Bonanza" theme for the Ponderosa. I try to make it pretty obvious, because I don't want the fans to be scratching their heads. I'm always thinking about what to play. When the Cubs signed Milton Bradley, my first thought wasn't if could he play right field, but what song would I play? I settled on "Games People Play" by the Spinners.

I do listen to other organists, but no, we don't really have a club. We have another great organist here in Chicago in Nancy Faust. I've filled in for her at other venues. She's great. We're great friends, and I sure hope we get to do a duet at the World Series some day! I listened to organists in the background when I had games on the radio as a kid.

We don't get many foul balls in our booth, but the last one came in and broke our fax machine in 2004. I know how to duck for cover if I have to. It was busier my first year when we were down a level where the suites are now. That was like a shooting gallery when we were down there. Keith Morcland would always hit foul balls up there.

It was very touching when I was asked to play the organ at Jack Brick-house's funeral in 1998. He was the voice I grew up with. I played "Hey Hey, Holy Mackerel" and then "The Impossible Dream," which was so fitting. I was truly honored when Pat Brickhouse asked me to do that.

In 1990 we had a game with the Atlanta Braves that never even started because of the rain, but wasn't called until around 3:30, so I was banging away for over two hours. Don Sutton was the Braves' broadcaster, and he told me I was named their player of the game and that they would send me a watch. It's a Wittnauer gold watch, and the engraving reads, "Atlanta Braves Player of the Game." I still have that, and every time I see Don I thank him for it. Rain delays keep me busy, because I have to keep plugging away.

207

When it is your life's dream to do something like this, it's amazing. We're in an era where parks use more and more CD music, and there aren't many ballparks that still have an organ. I am so fortunate to be with the Cubs in Wrigley Field playing on WGN and Comcast. As Lou Gehrig would say, I'm the luckiest man on the face of the earth. I get to go to the place of my dreams 81 times a year. There might be a few days when I don't feel great, but those fans really get me going. We can be in first or last, it doesn't matter. I'm playing at Wrigley Field.

Wrigley Field was the first ballpark to feature organ music, beginning in 1941. Gary Pressy was hired as the Cubs' organist in 1987 and is currently working on a consecutive games streak of more than 1,800 games.

VANCE LAW
THIRD BASEMAN
1988–1989

WHEN I BECAME A FREE AGENT after the 1987 season, it was right in the heart of the collusion era. I had a decent year with the Expos that year, and they were going to cut me and offer me 40 percent of my salary for the next year. I said, "You're not going to do that to me. I'll go anywhere for less money than you're offering me, because you don't treat people that way." The Cubs came in with roughly the same offer, and I decided that I loved Chicago and would try the North Side. It turned out to be a great blessing for me to get to back to Chicago. It was another club with great chemistry and a great bunch of guys. I was reunited with Andre Dawson, whom I had played with in Montreal and who had become a very good friend of mine. I got to know some wonderful guys who became good friends, too.

I made the All-Star Game in '88, and it was a bit of validation. Early in my career, there were some scouts who doubted me, and I remember one guy with the Pirates who said I would never be more than a backup player on a second-division team. To be selected as a National League All-Star was a great honor, and I almost felt like calling that scout and saying, "What do you think of me now?" I was never one to vocalize that kind of thing, but it certainly made me proud to think I had come a long way from where some people thought I would be. It was a great experience to go to Cincinnati with five of my teammates: Hawk [Andre Dawson] is about to go into the Hall of Fame; Sandberg already is in; and Maddux will be there. Rafael Palmeiro had

Cubs third baseman Vance Law is safe at first after a wild throw to Dodgers first baseman Mike Marshall during a game on April 26, 1988, at Dodger Stadium.

a great career, and I don't know what will happen with him. Shawon Dunston was the other guy who went, and I loved playing with him next to me. He was a fun, fun teammate.

The first night game that year came with so much controversy around the lights that I wasn't sure it was a good thing. There were so many people down on the idea. Frankly, we had a couple of practices there to test them out and see if you could see down the lines in the corners, because they weren't sure if there would be enough light down there because of the high walls. I thought it was a little dark, but it didn't matter what we thought—it was going to happen whether we liked it or not. I don't know what they did, but the lighting got better. I don't know if they added more or how they did it. That first game was really exciting. We got rained out in the first one against the Phillies on 8/8/88, but we won the next night against the Mets.

In '89 Zim never panicked. At the start of the year, our pitchers were having a tough time throwing strikes and were walking a ton of people. He had a meeting and said, "You know I'm tired of the media talking about the walks. I'm tired of talking about it, too. Get out there and throw strikes. Forget about the outside distractions you can't control. Just go throw strikes, forget about this stuff, and move on." Sure enough, our pitchers started throwing strikes, and we got some new blood to come in. Jeff Pico, Les Lancaster, and Steve Wilson were so-called no-name guys who came and really did a good job out of the bullpen for us. Mike Bielecki had a great year, and everybody knew that Sutcliffe and Maddux would be stalwarts, along with Scott Sanderson. Mitch Williams was there, causing all kinds of heart attacks not only in the stands but on the field. I remember his first game against the Phillies, he came in with a one-run lead, loaded the bases, then struck out the side. I was thinking, *Hey, this isn't the way it's supposed to be!* It turned out to be a great move for the Cubs.

It was fun to be a part of a team that wasn't expected to do much. Zim did a great job of downplaying all the outside distractions and just let us go and do our jobs. In mid-July, we were right in the thick of it, and I looked around our division and thought, *There's nobody that's any better than us. We might as well go ahead and win this thing.* The Mets were the one team I was most afraid of because of their pitching, but I thought offensively we could compete with anybody. It was just a matter of whether our bullpen could keep us in ballgames if our starters faltered at all. They certainly did their part to get us to the postseason.

Unfortunately, we didn't play very well in the playoffs. The Giants were a very good team, and I didn't feel like we played up to our potential in that series. It was certainly a fun ride getting there. I don't think we were the best team that year, but we played the best baseball.

I got a call from general manager Jim Frey that winter, and he said, "Have you ever thought about going to Japan to play?" I told him that I was only a year removed from being an All-Star, and I wasn't done. He told me I should really think about it, but I told them to release me if they didn't want me. They had gotten Luis Salazar late in the season. I asked him to trade me, but he said there were no takers. He didn't want to release me, and I had to think about the offer to play in Japan, so I ended up signing with the Chunichi Dragons. Once I got over there, I found out they had bought my contract for $400,000 or $500,000 from the Cubs. That's the story I got when I got over there. Whether that's what the Cubs would say, I have no idea. I was pretty bitter about it. I did not want to leave. I loved Chicago and loved playing for the Cubs. During '89 I had played with a bone spur in my neck and altered my stance so that I could turn my neck and see the pitcher. I didn't have the year I had in '88. Toward the end of the season, I started getting hot just before they picked up Salazar and was starting to feel more normal, but I didn't play a lot down the stretch.

I went to Japan and stuck it out for a year, then bought my way out of the contract. I had a good year there, and they wanted me to stay, but playing Japanese baseball and playing in the big leagues is a big, big difference.

I consider myself extremely fortunate. I couldn't have asked for a greater reception from both sides of town. I was very, very lucky to be able to play in Chicago during that period. I really enjoyed my teammates with the Cubs. I was fortunate to play on winners on both sides of town and feel like when I'm back in Chicago, people recognize my name, which is very flattering.

The son of pitcher Vern Law, Vance Law played on the South Side as the White Sox's third baseman from 1982 to 1984 and signed with the Cubs on December 14, 1987. He had a strong debut season in 1988 with a .293 average, 11 home runs, and 78 RBIs, and was named to the NL All-Star team. In 1989 a neck injury slowed him, and he slumped to a .235 average but remained a key contributor as the team won the NL East that season. Law spent the 1990 season in Japan with the Chunichi Dragons and played his final season in 1991 with the Oakland A's. He is currently the head baseball coach at his alma mater, Brigham Young University.

DON ZIMMER
SECOND BASEMAN
1960–1961
MANAGER
1988–1991

I WAS TRADED TO THE CUBS IN 1960, when they had that College of Coaches. It was a revolving door. The Cubs were good to me, but the last day of the year in 1961, Lou Boudreau had me on his pregame radio show and asked me what I thought of the situation. I said that I didn't want to involve any other player or coaches, but in my opinion, we had lost 90 games, yet the organization said the coaches' experiment worked. I thought that was the biggest joke in the world to have those revolving coaches, and I said to Boudreau that I only had a couple years left and I'd rather be elsewhere. We were going into the dugout, and Charlie Grimm said to me, "You said everything right, but you will be gone." The league was expanding by adding two teams, and each club had to put seven guys on a $75,000 list, two guys on a bonus list where you could only lose one guy for $125,000. I wasn't on either list, but they put Barney Schultz and Don Elston on the bonus list, then at the last minute they took Elston off and put me on when I said what I did. I was picked by the Mets. I loved Chicago, but it was tough.

Cubs manager Don Zimmer returns from the clubhouse to acknowledge the fans at Wrigley Field on the last home game of the regular season in 1989, a 4–2 win over the Pirates, after leading the Cubs to an improbable NL East title.

Santo was a rookie, and one coach would tell him to move in, one would say move over, and one would say move back. For a while, he didn't know which way to go. It was a popularity contest. One guy would be the head coach for two weeks, and you would be in the lineup, then another coach would take over, and you wouldn't play. I didn't think it had a chance of working.

I came back to Chicago when Jim Frey hired me as his third-base coach in 1984. We won the division that year, and that's when the whole Cubs thing exploded. It's gotten even bigger ever since. That team wasn't very good in spring training, but when we got Gary Matthews and Bob Dernier, our season turned around. Then we got Dennis Eckersley and Rick Sutcliffe to help our pitching staff, and we were really in it. I thought we were going to the World Series, but it didn't work out. Then, everyone got hurt, and we were a fourth-place team the next year. Eighty-six wasn't any better, and we got fired.

When the Cubs managing job came open after the '87 season, it was like a lottery. Every day the papers had a different guy managing the Cubs, with three or four names, and each day a different one would be the leader. I got tired of it, so I told my wife not to tell anyone, but I was going to Las Vegas. I was tired of listening to all of it. I knew a guy running a hotel out there, and we were having dinner, when I excused myself to go back and check if I had any calls. I had told my wife, if Jim Frey called, to tell him where to find me. Sure enough, there was a message from Frey. I called him back, and I remember to this day, he said, "Do you want to be the Cubs' manager?" I said, "Who the hell wouldn't want to be the Cubs' manager?" That's just what I said. He said, "You make reservations to get in around noon tomorrow, and we'll have a press conference at Wrigley Field. Take a cab to the Westin Hotel when you get in." We never discussed money or length of contract—nothing. Peter Durso, the traveling secretary, picked me up and took me to the hotel. Everybody there asked me if I was going to be the manager, and I said, "I hope so!"

I went to Wrigley Field, and they announced me as the manager. I still didn't know what I was making or how long my contract was. Frey often told the story about doing that and how unusual it was. I didn't need to know. I wanted to manage the Cubs.

I'll tell you what I've told people all my life—the greatest thrill I've had was in Chicago when we clinched the Eastern Division in 1989. That covers a lot of territory because I've done so much in baseball, including winning

World Series, but that moment in Montreal means so much because we were a team that came out of nowhere. When I was with the Red Sox, we were expected to win, and we always finished second. In 1989 we went to spring training, and I think everybody in America picked us to finish last. Before you knew it, it was the All-Star break, and we were right there close to first place. I said, "If we're this close halfway through, why can't we win it?" We had four rookies in the lineup—Joe Girardi, Jerome Walton, Dwight Smith, and Mark Grace. I can remember the press saying we couldn't win with a rookie catcher. Girardi could play, and having an inexperienced catcher was the least of my worries, because he was a bright kid. We kept winning, and those guys that year played so well. When we won it, I can remember hugging Jim Frey in Montreal, and we went upstairs with Ned Colletti to celebrate. We let the players do their thing, and we did ours. It was a big thrill.

I called the shots, but the shots aren't any good if your players don't execute them. You get lucky. Managing is like betting a race horse. You get lucky on a few races and win them all. It's the same way with managing, where you go along and you do things for two weeks where everything works. You walk a man and the next guy hits into a double play. You don't walk him and he pops up. Then, if things go bad for two weeks, you start to shut it down a little bit until things turn around. That was a year when everything went right. The players made all the plays. You have to be awful lucky—like on a suicide squeeze, you need a good pitch, and you have to get the bunt down.

After we lost to San Francisco, I felt like I let the players down. I had a goofy meeting during the season. It seemed like once a week, someone would write that Zimmer was a genius. To me, that was a joke. I was getting the credit for what my players were doing. I told them, "Guys, they are calling me a genius. No, it's the opposite. Every time I call for something, you guys are executing it. Not me. I haven't swung a bat or thrown a pitch." All I did was call the shots, and they did the right thing.

What can I say about the Chicago Cubs and the fans at Wrigley Field? If you're sitting in the dugout, you can't really hear anything going on behind you. One time, Shawon Dunston made an error, and as he came in the dugout, somebody said something nasty to him, and he yelled back. I grabbed him by the arm and pulled him into the dugout. I didn't like what he said, even though I could understand it, and I said to him, "Shawon, we have the greatest fans in the world. You have mothers and children sitting up there. For you to lash back at somebody like that, let me tell you something. You

215

will play for a lot of clubs, but you will never play for fans as good as the Cubs fans." He and I never had a problem again. That's the way I felt. I had fans boo me when I managed, and if they yelled, "Zimmer, you're a bum," I usually said, "You might be right." After that, they never knew what to say. If you argue with them, you have a war you don't want.

My wife and I lived in a high rise you can see when you look over the center-field fence at Wrigley. Every morning, I would get up around 7:00, and the first thing I would do is go to the window and look at the foul pole to see which way the flags were blowing. It's two different games when the wind is blowing in and when it's blowing out. You had to manage differently depending on the wind.

I came to Chicago and watched a game on a rooftop in 2007. I told Lou Piniella and Matt Sinatro I was going to be at the game watching on a roof. I looked down at them, and they were craning and looking out at right field, but I was in left field so they were looking the wrong way. I never expected to ever be up there outside Wrigley Field, but I made it one day. I had fun.

I can't say enough about the Cubs and Wrigley Field and the fans. I had a great time in New York, and I've been so lucky to play and manage in great cities, but Chicago is my favorite.

Don Zimmer was traded from the Dodgers to the Cubs in 1960. He played two seasons at second base in Chicago before being drafted by the Mets in the 1961 expansion draft. Zimmer served as Jim Frey's third-base coach from 1984 to 1986. When he took over as general manager, Frey hired Zimmer to manage the Cubs in 1988. After going 77–85 in his first season, Zimmer led the Cubs to a surprising 93–69 mark and the NL East title in 1989. Zimmer pushed every button imaginable that season, at one point successfully calling seven straight pitchouts and utilizing the suicide squeeze play 11 times. The Cubs' luck ran out in the NLCS, when they were beaten by the San Francisco Giants four games to one. The Cubs were only 77–85 in 1990, and when the club sputtered early in 1991, Zimmer clashed with Tribune executives and was gone 37 games into the season. Zimmer earned four World Series rings as Joe Torre's bench coach with the Yankees from 1996 to 2004 and currently serves as a senior baseball advisor for the Tampa Bay Rays.

The
NINETIES

GREG MADDUX

PITCHER

1986–1992 ★ 2004–2006

I WAS VERY FORTUNATE THAT when I was 15 or 16, my pitching coach Ralph Medard taught me that movement was more important than velocity. I believed him. I don't know why I believed him, but I believed him. You are only as smart as the advice you receive, and I was learning how to get movement on the baseball. Changing speeds was more important than velocity. Location was more important than velocity. You make up your stuff as you go along, try to add a little something here or there, and hope that it works.

The Cubs drafted me, and I didn't spend my bonus. When you sign out of high school, you don't know what's going to happen. I was going to save my bonus for college or whatever, in case baseball didn't work out. Luckily, it worked out pretty well for me.

I think it was Gene Michael who thought I was a batboy when I first came up. I'm sure he knew my name, but I don't think he knew what I looked like. So there I was, sitting on his bench, and I don't think he realized I was one of his players. I was called up in September 1986. Rick Sutcliffe, Scott Sanderson, Steve Trout, and Ed Lynch—the starting pitchers—all kind of took me in. Believe it or not, Lee Smith did also. They were pretty good to me. They showed me the way to do it—not only how to play the game, but to respect the game and respect your teammates. They were great players who gave me great lessons my first couple years in Chicago.

Greg Maddux pitches against the Pirates in a game at Wrigley Field on September 30, 1992. It would be the last game in his first stint with the Cubs and his first of four consecutive Cy Young Award–winning seasons. *Photo courtesy of Getty Images*

It was pretty cool when I faced my brother Mike in September that year. I had grown up playing against my brother an awful lot, and to do it on that stage in Philadelphia that night was something special. It was very special for my parents as well, and, yes, my team won.

Dick Pole taught me everything, really. I was a brain-dead heaver when I was in Double A. I reared back and threw it as hard as I could. I didn't really understand pitching as an art. Dick got me to understand that usually there is a right pitch to throw and there's also a lot of wrong pitches to throw, too. If you know the wrong pitch, it's just as valuable as knowing the right pitch at times. Dick was really good at helping me understand hitters and understanding myself as a pitcher. He taught me how to set hitters up, and how to not hurt myself was another important lesson he taught me. Always try to throw the high-percentage pitch, the pitch that can cause the least damage in a given situation, and understand all that may depend on what type of game you are in at the time.

When Eric Show hit Andre Dawson, I was pitching and hit Benito Santiago in return. I was afraid not to, to be honest with you. Don Zimmer was the manager then and said, "When you see this, you do this. Or else." I didn't understand it as much at the time as I would now, but I understood my manager wanted me to do something, and I probably better do it or I'll be going back to Iowa. I was happy to do it. I think we won that game, but the best thing was Hawk was okay. He got hurt pretty bad, but he rebounded fine, and we were glad to have him back.

What got me over the hump as a pitcher was when I finally took a chance to try something totally different because I thought it would work. I had a pitch like that when I was in Montreal and Delino DeShields was batting. I had him 1–2, but I was struggling with my fastball in at the time. The catcher called a fastball in, and I shook him off because I wasn't throwing that pitch well. I remember that I took a little two- or three-second break, yelled at myself, and called myself a few names. I got back on the mound and threw a quick pitch. It wasn't necessarily the pitch I had the most confidence in throwing, but it was the correct pitch to throw. I threw it, made a good pitch with it, and got the nicest little three-hopper back to me you will ever see. That one pitch made me realize I'd better start trusting what I see. Don't worry about how you feel, just do it right, and you will have success. That's when it all started for me personally as far as mentally getting over that hump to not be afraid to throw any pitch to any hitter at any time.

In 1988 I got off to a great start and had learned how to throw my change-up better. I was understanding that you have to be able to change speeds in order to have success as a pitcher. My first year I didn't change speeds well. I located my fastball okay, but I didn't change speeds well. I headed to winter ball with Dick after my first season, and he reminded me and taught me how to throw my change-up again. That was a great pitch for me for a long time.

Jim Frey and Don Zimmer said in 1989 if we played .500 ball, they would drink champagne, then they did because we ended up winning our division. It would have been nice to do better in the playoffs against the Giants, but that pennant race in September was something special. I still remember Mitch Williams getting that final out in Montreal, and the plane ride back with everyone greeting us at the airport was incredible. I remember thinking, *So this is what winning is all about.* It was pretty special. I did start that clinching game, and I remember Zim saying, "I've been making moves all year, and I've got one more to make." He grabbed the ball from me and brought Mitch in. That was pretty cool.

When I started Game 1 against the Giants, I think I tried to do too much. I think I tried to throw 100 mph when I could only throw 90. I really tried too hard. I rushed, I was anxious, I was tense, I was on edge, and I didn't think properly. It affected my mental game as bad as it could get back then. I turned into a brain-dead heaver and started chucking everything. Luckily, I didn't have a whole lot of other games like that after those two playoff starts.

The one thing that I do know about baseball is that you don't have to win to enjoy it. Winning definitely does make it more enjoyable, 100 percent more enjoyable, no doubt about it. We didn't win in those next years, but it was still fun. It was still fun going out there and playing the game. Getting paid to do something you love is unbelievable. It would have been nice to win more than we did after '89. We were ready to play every day, but it just didn't work out for us.

Winning my 20th game at Wrigley Field in 1992 was pretty special. As a young player, you always set personal goals. My goals were to win 20 games and to pitch in a World Series. To be able to accomplish one of those that year was very special for me.

It was real hard to leave for Atlanta after that season. That was just a big mess that went on, and that's when I started learning there was a business side to the game. I didn't want to go at the time, but it worked out for me. I had

221

a chance to pitch in the World Series several times and win one with Atlanta. It was even better that I got a chance to come back to Chicago.

It was great to play here again. It was so flattering the way I was received when I came back to play a second time. Being away for 11 years and leaving on bad terms the way it was back then—I guess time heals all wounds. It took a while, but to be accepted the way I was 11 years later, I can't thank the city and fans enough.

When I won my 300th game in 2005, the pressure that was on was all about the pennant race that year. This game has given me so much, I'd love to see the Cubs win a World Series, and I'd love to be a part of it. At the time, I knew I was going to win 300 sooner or later. It was about getting to the postseason and about getting the Cubs to have the chance to finally win that World Series ring. I was more concerned with that than I was with winning No. 300. I always figured they were going to score 10 runs for me sooner or later, so it didn't matter how I pitched, I'd get the win! I wanted the team to win, and we did win a lot of games down the stretch that year, but didn't get in.

My 3,000th strikeout was a very nice moment. I never really considered myself a strikeout pitcher. I've always thought strikeouts were overrated, to be honest with you. You've got to get 27 outs. You don't have to get 12 strike-outs and give up five runs to do it, you know what I mean? Strikeouts to me have always been overrated. To pitch long enough to get that many strikeouts is special, and I'm just kind of glad I hung around for as long as I did.

Before video, hitters remembered success. They remember a lot of some success, but only some of the failure. Now the with the way video is, you can play your last 10 at-bats against a pitcher and, in literally 10 seconds, watch him during the first inning if you are hitting in the second or third. I just think before the video got to the way it is now, hitters never remembered the 2–1 pitch they grounded to second, but they always remembered the 1–0 pitch they hit off the wall for a double.

I sat on the bench during batting practice because it was relaxing. It was also the best seat in the house at Wrigley Field. I've always enjoyed sitting on the bench at Wrigley more than I have enjoyed sitting in the clubhouse. I think the notion that I was watching the other hitters started because I just like to be sitting there a lot more than I did sitting in the clubhouse watching TV. It was more about being where I wanted to be, but I did see things. I noticed how guys practiced. I noticed how players took ground balls, how they took fly balls, and how they ran the bases. I learned some things about how seriously different guys took that hour before the game.

I think it's important to play all aspects of the game. I always thought if I was going to get 70 to 100 at-bats a year, if I could hit better than the guy I was facing, I might win one or two more games. Same with fielding my position and being able to run the bases correctly. You play the game, and if you can do other things than pitch, you stand a better chance of winning.

With the walks, I knew I had to stay under 1,000. I knew Fergie was the only other one that did it. Hey, I'll admit, I thought about it in L.A. those last few starts, "Hey, I can't walk anybody!" I always had goals and always reset my goals. Definitely, that last month of my career, one of my goals was to limit my walks, unless the situation called for it.

As far as teaching goes, I think you just talk about pitching. When a player asks you a certain question about something, you relay your past experience. It's up to that player to learn and gain from it. Showing a different way to look at things is something I can pass on. The player has to want to hear, and the player has to also want to do it on the mound. It's easy to talk about things in the clubhouse, but, hey, when there are runners on second and third with a 2–1 count, it's easy to go back to what's more comfortable, and that's usually what you see.

My last Cubs game at Wrigley was against the Cardinals near the trade deadline. There were some rumblings about me going to a contender. The team at the time was going nowhere. Jim Hendry was nice enough to give me a chance to pitch in the postseason with the Dodgers. Hopefully, they got a good player back in return. I think it was a win-win for the Cubs to get a better player and, at the same time, for me to pitch closer to home and in the postseason that year. I thought it was a class act for Jim to do that for me. What the fans did for me that day was special. There were so many moments like that. You kind of feel guilty sometimes. I am very appreciative of what they have done for me over the last 25 years.

It's really cool to have my number retired. It's a tremendous honor, and to be able to share it with Fergie is also amazing. I'm very grateful that the Cubs thought enough of me to do something like this. I think it's pretty special, especially when I come back in 10 or 20 years and get the chance to look at it again.

Looking back, it was a blast. One of my coaches gave me some of the best advice I ever got. Tom Trebelhorn told me, "You know what the problem is with players these days?" I said, "What's that?" He said, "They are always looking forward to something. They're never trying to do something today. They're always looking forward to the next off-day, the All-Star break, the end of the season. They never stop and enjoy the day that's here." I kind of thought about that, and I did that. I did do that. I couldn't wait for each off day and the All-Star break. I started enjoying each day as it was here and really started loving the games from that day on.

Greg Maddux was arguably the greatest pitcher of the modern era. The Cubs' second-round pick in 1984 joined the club in 1986 at age 20 as the youngest player in the majors. On September 29 that year, he started against his brother Mike and beat the Phillies 8–3. Maddux went on to post 355 victories, 133 of which came during his 10 seasons with the Cubs, which included two of his eight All-Star appearances and six of his major league–record 18 Gold Gloves. He won his first Cy Young Award with the Cubs in 1992, when he posted a 20–11 record with a 2.18 ERA. In December 1992 Maddux signed a free-agent contract with the Braves. He returned to the Cubs on March 23, 2004, and pitched three seasons with the team before being traded to the Los Angeles Dodgers for Cesar Izturis on July 31, 2006. He also pitched in San Diego and again with the Dodgers before retiring after the 2008 season, and finished his career with 3,371 strikeouts and 999 walks. He is the only pitcher in MLB history to record 15 or more wins for 17 consecutive seasons. On January 11, 2010, Maddux rejoined the Cubs as an assistant to general manager Jim Hendry.

DOUG DASCENZO

OUTFIELDER

1988–1992

I WAS DRAFTED BY THE CUBS, but I didn't know what it would be like until I got here. When you get to the city of Chicago, especially being from Pennsylvania, seeing the tall buildings along with the passion of the fans, I enjoyed my time here, no doubt about it.

There were about four or five of us who got called up in September 1988. We had just finished an extra-inning game in Des Moines, then got on the road, and arrived in Chicago at about 7:30 AM. I laid down at the hotel for about an hour, then crawled into the clubhouse, set my bag down next to Jody Davis' locker, and within an hour, saw my name on the lineup card leading off that day. I crawled down the steps, and I think I took a nap at my locker. I was very tired—so tired I didn't have the chance to get excited. At the end of the day, it all went well. Everything was flying by, and I just wanted to make sure I got my uniform on and got off to a good start.

I was up there for my defense, and I started my career with 242 games without an error, but those weren't full games. I was in there late for Andre or whoever came out for defense. For any young player coming up, being able to sit and watch how guys like Andre and Ryno played and acted was nice because you could learn a lot. They weren't as vocal as you might think, but just watching their actions, I learned a lot.

It's a transition if you are a role player. Once your body gets used to that, you know what to expect. When you're a little kid growing up and your

Cubs outfielder Doug Dascenzo, running the bases in a June 1989 game at Wrigley Field, was beloved by fans for his hustle and his defense, not to mention his career 0.00 ERA as an occassional relief pitcher. *Photo courtesy of Getty Images*

dream is to play at the major league level, and your passion is to play in a great city like Chicago, you do whatever you need to do. That's what my job was.

Harry Caray liked everybody and wasn't afraid to speak his mind. He liked me a lot. Guys come in and play as hard as they can and give it all they've got. That's what the fans want. We're here doing it for them. We had a good group of guys, and that's what we tried to do.

I could hear all the fans in the bleachers. I remember one guy yelling at me that they should trade me to Montreal for an old pair of shoes. You have that closeness to them. Maybe because of my small stature and the fact that I played hard, they liked me. I have Dawson and Sandberg to thank for that, because it went a long way.

I'll never forget clinching the East title in Montreal in 1989. You're there as a group trying to accomplish a goal, and when you do that, it's a very, very, special thing. We'd like to have been able to clinch it at Wrigley, but when you have all 25 guys working for one goal, that's the ultimate accomplishment.

As for my pitching, I say it stems from my career batting average of .230! I wasn't playing, and I used to throw batting practice to the guys throughout the season. The first time I pitched, we were getting beaten by a lot, and Zim asked me if I could go out and pitch. I said I'd try, and the fans loved it. We saved the bullpen for that day, and I moved on to the next day.

I made four relief appearances in my career, and one of them was a two-inning stint that is probably to blame for the four holes I have in my elbow. It was for the team, and that's what I tried to do throughout my career. When I come to the Convention or see the guys, you bet my 0.00 career ERA comes up, especially when these guys start talking about pitching. I make sure they know that.

In a perfect world, you would like no wind and 70-degree weather every time out like in San Diego, but that's not Wrigley Field. What I liked about playing there was that stadium was always filled   there was never a game where you would wonder where everybody was. There was an electricity, and you looked forward to coming to the ballpark every single day. I don't know if there was anything I disliked, because you get used to the wind and used to the cold when it's blowing off the lake, and you adjust. I wouldn't change it for the world.

I did mess with the ivy and bricks a few times. I can remember Tony Pena hit a drive to left-center field, and I tried to grab it. The ivy wasn't in full bloom, and I hit the wall pretty good and didn't get it. I told the younger guys who came up after me to remember there were bricks behind the ivy. There were a couple times where the ball went into the ivy and I wanted to scoop it out, because your natural reaction is to go in it, but you have to put your hands up and leave it as a ground-rule double.

When Rob Dibble hit me, we were trying to tack on an additional run in a game where we had a lead. Zim put the squeeze on, and I executed it perfectly and got the bunt down. I guess Dibble's personality at the time was that he didn't care for it, so he let me go down the line and then took it out on me by hitting me in the back on his throw to first. We dealt with it then and let it go. We won the game, and that's what counts. That's what you want to do every day.

227

These fans are unbelievable. I only played four and a half years here in Chicago, and I didn't play a whole lot, except for the last three. But 20 years later to be received here as I am says something about the loyalty of these fans. Everybody knows who the Cubs players are across the country and the world because of WGN-TV. I enjoyed it.

I've brought my kids to the Cubs Convention, and they are astounded and can't believe what's going on. I'm sure it will never change. It's unbelievable, and I'm very fortunate. I don't know any other place anyone would want to play.

Doug Dascenzo was drafted by the Cubs in 1985 and made his debut with the team on September 2, 1988, with a 3-for-5 day against the Reds at Wrigley Field. Dascenzo was an outstanding defensive outfielder who was beloved by Cubs fans for his small stature and all-out hustle. In 1990 and 1991 he made four appearances as a relief pitcher and threw a total of five innings without allowing a run. He signed with the Texas Rangers as a free agent after the 1992 season.

MARK GRACE
FIRST BASEMAN
1988–2000

I HAD 13 YEARS IN CHICAGO, 13 great years, and I loved playing for the Chicago Cubs. I can't get enough of this city, and it's always great to come back.

There's nothing close to the love affair between the Cubs and their fans in the National League. The Yankees and Red Sox come to mind in the American League, a love affair and a nation of fans, and it's the same thing with the Chicago Cubs. It's absolutely insane, that's what it is, but in a great way. I was lucky to be a part of their adoration for 13 years. I look back on my days in Chicago and wish they never ended. I couldn't wait to get to the ballpark every day to not only play the game of baseball at the professional level, but to play in front of the most adoring, most faithful fans that I could ever imagine.

Our fans identified with a blue-collar work ethic. That's what I think I was, Ryne Sandberg was. We were guys—Andre Dawson comes to mind, Sutcliffe—who just came to work every day, did the best we possibly could, and played for some bad teams. There were some great times, there just wasn't a whole lot of talent there. But you wouldn't know from watching us play because, God, we gave it everything we had, every single day. We dove, slid hard, took people out, and did everything we possibly could to try to win that baseball game. I think the fans saw that and just the blue-collar type of guys we were. We called ourselves lunch-pail guys. We would clock in, wear our hard hats, bring our lunch pail, and go to work. And when the game was over, it was time to have a good time, and the fans certainly saw that. I didn't travel with a posse. I didn't need bodyguards. I was one of the Chicagoans. I was one of the Chicago faithful who said, "You know what? Let's go have some food and a couple of beverages and talk about things."

There's just so many nuances to Wrigley Field that come in to play. Which way the wind is blowing makes such a difference here. It has the longest grass—infield and outfield grass—so the ball's not going anywhere on the ground. I love the manual scoreboard, the rooftops—there's just so many things that go on here at Wrigley Field that don't go on anywhere else. You realize the people who have watched games here and brought their families. Probably three and four generations of families have been coming to this ballpark and loving the Cubs. A century's worth of ballplayers have been playing right out there on that field. It kind of gives you the chills just thinking about it that way.

When we had the first night game in '88, it rained, wouldn't you know it? Of course, because God didn't want lights at Wrigley Field. Morganna the kissing bandit came out and kissed Ryno in the first inning. I was on deck and was jealous because I wanted her to come and kiss me. And then the rains came and washed away that game, so we did it again the next night against the New York Mets and ended up winning. Mike Bielecki pitched for us, and Sid Fernandez pitched for the New York Mets, and I ended up getting the first base hit in that game. It was awfully cool. That ball is in the Hall of Fame. It should be in my house. No, it's in the Hall of Fame, and that's where it should be.

Nineteen eighty-nine was such a magical year. The '89 playoffs go down for me as a thrill. I was locked in, no doubt about it, and my first at-bat I had a home run. That really got me going. I hit some good pitches, and Will Clark was hitting everything on the other side. It was tough to lose after the season we'd had.

Ninety-eight was an unbelievable year for us. We were thinking we'd be around .500 and, you know, back in the '80s and '90s, let's not kid ourselves, .500 was pretty good for those teams. We ended up winning the wild-card, but I remember that Milwaukee series in September was just wild, it was nuts. I ended up hitting a walkoff home run in the last game of that series. Sammy was obviously on a home-run roll. He had hit 61 and 62, and we ended up winning some big games. That was just as loud as I've ever heard this place, it was awesome.

Cubs first baseman Mark Grace watches his three-run home run sail over the right-field wall in the first inning of a game against the Pittsburgh Pirates at Wrigley Field on September 9, 1998. The blast drove in Lance Johnson and Sammy Sosa.

A big thrill was that one-game playoff that year when we beat the Giants. Gary Gaetti hit a big home run, and Steve Trachsel took a no-hitter into the seventh inning. People forget about that. We ended up beating the Giants. Rod Beck came in and got the final out, the late Rod Beck, unfortunately. He got Joe Carter to pop up to me, I caught it, and it was pandemonium. We didn't quit partying for a while. The fans deserved it. I remember I went into the stands, and it was just a big lovefest. It was awesome.

I was fortunate that maybe the fans thought they could live vicariously through me. They thought I was one of them, and I tried to be one of them. I never had a private booth at a club, I hung out with the common folk, because I am a common folk. They realized I was a normal guy, and about 40,000 normal people come out here every day. That's why I became a popular player.

If anybody deserves a title, it's this city. They got it on the South Side. If it happened on the North Side, it would be like Mrs. O'Leary's cow kicked the lantern again. It would be another Great Chicago Fire, but it would burn with joy and adulation. It wouldn't be rioting, it would be just dancing in the streets. I think Chicago Cubs fans would just fiddle while it burned. I would be right here. I would be right here enjoying it, because the Cubs deserve it, and it didn't happen in my 13 years here, but God, I wouldn't trade those 13 years for anything.

Mark Grace was a 24th-round pick of the Cubs in the 1985 amateur draft. He joined the big-league club in 1988 and finished the season with a .296 average. Grace helped the Cubs to a division title in 1989 with a .314 average and was outstanding in the NLCS when he hit .647 and drove in eight runs in the five-game loss to the Giants. He was a model of consistency each year, driving in 1,004 runs with 2,201 hits in his 13-year Cubs career. Grace was a three-time NL All-Star and won four Gold Gloves for his outstanding play at first base. He led the NL in hits (1,754) during the '90s, and his .308 career average as a Cub is the team's highest for a left-hander. Grace was also named to the Cubs All-Century Team in 1999. He signed with the Arizona Diamondbacks as a free agent in December 2000 and was an integral part of the D-backs' 2001 World Series championship. Grace retired after the 2003 season and currently works as a television broadcaster for the Diamondbacks and Fox Network.

DAN PLESAC

PITCHER

1993–1994

My team was the White Sox when I was growing up in Gary, but the first game I ever went to was a Cubs-Cardinals game in 1967 or '68, and I'll never forget it. My dad and my older brother Joe went with me, and in order to beat traffic on the way home, we left in the eighth inning. We were sitting in the right-field bleachers, and as soon as we got up to walk out, we heard a roar, and there was a Cubs home run that landed right in the section where we were sitting. We sat there for two and a half hours with nothing, and as soon as we got up to leave, the Cardinals' Orlando Cepeda hit a home run that landed in our seats.

You get to a point in Chicago where you can't be a fan of both the Sox and the Cubs. It has to be one or the other. I was such a White Sox fan as a kid, but as I got older that changed. In 1992 I was with the Brewers in the American League, and we had an exhibition game in Wrigley Field before the season started. I had never played there. I remember going on the field that day thinking, *Wow, this is some kind of neat place.* Right then, I was thinking that I couldn't let anybody know that, because I grew up a Sox fan. I couldn't call my brothers and friends and let know what a cool place Wrigley was, so I had to play it off as, "Old Comiskey was better!"

When I was a free agent at the end of the '92 season, I wanted to play so badly for one of the Chicago teams. I had it narrowed down and was close to terms with the Reds, Jays, or the Dodgers. Right at the last minute, Larry

Cubs left-handed relief pitcher Dan Plesac spent two seasons on the North Side and appeared in 111 games before signing with the Pirates. He also worked as a Cubs studio analyst for Comcast SportsNet for four years before joining the MLB Network in 2009. *Photo courtesy of Comcast SportsNet Chicago*

234

Himes called my agent and asked if I'd be interested in playing for the Cubs. It was an immediate slam on the brakes with the other deals, and I told my agent to get me a two-year offer that was anywhere in the ballpark with the other offers, so I could play in Chicago. Unfortunately, they weren't the best two years of my career, but they were without a doubt the most memorable two years that I played. To get a chance to play at home, to have my friends and family there, even guys I played little league with, was the neatest thing.

My first year in '93 was difficult. That was the first year Greg Maddux had left for the Braves in free agency. I was kind of sheltered, playing for seven years with the Brewers in more of a football town. I'll never forget when the Braves came in for the first time and how they booed Maddux in his first start. I was in the bullpen thinking, *Wow, these people want blood here*. The first foul ball hit in the stands by the Cubs was thrown back on the field. They didn't even want a foul ball thrown by Maddux. That's when I knew it was going to be different from Milwaukee. We were at or over .500 all season, but Jim Lefebrve was fired at the end of the year.

Tom Trebelhorn took over, and there was a lot of turmoil the next year. There were new coaches, some whom Trebelhorn wanted, and some Larry

Himes wanted him to have. When I look back on it now, it wasn't a smooth transition for a new manager. It was a very uncomfortable season, and we didn't even finish it due to the strike. We weren't that good, and the expectations were that we weren't going to be any good. We had injuries, and it turned out to be a long, long season.

When you pitch at Wrigley, it's hard to ignore the flags and where the wind is blowing. Any guy who tells you he drives into the ballpark and doesn't look at the flags is not telling you the truth. You can't change the way you pitch, but when you pull in and the wind is howling out, you know it could be a 15–14 game that day. I tell people all the time that it can be the greatest ballpark in the world to pitch in during April and September with the wind blowing in, because you could stand at second base and not hit one out with a fungo bat. When it warms up and the wind starts blowing out, it can be the worst place to pitch and a free-for-all. And it can change from day to day.

You learn a lot of things sitting in the Wrigley bullpen. The thing I noticed most is the difference in the fans between the day games and night games. The day crowd was more laid back with people skipping a few hours of work, a lot of families, and a lot of kids. The night crowd was the rowdy crowd. If you pitched bad or messed up in a night game, you were going to hear about it. But in the day games, it wasn't as bad.

235

I was spoiled the four years I did the Cubs pre- and postgame shows. Everybody was great to me, and I got to go to Wrigley quite a bit. When I came back and did a game in 2009 with the MLB Network, I was struck again by what a nice ballpark Wrigley is. It's nicer than Fenway Park. It's just different than going to any other park because of the atmosphere around the park, and there's so much more than just the game. All the things that make up the tradition there, from the ivy to the sunshine to Harry, just grab you when you walk in there.

I took my daughter to the first playoff game in 2008, and that was as excited as I've been going to a sporting event since I played. The passion that Cubs fans have makes for a different kind of fan base. They love their team, they want them to be good. Since the 2003 series with the Marlins, the culture has changed. The expectation level has gone up. The caliber of player they're bringing in there has gotten better. Cubs fans won't accept just being over .500. The 2003 playoff loss was a bitter pill to swallow, but the fans got a taste of what winning would be like. I really didn't understand it until the last two years when I was doing the pre- and postgame shows on Comcast.

Being at the park during the playoff series and hearing, "Is this the year, Dan?" reminded me of how badly Cubs fans want it. It's almost not fair that an expansion team like the Marlins has won it twice. The Cubs are right there with the Yankees and Red Sox with the faithfulness and sheer number of fans, but they don't have the wins to show for it yet.

My theory on what the Cubs are going through now is what the Red Sox went through until they won it in 2004 to get the monkey off their back. Until they win it all, they are going to have a gorilla on their back. The Cubs in '08 were by far the best team in the National League, and I didn't think they could lose that series to the Dodgers that year if they tried. When DeRosa homered to give them the lead in Game 1, the place was nuts, but when L.A. got a grand slam to take the lead, the air went out of the balloon. It was almost like 41,000 people all said at once, "Oh, no, here we go again." I would always tell people not to think like that, but even I went, "Oh, no, this is going to happen again." They have to win it all, and there is a lot of pressure playing there now. The questions start in April about, "Will this be the year?" The only question is whether the Cubs will win it all, and it doesn't get asked that way in other cities. Cubs fans are tired of waiting for next year.

I agree that every player should play for the Cubs at some point. I had a great time. The people that go to the Cubs games so badly want the Cubs to win. If you were able to be there when they go on that magical ride, you would see a city come to total gridlock. That town is waiting for the Cubs to win. It would be the greatest experience a player could go through if you could win it all with the Cubs. It will happen. When, I don't know, but it will happen.

236

After seven seasons and three All-Star appearances with the Milwaukee Brewers, Dan Plesac signed as a free agent with the Cubs in December 1992. He appeared in 57 and 54 games in his two seasons on the North Side. He signed with the Pirates after the '94 season and also pitched with the Blue Jays, Diamondbacks, and Phillies. Plesac finished with 158 saves in his 18-year career, and his 1,064 games pitched ranks sixth on the all-time MLB list. After his retirement, Plesac transitioned seamlessly to the broadcast booth. He worked as a Cubs studio analyst for Comcast SportsNet for four seasons, and in 2009 he joined the MLB Network as a studio analyst.

GLENALLEN HILL

OUTFIELDER

1993–1994 ★ 1998–2000

W HEN I WAS TRADED TO THE CUBS in 1993, I didn't think much of it. I had watched the Cubs on TV and just knew that they were on TV a lot. I had heard that Wrigley Field was a great ballpark to play in. When I re-signed, I was attracted to the team because it was a job.

Personally, I think that Wrigley Field is one of the best ballparks in the game now. I've always enjoyed playing there. There is no instant replay, so fans actually have to stay and watch and pay close attention, and they do.

I would love to talk about that first season, but in my mind, I don't remember those things. My career was a blur, and it happened really fast. I know that I enjoyed my time as a Cub and that the fans are probably among the top three teams in all of baseball. They appreciate hard work, and they let you know. It's a great, great place to play baseball.

One game I do remember was that wild-card game in 1998. We were playing the Giants. I only remember that game because Dusty Baker is a good friend of mine, and I had played for the Giants. After that game, Dusty told me he knew they were doomed in the seventh inning, when a big balloon of Harry Caray came up behind left field.

When I hit the roof across the street with a home run, I wasn't surprised. It was nothing unusual for me to hit a ball that hard, and so it was more the situation. Steve Woodard of the Brewers was pitching, and it was a process

238

As a part-time player with the Cubs over five seasons, Glenallen Hill hit .304 with 167 RBIs and 59 home runs, including one shot that landed on a rooftop on Waveland Avenue in 2000. *Photo courtesy of Getty Images*

of elimination. I knew that he was only going to try to throw one pitch, and I was totally committed to that pitch. He threw it right in my loop.

What people don't know, but the true Wrigley fans know, is that I used to hit balls over the Budweiser house every day, so hitting a ball on the roof in a game was not a surprise to a lot of people who watched the Cubs take batting practice every day. Yeah, there were several balls that went that far.

I think most players who are fortunate to make it to the major leagues and experience the major leagues have a blessing in itself. If you get the opportunity to play for the Chicago Cubs, then you will know what a lot players know once they leave there. It is a great place to play because the fans love you dearly.

Once a Chicago Cub, always a Chicago Cub. I think it's important that people know that you have to play hard, and fans respect those players that leave it on the field. Fortunately, I was one of those players, and the Cubs fans appreciate that. I think one of the things that they remember about me, more than the home run, is how I played. They appreciate that, and it's an honor to be appreciated by the Cubs fans because they're not easy. You can't fool them.

239

Glenallen Hill was acquired from the Cleveland Indians for Candy Maldonado on August 19, 1993, and saw part-time action for the next two seasons before leaving as a free agent. Hill was claimed by the Cubs off waivers from the Mariners on July 6, 1998, and was instrumental in the wild-card stretch drive with eight homers and 23 RBIs. In 1999 he hit 20 home runs in just 99 games. On May 11, 2000, Hill hit one of the longest home runs in Cubs history when he blasted a pitch from Milwaukee's Steve Woodard onto a rooftop at Waveland and Sheffield across from the left-field bleachers, a feat made more impressive by the fact that there was not a breeze blowing out that day. In July 21, 2000, he was traded to the Yankees. Hill is currently the first-base coach for the Colorado Rockies.

JIM RIGGLEMAN

MANAGER

1995–1999

IWAS IN SAN DIEGO getting my first chance to manage, and I loved it there. It was a great city, but new ownership came in. I was told I could have another year on my contract, but that the Cubs had called and wanted to talk to me. The Cubs offered me two years, so I did the math and said, "I'd better go!" That's how I came to Chicago.

You manage the ballclub and try to manage its assets. If you have deficiencies, you try to improve those. As far as any home and away stuff, I really didn't do anything different. The things I tried to express to our ballclub was that it was windy at Wrigley Field, it's cold, it can be uncomfortable to the players, but we have to use that to our advantage. The players come in here, and maybe they don't know the wind as well or the little slope we had back behind the infield toward the outfield, that we should be aware of the little nooks and crannies in our outfield. We could not be fooled by that. Maybe the other club will, and we can take advantage of that.

In '95 and '96 we were in the hunt pretty well. In '95 we were eliminated with two days to go. A lot of things would have to have happened for us to get in. We were counting on some other teams losing more than just us winning. In '96 we were in it right into September. We went into St. Louis with a chance to pick up some ground, and I think we were swept. That really set us back.

Jim Riggleman managed the Cubs from 1995 to 1999, compiled a 374–419 record, and led the team to a wild-card playoff berth in 1998. *Photo courtesy of Getty Images*

Nineteen ninety-eight was a very special year with a great ballclub and great individuals on that ballclub. We did some great things. Everybody knows what Sammy did, but there were so many great things from the other guys—Morandini, Grace, Tapani, Trachsel, Wood, Gaetti, Hernandez. All the guys were such great contributors on that club.

It was really great how Sammy handled the home-run race, because there was so much attention on him. Every day, there was a press conference before the game to talk to Sammy. That allowed a lot of the other ballplayers to just go about their business and get ready to play the game without having to answer too many questions. Grace, Woody, Beck, and some of the guys were always going to get some demands on them, but I would say 75 percent of our attention was on Sammy, and he just handled it so well. It didn't bother him. He liked it, and it allowed everybody else to just do their thing.

Kerry Wood was our most dominant pitcher in spring training that year. We made the determination that he was going to start the year in the minor leagues. We stuck with that, then we had an injury to Bob Patterson, who was a reliever. So Ed Lynch called me and said we would put Terry Mulholland in the bullpen to cover the left-handed spot and bring Kerry up. He came up, and we were in such important games all year trying to get into the post-season that we put a lot of demands on Kerry. Looking back on it, it might have been better for a young pitcher to come into it where we weren't trying to win so much. If it had been one of those years where we weren't going to win and get into the playoffs, we would have cut him down to 90 pitches and gotten him out of there after five innings win, lose, or draw. With Kerry, he was on a club that was trying to win, and he had to be part of that.

It kind of rolls off your tongue sometimes that Rod Beck had 51 saves. You can dismiss that like it's just a number, but then you think about: how many guys have ever had 50 saves in a season? Rod was doing it because he was Rod Beck. He had guts and guile, and he challenged hitters with what was at that point probably an 87 mph fastball. He had very good control and a nice slider, but he wasn't scared. It was amazing that he was able to get 51 saves for us, and if we didn't have him, we wouldn't have been contending.

That last week was something. I loved Brant Brown and how he competed for us. We were in Milwaukee when he let that last-out fly ball get away, and I got the club together and said, "Hey, we're not where we are without this guy." He played center field for us when Lance Johnson was hurt and did a great job for us out there. He filled in for Mark Grace at first base and did a good job. How many guys can fill in at both first and center field? I reminded the club that it was a tough loss, but I reminded them that without Brant Brown, we wouldn't have been competing, just like we couldn't compete without Mark Grace, Sammy Sosa, Rod Beck, or anybody. We regrouped and won enough ballgames to get in when Neifi Perez hit that ball out for Colorado against San Francisco and forced the 163rd game.

That was the most exciting game I've ever had the chance to manage in. To manage in the big leagues is a great privilege. There's not too many times when I can point to a particular situation, but that one was the most special game I've ever been able to manage in. It was a great night at Wrigley Field with great individual performances. I'd be fired if I did today one of the things I did in that game. Mulholland had thrown 118 pitches the day before yet insisted he could pitch in relief that night, and he came in and got Barry Bonds out for us. You can't do that in today's world. Steve Trachsel had a no-hitter into the seventh, Gary Gaetti hit a home run to give us a lead, Kevin Tapani pitched in relief for us, and rightly so, Rod Beck got the save.

If we had gotten into the playoffs on a normal schedule, we would have opened up with Trachsel, who had won 15 games for us, then the next day would have been Tapani. Because we used Steve in the 163rd game, we opened up with Mark Clark, who was pitching on a bad knee all year. He gave us a good effort in Atlanta, but they beat him. Then the next night, Tapani had them down 1–0 in the ninth when Javy Lopez hit a homer to tie it. We missed a chance in the tenth when we had first and third with one out and didn't score, then they scored in the bottom of the tenth. Then we came home, and they beat us again for the sweep.

The next year was terrible. It was an unbelievable year. We got off to a good start and were 32–23. When it started going south, I remember standing on the field with Andy MacPhail, and we were going backward and had fallen to .500. He looked at me and said, "I've never felt so bad about a .500 ballclub in my life." I knew it was going to be hard to turn that around. We got old fast, Tapani's back was bothering him, Woody wasn't with us, Beck's elbow was barking, and there were just so many things. Anything that could go wrong was going wrong. We had gone out and gotten Benito Santiago to catch, and he was coming off a bad car accident and really was about a year away from being the real Benito. That was a mistake on my part, because I really lobbied over the winter to get him, and it didn't work. It started going bad, and there was no turning it around.

I rode the CTA to work because it was cheap! The El was right there where I lived, and I could jump on and read the paper on my way in. It worked for me, and nobody bothered me. It was a normal way for me to get to work.

People here were so good to me. The fans and media were good to me. Andy MacPhail and Ed Lynch, we all left on good terms. They treated me great. A change needed to be made. I say that reluctantly because I love to manage. When you've been saying stuff for five years and don't get to the promised land in that time, it starts falling on deaf ears. I'm sure Don Baylor came in and was giving the same message I was giving, but it was a different

243

voice, and it had a chance. When the same person keeps saying the same thing and you're not getting results, somebody else is going to have to say it. They recognized that. Andy and Ed felt a change needed to be made, and I said that I'd love to continue to manage the club if they would let me, but I understood where they were coming from.

For me, the players made the success we had. It was Sammy, Mark Grace's personality, Rod Beck, all of them who did it. The players really united, and I think the fans sensed they were all in it together. I just happened to be here. The city really rallied around those guys. When you think about Michael Jordan in this city, Sammy was actually a bigger personality, and that's really saying something. It was all great.

After managing for two-plus seasons in San Diego, Jim Riggleman became the manager of the Cubs in 1995. His first team finished 73–71 but in 1996 faltered, ending up 76–86. After a last-place, 68–94 record in 1997, the following year was one of the most wildly entertaining seasons in Cubs history. In 1998 Riggleman presided over Kerry Wood's 20-strikeout game, Sammy Sosa's 66 home runs, Rod Beck's 51 saves, and a harrowing Game 163 win at Wrigley Field to win the wild-card spot. The Cubs were running on empty and were swept in three games by the Braves in the NLDS. The Cubs started 32–23 in 1999, but the bottom fell out, and Riggleman was let go when the team finished 67–95. He is currently the manager of the Washington Nationals.

DOUG GLANVILLE

OUTFIELDER

1996–1997 ★ 2003

W HEN THE CUBS DRAFTED ME in 1991, it was a stressful and crazy time because I didn't know where I would fall. I kept hearing rumors, and the Cubs called to tell me I was the 12th pick overall. It was exciting to hear them talk to the media about why I was such a good choice. As soon as they get away from the press, though, they tell you all the things you can't do, because they are about to negotiate with you for your signing bonus! It was a shock as a 20-year-old to hear all these people talking about me who hadn't even met me.

I knew there was a lot of history here. I was a Phillies fan growing up, and I remembered the Phillies making all the trades with the Cubs and Dallas Green. They called it "Phillies West." I paid a lot of attention to the Cubs' personnel because of all the Phillies like Keith Moreland, Gary Matthews, Larry Bowa, and John Vukovich who were there.

I was picked one spot ahead of Manny Ramirez. Alan Schwarz is a friend of mine who writes for the *New York Times*, and he was going through that draft about four years before I was finished playing and said, "Oh, I don't know if a lot came out of this draft." I told him he had to wait and see, and certainly Manny was the most notable. I feel good about being picked then because I did a lot of different things on the field. He was a stone cold hitter, but I was known for speed, defense, getting the bunt down, making contact, and hitting a little for average. The Cubs said I was more of a "turf player" than they might have chosen because I hit the ball on the ground. I'm proud I did it all clean and never went down the steroid route.

The only time I had been to Wrigley before that was during the off-season. I came one time, and I remember seeing snow on the field. I hadn't been on the field before. It was interesting, because usually they gave the top draft picks the red-carpet treatment and flew them out to take batting practice, but they were annoyed at me because I held out for six weeks and wanted to get me going in the minor league season. So they signed me and sent me right to Niagara Falls, where the Geneva Cubs were playing in A ball.

In '96 I had a really good spring and got sent down. Mike Morgan pulled me aside and told me, "Hey, you'll be here. You played well. Keep doing what you're doing, focus in Triple A, and you'll be right back here." That was something I really appreciated, and I ended up saying the same thing to Chase Utley about 10 years later with the Phillies.

I was in Triple A with Iowa when I got called up, and I was a little suspicious because they started me that night in left field. I hadn't played left field a single game in my minor league career. My Triple A manager and I were like oil and water, and there was no semblance of us getting along, which was unusual in my career. He called Mike Hubbard, Terry Shumpert, and me into his office. He told Mike he had done a great job and deserved to be there and told Terry, "You've been there before. You're an established player. Just do what you do and you know what you're doing." Then he turned to me and said, "If you make the same mistakes you made down here when you get up there, you'll be right back here." That was my send-off. I knew at that moment I was kind of on my own.

I packed all night, and one of my friends, Jeff Miller, had promised me that he would be at my first big-league game, no matter where it was. I called him at 4:00 AM in Washington, D.C., and sure enough, he and another Penn friend got a ticket and came to my first game. It was freezing, even though it was June 9, but I didn't feel a thing. I saw my name on the lineup card with Sosa, Sandberg, and Grace, and it was mind-blowing. Plus, to do it at Wrigley Field, which is the cathedral of the game, was even more majestic. I didn't get any hits that day, but I didn't feel a thing. We were playing the Expos, and the first ball I hit went to the warning track, but it wasn't to be. I got my first big-league hit the next day in Philadelphia.

Shawon Dunston was a huge mentor to me. He took me under his wing and gave me a heads up about a lot of things and how to go about your

Cubs outfielder Doug Glanville drives in Kenny Lofton with a game-winning triple against the Florida Marlins in Game 3 of the NLCS on October 10, 2003, at Pro Player Stadium in Miami. *Photo courtesy of Getty Images*

247

business. The one thing that really stood out for me was when he was older, I remember seeing him pop up to second base, but by the time the ball came down, he was on second. He hustled right out of the batter's box every time. I was thinking, *Wow, I'm 28. There's no excuse for me to not hustle. Here's a player who's experienced who goes full-out every day.* He influenced me about playing hard and understanding office politics.

I enjoyed listening to Dunston and Grace argue all the time. They never agreed on anything, except that Barry Bonds was the greatest player they had ever seen. They were really funny about it, but they were always going back and forth about something or other. You didn't have to instigate it, they were

always on. They had such opposite backgrounds growing up, so it was interesting to see that they were good friends and were very open with each
other. I appreciated the honesty they had in their conversations, and they
touched on every issue, from race to umpires to being on the disabled list.
They talked a lot about the game and the life elements around the game. I
learned a lot from that.

Playing the outfield at Wrigley was a matter of getting out there and doing
it. It's the hardest outfield to play in the game in my opinion, because you
were dealing with the fact that it used to slope downhill, the grass was a mile
high, and if you dared deal with the wall, it was brick. If you were allergic
to ivy, that was another problem. You had the wind swirling and the sun in
your eyes part of the time. As a young outfielder, it was work getting adjusted
to that. I would watch guys like Brian McRae prepare, and they would
always take at least one round of batting practice going after balls in the outfield like it was a game. That really helped me. Wrigley was so mysterious,
with the shadows and other things, that it was a difficult outfield. In the end,
I felt comfortable—well, as comfortable as you could be, anyway.

After '97 there were some rumors going around about if they would pro-
tect me in expansion. I heard rumors about going to Tampa Bay or Boston. I
didn't really know where I'd be, but I did have a sense they were shopping
me. Even then, it doesn't prepare you for the day you get the call. It was brief,
and you feel like a set of steak knives. My grandfather had passed away about
an hour before Ed Lynch called to tell me, so I was a little out of it. It took
me a bit to realize that the glass was kind of half-full, and I was going to
Philly, where they needed my services. I think in the end I kind of realized
the Cubs did me a favor by not keeping me stuck there as a fourth outfielder,
though I didn't feel that way then. I did try to beat the Cubs to a pulp when
we played them to show them they made a mistake. Nothing gave me more
pleasure than when I got my 200th hit of the season against the Cubs on a
home run in 1999. That was poetic justice, I guess.

When the Cubs got me back in 2003, my GM in Texas, John Hart, called
me. He was all cryptic and told me they had traded me back to my old organization, and I thought he meant the Phillies. I had arguably been playing the
best baseball of my career that July and had come back from an injury. I
wanted to get back in the saddle full-time, but the Rangers were out of it, so
it made sense for them to trade a salary. I wanted to go to a contender, but the
flip side of it was that I was going to be a free agent, so I didn't want to be

rotting on the bench going into free agency. I had mixed feelings and wasn't really prepared to be a role player. The Cubs had made a lot of moves to get some veteran players, so ego management was a key, and Dusty did a great job with that.

When I got here, we weren't a shoo-in by any means. We were only a couple games over .500. The series against the Cardinals at the start of September was the best I ever played in. The intensity was amazing. We clinched without a moment to spare on the next-to-last day of the season when the Astros lost and we swept a doubleheader.

That was my only playoff experience. I was 31, so I appreciated pouring the champagne and all that. I really enjoyed that team, and it was a very self-less group that respected Dusty's decisions. We had guys, like Eric Karros, who had played every day and now were role players, so it was hard. We made a great run and pulled it off.

We were on a high in Florida after I got the game-winning hit in Game 3, then we took Game 4 and were up 3–1. Then Beckett was unhittable, so you tip your cap, but we were still in the driver's seat. Then we came home feeling pretty good with Prior and Wood, so we could taste it and had high expectations. The thing about the playoffs is you have to get your tickets in advance for the next round, so you're thinking about the World Series. I was thinking about how great it would be to play the Yankees, because I grew up 15 minutes from Yankee Stadium. I was in that mode, and certainly the odds were in our favor, so we were stunned like everyone else.

I feel extremely fortunate that I've maintained so many positive relation-ships in the city of Chicago. What was special was that once I made it, and I had overcome a lot of things in the minors, I was the underdog, even though I was a first-round pick. The press embraced me and said I should be playing more. I kept my head down, played hard, and did my job. That created an environment of people backing me. After I was traded, there was the mys-tery of why I hadn't gotten the everyday job when I was now playing well. Plus they knew I hadn't wanted to leave. When I was with the Phillies, I had a great time with the Bleacher Bums. They were giving me a hard time one of my first times back, and I went over to left-center and said to them, "Hey, don't be giving me a hard time. You traded me. I didn't want to leave!" After that, I had nothing but love the rest of the series.

I loved how positive the fans were. I remember Frank Castillo starting off a year something like 0–9. He was running his sprints in the outfield as the gates opened. A fan in the bleachers was hollering, "That's okay, Frank. After today, you'll be 1–9. Don't worry about it." That doesn't happen on the East Coast. I enjoyed that environment. I moved to Chicago after my career and have had a great time with business and being an ambassador for the game.

Doug Glanville was selected by the Cubs with the 12th overall pick in the 1991 amateur draft. He made his major league debut at Wrigley Field on June 9, 1996, and hit .300 in his first full season the next year. On December 23, 1997, he was traded to the Phillies for Mickey Morandini, where he spent five seasons as their regular center fielder. He posted career highs with 204 hits and a .325 batting average in 1999. Glanville moved to the Texas Rangers as a free agent in 2003, but was traded back to the Cubs on July 30 and saw limited duty down the stretch as a pinch-hitter and defensive replacement. His eleventh-inning, pinch-hit triple off Braden Looper won Game 3 of the NLCS over the Florida Marlins. Glanville played one more season with the Phillies before retiring in 2005. He currently lives in Chicago and is involved in several businesses ventures. He writes op-ed pieces for the *New York Times* and does analyst work for XM Radio and Comcast SportsNet Chicago.

BRANT BROWN

OUTFIELDER/FIRST BASEMAN

1996–1998 ★ 2000

I NEVER REALLY FOLLOWED THE CUBS growing up. My uncle had played in the Dodgers organization, so I was always a Dodgers fan. I really didn't hear much from the Cubs before the draft. The guy who ended up talking to me was someone I had never heard from, and I talked to him only two days before the draft. I met him at a baseball game near my hometown, and he never called before then. The next thing you know, two days later, he's calling me to tell me the Cubs had drafted me.

My maturation process was kind of good, bad, good. I had a real tough time for some reason in Double A, maybe because of the weather or travel, I don't know. What I do know is that the staff members of the Cubs system were very important in my development, and that includes Dave Trembley, Bruce Kimm, Tim Johnson, and Ron Clark. They were all my managers, and we just kind of got along—that core of people, along with Chris Speier and Glenn Adams. It seemed like when I made that shift from Double A to Triple A is when I started to make the change from going up and down to going up.

When I got called up, we had just flown that morning from Nashville, and my roommate, David Swartzbaugh, and I were taking a nap. We had gotten in very early, gotten our room, and had gone to sleep. Our manager, Ron Clark, called and said, "You need to come down to my room." I went down there, and he told me Mark Grace had a hamstring injury, and I was being called up. He told me to do him a favor and have one drink on the plane on the way in.

Brant Brown connects on a pitch during a game against the San Francisco Giants on May 9, 1998, at Wrigley Field. *Photo courtesy of Getty Images*

Nineteen ninety-eight was a fun year. The Cubs hadn't been in a race in a while, and the wild-card was so close all season. It made every day exciting. For a player, when you are fighting like that, you get to the park earlier and don't feel tired, because you are running on adrenaline. It was my first full year, and I was getting the chance to play a lot. I was just there, saying, "This is great. This is what it's all about."

The day Kerry Wood struck out 20, it was a little bit cold, windy, and rainy. He had a curveball and slider that were just unbelievably wicked. His fastball was just as hard as he could throw it, and he could locate it where he wanted. I was playing center field that day, and I always tell everyone that all I did was turn to the other outfielders and signal one or two outs, then jog in at the end of the inning. I didn't have anything to do, because he struck everyone out!

Sammy Sosa brought added excitement that year, and if he wasn't in the home-run race, we probably wouldn't have been where we were. He damn near carried us for the whole summer, and it was an integral part of how we made the playoffs. Plus it was just so fun to watch. I'm sure it had to be a burden for him after a while, because the media attention was just ungodly. For me, as an outsider, to watch him hit a home run every day, it was just ridiculous. It just added to that whole ambience of electricity generated in the summer of '98.

I played first base and all the outfield positions. I was lucky that I could run for a white guy, at least that's what I always tell people. During spring training of '98 Lance Johnson was hurt, and I had been playing the corner outfield positions. So I asked Jim Riggleman if I could take some reps in center field to see how I would do. I was also hitting well, and I started off so hot that I got to play out there against right-handers. I was so locked in that first half until I hurt my shoulder, every day really came easy to me. It was such a joy.

I had two walk-off home runs that year in a seven-day span. One was against John Rocker of the Braves, and one came off Tony Castillo of the White Sox—both of them were left-handers. My favorite game was probably when I hit three home runs against the Phillies.

When I dropped the ball against the Brewers, after the game I was crying in Jim Riggleman's office. It was so upsetting to me because I am such a perfectionist. I wanted to go to the playoffs more than anyone, and I certainly didn't want that to mean that we weren't going to go to the playoffs. That's why I always say my favorite player is Neifi Perez for hitting that home run against the Giants on the last day. I got asked about it so much that I tried to turn it into a positive and say that we still made the playoffs, and there was an extra game in Chicago because of it. So I made the Cubs and the city of Chicago a lot of money.

Riggleman put me back in right after that when we went to the Astrodome, and then I got chased by a pigeon. Charlie Steiner asked me there how I was doing, and I remember telling him, "My hotel room does have a balcony, but I'm still here, so I must be doing okay."

One of the determining factors in our winning the wild-card game was that we thought we were out of it on Sunday, then suddenly were back in, while the Giants thought they had won it and suddenly had it taken away. That emotional value of them going down and us going up really helped us, as did playing in Chicago. Before we even started that game, our sense of what was going to happen was much better than theirs.

I would have loved to spend my whole career with the Cubs. I loved the city of Chicago. I'm a morning person, and I loved getting up early and taking the El to the park. I used to have fun walking down Michigan Avenue and finding a family, asking them if they wanted to go to a Cubs game, then leaving them tickets. I just enjoyed every part of that city.

The premise of being traded to Pittsburgh was that I was going to get to play every day and have 500 at-bats, but that didn't work out. Then, I went to the Marlins and sat on the bench all the time. I got traded back to Chicago, and I thought, *Here we go. This is the way it's supposed to be. I can finish my career here as a utility player.* I just didn't perform, though. I love Chicago. It's so clean and pretty, and I loved it there.

254

The Cubs drafted Brant Brown in the third round of the 1992 amateur draft. After brief stints with the team in 1996 and 1997, Brown played in 124 games for the Cubs in 1998, hit 14 home runs, drove in 48, and batted .291. On September 23 in Milwaukee that season, Brown dropped a two-out fly ball in left field that allowed two runs to score in the bottom of the ninth and cost the Cubs the game. Brown's gaffe occurred on the 90th anniversary of "Merkle's Boner," which helped the Cubs win the pennant in 1908. The Cubs recovered and won the National League wild-card in a one-game playoff against the Giants a few days later. After 1998 the Cubs traded Brown to Pittsburgh for pitcher Jon Lieber. He played with the Pirates in 1999, then finished his career with the Marlins and Cubs in 2000. Brown is currently the hitting coach for the Frisco Rough Riders, the Texas Rangers' Double A affiliate.

PAT HUGHES

BROADCASTER
1996–Present

I JOINED THE CUBS IN 1996. The radio job was open, and I applied. I sent a tape, hoped to hear from the Cubs and WGN Radio, and I did. I knew I was a candidate in the top 10 or 20 fairly early on, then found out they had narrowed it to three or four announcers. I had a dinner with Ron Santo, John McDonough of the Cubs, a few others, and things went pretty well. I got down to the final two, and in late November 1995, I got the call that I was going to join Ron Santo on WGN Radio to become the play-by-play voice of the Chicago Cubs, and that was one of the great thrills of my life.

This is one of the best jobs in all of sports. The Cubs are one of the classic American sports franchises. In baseball, you have the Yankees, Red Sox, Dodgers, Giants, Cubs, Cardinals, and a few others. The Cubs are one of those special franchises, and I grew up wanting to be the voice of one of those great franchises. I've been fortunate enough to have one of those jobs.

It was a little overwhelming at the start because of the newness and immensity of it all, the number of people listening, and the size of WGN Radio. It goes into 25 or 30 states at one time, so the audience is much greater than the Milwaukee audience I had with the Brewers. The interest level of the fans and media here is huge. When Len Kasper got the TV job, I told him, "Len, it's never easy being the voice of the Cubs, but it's never boring!"

As a high school and college basketball player, I always liked being part of a good team, and as a broadcaster, I feel the same way. Ron Santo and I have achieved a certain level of popularity and notoriety, and I'm very proud of that. It's an evolutionary process. Our chemistry did not happen right away, but after being around each other day after day, we learned each other, what to do and when to say it, and what might bring out some outrageous comments from him. I give him a world of credit, as well. Our partnership is like a marriage—not every day is going to be great, but most of the days are very pleasant.

I think every broadcaster in any sport should have played a sport at the highest level possible, just to try to relate to what the athletes are going through. I tell people there is a big difference between performing, which is what I do, and competing, which is what the athletes do. Every single minute they are out there, somebody on the other side is trying to make them look bad. I always try to remember that and remember what it was like in college basketball driving to the basket and having someone block my shot to humiliate me in front of all the fans. It's no fun. It's not fun to stand up there and try to hit a fastball when a guy is throwing 90 or 92 mph. I can only imagine what it's like trying to hit a guy like Carlos Marmol with his fastball and breaking stuff. I do appreciate how difficult a big-league ballplayer's job is, and I'm glad that I played at least the high school and college level in athletics, because it really helped me a lot.

I'm proud I got to know Harry Caray. I loved him, and he treated me great. When I think back, I've been able to work with Ron Santo for 14 years, Bob Uecker for 12 years, Harry Caray for two years, and do Marquette basketball with Al McGuire. Out of all the play-by-play guys in America, how many would love to be able to say what I just said?

A home run call has to come naturally. You can't rip off someone else. It can't sound contrived or forced. When it's a really long home run, I'll say, "Get out the tape measure. It's long gone!" Generally, I'll say, "There's a swing and a long drive. That ball's got a chaaaance…" Really what I'm doing by extending the word "chance" is buying time. I'm waiting to see if the ball indeed is going to be caught, off the top of the wall, or in the stands. That's what I'm doing when I say, "This ball's got a chaaaaance…. Gone!" It's something that has to come naturally. You don't want to copy someone else, but if feels right to you, and the audience seems to like it, go with it.

The one broadcaster, far and away, who had the most influence on me was Bill King, the great radio man of the Golden State Warriors, Oakland Raiders, and Oakland A's. He is simply the best all-around radio sports

Pat Hughes calls a Cubs game in the radio booth at Wrigley Field while at the same time interviewing the guest conductor of "Take Me Out to the Ballgame."

play-by-play man in the history of our country. I really don't think anyone is close. He was amazingly prepared, was so descriptive, had a tremendous vocabulary, could build the drama in a game, and was just the best in the game. There were other announcers who influenced me, and I always felt you could learn a lot from everyone. Sometimes, you learn what not do. Vin Scully was great. Pat Summerall was wonderful. Dick Enberg was an excellent television play-by-play man. In the all-around category, Bob Costas is just amazing. You can't copy any of them, but you can learn a lot by listening to other guys.

I do have some favorite calls, but it's probably immodest to go into them. The one that I really like that I made was in the tail end of the 1998 season with the Great Home Run Chase between Sammy Sosa and Mark McGwire. It was late in the year in Milwaukee. Harry Caray had died in February of that year, and Jack Brickhouse passed away in August. All that year, I kept thinking how much both men would have loved that season. Kerry Wood had 20 strikeouts against Houston, and Sosa had 20 home runs in the month of June. The Cubs were in the wild-card hunt, but it was that homer chase that made it special, so when Sosa hit his 64th home run in Milwaukee, I said, "Deep drive for Sosa, gone! 'Holy Cow' and 'Hey Hey' for Harry and Jack!" I just wanted to pay tribute to Harry Caray and Jack Brickhouse at that moment in the season because I loved those guys, and I knew they would have loved that Cubs team.

The season is a grind, six months, seven if you get to the playoffs, and you have to take care of yourself. You have to get your workouts in, get your rest, eat right, lay off the pizza at midnight, all the common-sense stuff. It's a grind, but I love baseball. If you're going to go into baseball announcing, that is the number-one prerequisite. You have got to love the game, because you're not always going to win. Harry Caray told me, when the team wins, your job is fun. You have comebacks, rallies, fans, and magic numbers. When you're 35 games out of first on August 5 and there are still 55 games to go, that's when you really have to bear down. You still have to perform. Harry also told me that when the team is losing, you have to try other things. Tell stories, have some fun, and work with your partner. You hope your team is good, but I always tell people that, as a baseball announcer, you are in the passenger seat of life. You don't dictate which road you take. You want it to be a great, pleasant drive, but there is no guarantee.

I do think about what it will be like when the Cubs win the World Series. Not only do I think about what I may do at that time, I'm not going to rehearse anything for sure, because I want it to be as spontaneous as possible, but I might try to think of a couple of things to add after the actual moment. It also occurs to me that Cubs fans have never heard somebody say, "The Cubs win the World Series!" The last time was in 1908, well before television or radio. If there's a tape that exists from when the Cubs won the pennant in 1945, I'm unaware of that. I don't think there's even an audio tape of a radio announcer saying, "The Cubs win the National League pennant!" That thought occurs to me that I am going to be the first, and I hope I am, and I always hope it will be this year.

It never gets old. That's exactly what it is. These fans love this franchise. They love to watch baseball. They've been heartbroken many, many times, but they still bounce back. I think being a Cubs fan teaches you a lot about life. You have to remain optimistic even though things are tough. Sometimes you feel like giving up, but you can't. If you give up, it's going to be a disaster. You've got to remain at least somewhat optimistic. If you're a Cubs fan, you have to remain *very* optimistic. One of these days, it will happen for these great fans. This team will win eventually. As long as they stay competitive and give themselves a chance, it will happen. Trust me.

Pat Hughes joined WGN Radio as the Cubs play-by-play announcer in 1996 after a 12-year stint as the radio voice of the Milwaukee Brewers. In their 13 seasons together, Pat and partner Ron Santo have turned "The Pat & Ron Show" into one of baseball's most entertaining and informative broadcasts. Pat has been honored as Illinois Sports Broadcaster of the Year five times. He has written, produced, and narrated a CD series of tributes to Hall of Fame broadcasters titled *Baseball Voices*.

MICKEY MORANDINI
SECOND BASEMAN
1998–1999

I WAS ON THE OLYMPIC TEAM that won in 1988, and it was awesome. The Games were in Seoul, but we also traveled to Italy, then Japan right before we went to South Korea. It was the first time out of the country for a lot of us. That's quite an experience to be away from home for an extended period of time, but it was a great group of guys on that team. It definitely prepared us for baseball away from home, and also we had a lot of media following us around, so it helped prepare us for that part of baseball, too.

In December of '97, right before Christmas, I was with the Phillies and got a call from Ed Wade, who was our GM. You know something is happening when he starts out, "You know we love you…" I was kind of torn about the trade. I loved Philadelphia, the organization, and the people, but if I had to get traded anywhere, the Cubs were a perfect fit for me, because I lived in this area. Even though I didn't want to leave Philly, the one place I was happy to go to was Chicago, so it worked out pretty well.

I loved the day games in Chicago. I felt like I had a regular nine-to-five job. I'd drive in, in the morning, play the game, and be home by 6:00 at night. That's what I really loved about playing the day games. It seemed like I had a little more family time and time to rest, much more like a normal person. I'd always heard it was hard to play so many day games, but I really enjoyed it. I didn't mind playing in the summer, even though people told me the heat might get to me. I don't buy the notion that the day games are the reason the

Second baseman Mickey Morandini, the Cubs' "Dandy Little Glove Man," tags out the Houston Astros' Bill Spiers on an attempted steal of second during a game at Wrigley Field on April 21, 1999. *Photo courtesy of Getty Images*

Cubs haven't won a championship in so long. You get your body into a routine playing day games, and it was never a problem.

Back then, the Cubs were still considered the Lovable Losers. We just put a good group of guys together. There were veterans on that team. They brought in Kevin Tapani, Henry Rodriguez, Jeff Blauser, and me—all guys who came from winning teams. We just put it all together that year and certainly rode the coattails of Sammy, with the way he was going. Mark Grace was still in his prime, and Kerry Wood came along all of a sudden from the minors. It was a lot of fun. We got off to a pretty good start, and at that time, the division wasn't super strong, and we hung in there. We played really good baseball at the end, had our battle with the Giants, and were fortunate enough to win the playoff game for the wild-card. It was a lot of fun that year and one of the best seasons I've ever had as a professional ballplayer.

The day Kerry struck out 20 Astros, you could tell early on his breaking ball was really moving, and with the velocity on his fastball, he was going to be tough to hit. I've never seen a curveball break as much as his was breaking that day. When you have good hitters coming up, and he's making them look pretty silly with his breaking stuff, you know that he's got some electric stuff going on. It was a pretty special day to see him do what he did.

Sammy's performance that year turned into a sideshow, but deservingly so. At that time in the aftermath of the strike, people were not really loving baseball as much as they had. It was sure fun to watch, I'll say that. It was fun to be a part of, and I do think it did take some pressure off everybody else on the team, because each game the media would all run to Sammy. We still had to go out and win ballgames, though.

I think I was a part of it, and that was a career year for me. People really wanted to get me out, because I had Grace and Sammy following me. I usually hit second behind Lance Johnson. That was a perfect spot for me because Lance was on a lot and could steal some bases. With Grace and Sammy behind me, they didn't want to put me on, so I saw a lot of fastballs. Other than a little slump in August, I was hitting well over .300 for most of the year. When I go out and speak now, I tell people that was the year Sammy and I combined for 74 home runs. He had 66, and I had eight! That was one of my better power years, and those eight were a career high for me. I probably had another handful that hit off the wall. It was just one of those years where I was seeing the ball really well, hitting good pitches, had a good eye for the strike zone, and put everything together.

Steve Stone and Chip Caray started calling me "the Dandy Little Glove Man," and that was fine. I took a lot of pride in my defense, and I had a couple of really good defensive years there with the Cubs. That didn't bother me, and I took it as a tribute to how well I caught the baseball with the Cubs. I appreciated the term and thrived on robbing hitters and seeing their faces after I made a great play.

The last day of the season was a weird day. We blew the game at Houston and were thinking, *Okay, we're done*. I remember looking at the scoreboard, and the Giants were tied with Colorado. We went up into our locker room to watch that game, and by the time we got to the clubhouse, we were told Neifi Perez had hit a home run to beat the Giants, and the Cubbies still had life. We went from being completely demoralized to, a minute or so later, being completely rejuvenated. That was a weird couple of minutes, for sure.

The playoff game was electric. I've been to and played in a lot of games at Wrigley, and that was the most electric I've ever seen it. The way we got there, with San Francisco losing the way they did, gave us new life, and we

262

were able to take advantage of that. Steve Trachsel gave us a real good pitching performance, and Shooter [Rod Beck] came in to close it down. It was a real emotional few days, for sure. To win that game and see how the city reacted was very memorable.

We felt good going into the division series against the Braves. I know we lost the first game, but in the second game we were winning late, and then they hit a home run to tie it and beat us. After losing that game, we were pretty down and knew we were in trouble. If we could have taken Game 2, I think that series would have gone the distance, at least.

The next season, we were 10 or 12 games above .500 going into early June. We went into Arizona and hit a wall, and it was a big hard one! We went from 10 or 12 games over to 10 or 12 under really, really fast. They started to make some changes, and it was a really disappointing month of baseball because we felt we had a team that could get back to the postseason. It didn't work out that way.

Two years went by quickly. You see the good part of Chicago, and then in '99 you saw the bad part of being a Cub when you're on a bad baseball team. I was part of both in my two years. I loved the fans, the city, and playing there. It was unfortunate that it didn't work out so I could stay there as a player longer.

The fans are still great to me. You can see that at the Cubs Convention when we all go back. A lot of ex-players there were only with the Cubs for a year or two, but still get the same response from the fans as the Graces and Sandbergs do. It's gratifying to come back and know they appreciate what you did, no matter how long you played there.

The Cubs acquired second baseman Mickey Morandini from the Phillies in exchange for Doug Glanville on December 23, 1997. The "Dandy Little Glove Man" shored up the Cubs defensively and was a fan favorite for his heady and aggressive play. Hitting second in the Cubs lineup, he scored 93 runs while hitting .296 with eight homers and 53 RBIs as the Cubs won the National League wild-card in 1998. Morandini slumped to .241 the next year and was granted free agency after the season. Morandini finished his career with the Phillies and Blue Jays before retiring after the 2000 season. He currently coaches high school baseball in Indiana.

KERRY WOOD

PITCHER

1998–2008

I REMEMBER WATCHING WGN coming home from school. I'd catch the last four innings of the game, and I was in Texas. WGN obviously helps the recognition of this team.

The 20 strikeouts was just one of those days. It happened, and it felt, honestly, like I was playing catch out there. The game just slowed down. I took in everything. I was able to look around and enjoy the fans who were doin' it up. Not too many times when you're out on the hill does the game slow down that much where you can really take it all in. For whatever reason, that day it seemed like everything was kind of in slow motion.

The one thing that sticks out in my mind is waking up and going to the ballpark, I really didn't feel that well. My energy level was way down, and I thought I might be getting sick. I went to the bullpen, started warming up, and thought, *This is going to be awful. It's only my fifth career start.* I couldn't throw a strike, and I thought it was going to be a bad day.

The game started, and before I knew it, I'd struck out the first three hitters. Then I looked up at the scoreboard, and we were in the fifth or sixth inning, and I felt like I had only pitched an inning or two. I felt like I got caught up in the moment and was so locked in I wasn't paying attention to anything that was going on around me. It was one of those days where it was my day.

The weather was pretty bad, and I remembered thinking they might have a chance to call it around the seventh when I slipped on the mound, but even then the ball kept going right where it needed to. Again, it was just my day.

The only hit was when I threw a hanging, back-up breaking ball to Ricky Gutierrez, and he jam-shot it toward left field between third and short. Believe me, when Ricky came here to play shortstop, I never heard the end of that. He brought it up at least twice a week!

I don't really remember if the guys were talking to me. I didn't know most of the guys, because I'd only been up for a couple of starts. I'm pretty sure they weren't. Sandy Martinez was my catcher that day, so we were speaking, but it was limited to that. I think that's the first game he caught me. Scott Servais was our regular catcher. I'm not sure what happened, but we were on the same page for a couple of hours.

Derek Bell made the last out, and we went back to Houston later in the season. He came up to me and said he wanted me to get it, and I called him on it. He said he wanted me to get it, and that's why he was swinging like that. I thought that was pretty funny. Bagwell and those guys, I respect what they have done in the game. When you respect the game, the veteran players tend to have a little respect for you. Those guys were great. Looking back on it, that was a pretty good lineup. At the time you don't think about it. I was young enough and dumb enough not to know what I was doing. Looking back on it, I'm glad I'll be able to show my son that tape.

265

About 45 seconds after I punched out the last guy, WGN-TV grabbed me for a postgame interview. My hand was shaking as I was holding the mike— I really didn't know what was going on. I didn't know I'd struck out 20 until Stoney [Steve Stone] mentioned it when he was interviewing me. I made the last pitch, got mobbed by my teammates, then I was trying to hold a microphone in my hands and earpiece in my ear while I tried to figure out what was going on. The adrenaline was still racing. I was lucky I didn't get the shaving cream treatment while doing the interview, but all my teammates were still on the field.

When we won the wild-card game that year, I was stuck in Arizona, knowing the guys for the first time in however long were celebrating, popping champagne, and there I was rehabbing, trying to get ready for the playoffs. That was definitely frustrating for me. I was ecstatic my rookie year to get a chance to pitch in the playoffs, and against Greg Maddux no less. Up

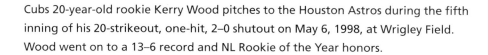

Cubs 20-year-old rookie Kerry Wood pitches to the Houston Astros during the fifth inning of his 20-strikeout, one-hit, 2–0 shutout on May 6, 1998, at Wrigley Field. Wood went on to a 13–6 record and NL Rookie of the Year honors.

until 2003, that was one of the most special moments for me, getting to pitch against a Hall of Famer at home in a playoff game. What a great experience!

The clincher against Pittsburgh in '03 was tough to get too excited at first, because I knew I was pitching the next day if we didn't win both games of the doubleheader that day and the Astros lost. Your mindset is that we'll split the doubleheader and go from there. You'll take a split, so it kind of caught us off guard. We took the first game, then it was the fifth inning or so in the second, and we were up, and I realized we could win it right there. It just happened, and it was awesome. We rode that high right into Atlanta for the playoffs.

When we walked out onto the field in Atlanta and heard how many Cubs fans were in that stadium, it felt like a home game. We rode that adrenaline throughout that series. I think I'll always remember the 2003 season, even though it didn't end the way we wanted it to. It's still as far as the Cubs have gotten in a long, long time, and it's a great memory for me.

The summer of 2008 was probably the most fun summer I've had playing the game of baseball. I changed roles and took pride in what I was doing, not that I hadn't before, but it was such a big change for me. I had a great time closing, we had a great team, and we had a fun summer. My son had a great time at Wrigley—he was at every game and got to see me on the field. He would wave and jump up and down, sing "Go Cubs Go" every time we got in the car; all those things made that summer special for me.

267

Getting into the postseason four of my 10 years with the Cubs was the most important thing to me. That's the reason we play the game. We were fortunate enough to get there four times in my time here. The atmosphere of Wrigley Field during the game is something I'll never forget. Playing here for so long and then going somewhere else, it's hard to duplicate the energy this stadium brings. It's exciting.

There really isn't anything like Wrigley. To have 40,000 people there on Monday, Tuesday, and Wednesday for a sellout is really something. It's a special place and will always have a special place in my heart, just the ins and outs of the clubhouse, going behind the scenes. The history in the stadium is obviously tremendous. Knowing that Fergie Jenkins, Billy Williams, Santo played here—roamin' the halls of the same stadium as these guys. It's a special place, it really is. I guess my favorite place obviously would be out there on the mound pitching, but I like the clubhouse and the concourse, the whole thing.

There's not a whole lot I would change with the things that were under my control. Obviously, missing a couple of years due to the injuries, I'd love to change that, but you can't do that. It happened, and 2008 wouldn't have been as rewarding as it was if I hadn't gone through those things. I was always passionate about my job, the team I was playing for, and the city I was playing in.

The fans were good to me, maybe because they knew me from the time I was drafted at 17. I was at the Cubs Conventions when I was 18 or 19, so I feel like they saw me grow up. I came here as a single teenager and left married with two kids. They've seen us, they know us, they've read about me for years, they've gone through a lot of ups and downs with me. The fans here in Chicago are special and one of a kind.

I appreciate what the organization did for me and my family during my entire time here. It was a great run, and I had a great time in Chicago. I was in that clubhouse for 10 years, saw guys come and go, and it just came time that it was my turn. This city has embraced us, and anything we can do to return the favor is great. This is the city where I want to be, even after baseball is long gone. I hope we can raise our kids here. This is our home, and I appreciate all the fan support for my career here and when I came back with the Indians. I appreciate all the kind words and all the great mail I've gotten. I spent 10 years in the greatest baseball town there is, and I enjoyed every minute of it.

Kerry Wood was selected by the Cubs with the fourth overall pick in the 1995 amateur draft. In just his fifth career start, Wood tied a major league record with 20 strikeouts on May 6, 1998, against the Houston Astros. Wood finished 13–6 that season and won the National League Rookie of the Year award. Injuries derailed much of his career in Chicago, but he led the Cubs to the division title in 2003 with a 14–11 record and 3.20 ERA. Wood was brilliant in the division series that year against the Braves, with two wins in Atlanta, including the deciding Game 5, as the Cubs won their first postseason series since 1908. In 2008 he moved to the bullpen and recorded 34 saves as the Cubs' closer. He was a free agent after that season and signed with the Cleveland Indians.

The
NEW
MILLENNIUM

CARLOS ZAMBRANO

PITCHER

2001–Present

I<small>T'S BEEN A LONG TIME</small> between being young and being a veteran. It's been good. Anything I can do to help out other players and the organization is good for me. I feel very proud of the Cubs organization. I always say this is the team that brought me up and the team that helped me grow up.

When I first came up, I looked at and talked to Jon Lieber. He was the kind of guy I admired. He was the main man here, and when he won 20 games, I was very happy. He taught me some big things. Then Greg Maddux came and helped me use what God gave me. I appreciate those two guys and the help I received from them.

Two thousand three was the year I broke out as a starter. I was a reliever and started some my first two years, but in '03 I faced a lot of good teams like the Atlanta Braves from back in the day. They had Andruw Jones, Chipper Jones, Javy Lopez, and those guys were raking! I faced those guys in the playoffs, threw a lot of scoreless innings, and after that I felt like I belonged up here.

I would say this: any time you can go to the playoffs, there is a chance to be the champion. You can see what the Atlanta Braves did 14 years in a row, and they went to the World Series a few times but only won one. Every time you put yourself as a team in the playoffs, anything can happen. You see teams that are nothing on paper, but then get to the playoffs and are a different team completely. Two thousand three was a great year for us, and we had great chemistry, but we have a bad taste from that year, as well as '07 and '08. We have to keep going to the playoffs and keep qualifying, then one of these years, the good news will come.

I don't get tired of being talked about. I always say that things happen for a reason. Here in baseball, some people will talk good about you, and some people will not. You are not a prisoner of everybody. You can be the man of the people you love and who love you. This is the situation, and a lot of people can talk about you because that is their right. You know who you are, and you have to know what position you are in with your friends and family, and that's it. From then, whatever your family and your friends think about you, that's what you are.

I enjoy this game a lot. I enjoy seeing my teammates hit a home run or make a great play or pitch a good game. So far, in eight years, they have been good to me. This thing is what I know how to do, and you have to enjoy it. That's it.

Wrigley Field is a great place to pitch—when the wind is blowing in! It's an old ballpark, but the people are friendly, at least with us as the Cubs. I remember in '06 we were struggling, really struggling. We were in last place, and you would still have 39,000 or 40,000 fans in this place. That's the special thing about Wrigley Field. I once saw a player from the Minnesota Twins, and he was completely in shock after seeing Wrigley Field. It is amazing to see the ivy on the wall, the people in the crowd, the dugouts. There are things that the Cubs need to repair and modernize, but otherwise Wrigley Field is a great place to be. It's home. It's my house, and I feel I will be here for a long time.

271

Everywhere we go, the Cubs fans are there, and we appreciate that. We feel like we're home in all those places. We appreciate when the fans are supporting us every time they cheer for us. That's the main thing, that the fans deserve a championship. The city of Chicago deserves the Cubs to be champions.

I work hard every day and come to the ballpark no matter the situation. When I come into the clubhouse, I'm a ballplayer.

My no-hitter against the Astros was a great experience. I haven't been in a World Series, which is my biggest goal, but I do have personal goals, and getting a no-hitter was one of them. It was an exciting night. We were close to Chicago, playing in Milwaukee, and there were so many Cubs fans there. It felt like a home game. A hurricane was hitting Houston, so we had to play somewhere, and they chose Milwaukee.

Barry Bonds told me once that even if he was 0-for-28 against someone, he went to the plate thinking that this was the time he would get a hit. I like

Playing the Astros in Milwaukee due to Hurricane Ike, Carlos Zambrano uncorks to
a Houston batter in the first inning of his no-hitter on September 14, 2008.

to think that even if a batter is 10-for-20 against me, in that moment, I can
still strike him out in a big situation.

I like to do things right and want to be the best professional I can be. I take
it all seriously, and being in the National League as a pitcher, I have to go to
the plate and give it my best. Every time I go out there, I want to put the ball
in play and do my best just the same as my pitching.

I love to hit. If I was done pitching, maybe I could be an outfielder. I would think about it. It may be a way to a better contract!

I got my first hit as a right-handed batter. At the time, the Cubs weren't letting me switch-hit because they were worried about someone hitting my arm. I got a double off Nelson Figueroa, and that was fun. I don't remember my first homer, but I remember one I hit off Todd Wellemeyer. He used to pitch for us, and before the game I told him, "I'm going to go deep. Don't throw a fastball right there if you get behind in the count. I will look for that fastball." He got behind me 3–1 and came in with a fastball, and I hit it good. That was fun. I looked at him while I was rounding the bases, and he said, "Carlos, nice shot!"

Cubs fans are great. I never want to play for another team. Every player I know that comes from another team tells me the Cubs fans are the best. We almost went to the World Series in 2003, then followed with a bad year in 2004, but there were still 38,000 fans there every day. That is really something.

Sometimes I get in trouble with the things I say, but I always want to tell the truth. When this contract is up in a few years, I will hang up my glove. That's what I feel. I'd like to see my daughters grow up and things in my family run smoothly. Before that, let's just talk about baseball and on the field. I don't want to talk about retirement. That will be in a few years.

I can only speak for myself, but I really don't feel any added pressure from the fans to win a World Series. We have had some good teams, and the Cubs keep investing in good players to try and get it done. The most important thing right now, though, is to win a World Series for the city.

Carlos Zambrano was signed by the Cubs as an amateur free agent from Venezuela in 1997. He made his big-league debut in 2001, split time as a starter and reliever in 2002, then moved into the starting rotation at age 22 with a 13–11 record and 3.11 ERA. Zambrano established himself as one of the most durable starters in baseball over the next five seasons, averaging 16 wins and 210 innings per year and making three All-Star teams. On September 14, 2008, Zambrano became the first Cub to throw a no-hitter since Milt Pappas in 1972, beating the Astros in a game that was moved from Houston to Milwaukee's Miller Park due to Hurricane Ike. Zambrano is one of the best-hitting pitchers in baseball and holds the Cubs' career record for home runs by a pitcher with 20.

JIM HENDRY
GENERAL MANAGER
2002–Present

WHEN I CAME TO THE CUBS in charge of the minor leagues in '95, it was a good experience. I thought I was kind of made for that job from my coaching and on-the-field background, which was a good fit. Then after one year, Andy MacPhail asked me to take over the draft, and I was a little concerned about whether I was capable of doing that, because I had only scouted with the Marlins for about three years and didn't have a scouting background. I told him that, but he said I'd be good at it and that it was more important than the minor league job. I did that for five years and ran five drafts here. Then, in the last two years of the five, I ran the minor leagues at the same time. So from the scouting and development mindset, I was prepared.

I think he did me a tremendous favor when he took over the GM position again and brought me in as his assistant. That's what I really needed, because all my experience in pro ball was not in the office. It was out in the field evaluating our minor league system or hiring coaches or running the draft when you are in a different city every day most of the year. I needed some apprenticeship, and Andy was very good at it. He was a tremendous guy in the office and probably wrote half the rules in MLB from his past pedigree. He told me that I was going to be the next GM, but the promotion wouldn't come until he felt I was ready to do that. Obviously, he was just tremendous to me in my career.

Cubs general manager Jim Hendry talks with Cubs manager Lou Piniella and White Sox skipper Ozzie Guillen before the Crosstown Classic on June 17, 2009, at Wrigley Field. *Photo courtesy of Getty Images*

He told me that unless I really screwed it up, I would be the next GM. I remember the night it happened. I was in Florida. At the time, I was traveling with the team as the assistant more than Andy traveled. I probably made three-quarters of the trips at that time. He called me late Wednesday night after we had played the Marlins and told me he was coming to Atlanta to meet the team on Friday. At 12:00 he was going to meet with Don Baylor and let him go as manager, and at 3:00 he was going to name me general manager. I was surprised at the timing of it and thought maybe he'd wait another year. It was a tough day for both of us, because Don was such a good man, but we felt we needed to make a change. As a human being, Don was a 10. Emotionally, three hours later, you know it's one of your dream days that you're now general manager of the Cubs. It was one of the strangest emotional days of my life. Literally, I felt bad at noon for what had to happen, but couldn't help but be ecstatic a few hours later at the position I now had.

In 2003, in the big scheme of things, the Marlins probably had the better team. That doesn't mean we shouldn't have won. When you get up three games to one, then three to two after Beckett beat us, and you're coming home having to win just one of two, I think we thought we were going to win. We had Wood and Prior ready to go. The Marlins were very good and proved that when they knocked out the Yankees. The one thing nobody talks about or remembers, because we all got caught up in Game 6, is that we were ahead in Game 1, 4–0 off Josh Beckett after a few innings. He probably never gave up another run after that. If we'd have won Game 1 here, we'd have swept them. I felt if we got past the Marlins, we were going to be the World Champions, just like they proved. It was one of those times when they caught the Yankees at the right time. Our advance scouts told us at the time that they were hoping the Giants would beat the Marlins, because they thought Florida would be a tougher battle for us, and obviously they were.

The expectations here are high, and I wouldn't want them to be any lower. Things can get out of line, and when you come in second, you catch more abuse than you would have at any other era in Cubs history. We're proud of the fact that we've won two of three division titles with Lou Piniella. That's something that if, looking forward, we could do every three years, I'd be thrilled. The Cardinals have been dominating us for years, and we finally got them twice, but now they're good again, too. That's what you want. I never wanted to be the GM of the Cubs and just make incremental improvement or just try to be .500 every now and then. That's not the way I would want the franchise to be looked upon. I would rather take the criticism when we come in second and people have higher expectations. I'd rather take that than be inching up the ladder from sixth to fifth to fourth and say maybe three years from now we'll be good when so-and-so gets here. It's a tough place to play. The bar has been raised. Expectations have never been higher, and not everybody can handle it. Some parts of my job are trying to keep mixing and matching. Some people on paper look like they are the answer, and it doesn't work out that way.

How you build and construct your team depends on the market and on ownership. We had a drastic change here when Andy left. The company knew they were going to sell and wanted to win right away. All of a sudden, we spent a lot more money than we used to, started backloading contracts, and the plan was to win now while the company still owned it. I don't think anyone at the Tribune Company felt that it would take two and a half years to complete the sale. Of course, you pay for some of those decisions down the road. Nobody in free agency hits bull's-eyes with eight out of eight or 10 out of 10. That philosophy to maybe win now while the company still owned it and not worry about who was going to own it next or what the payroll would be in five years made you make decisions that were good short-term, but if you're not careful, some of them can hurt you long-term.

How I spend my day just depends on the time of year, and you can't script it. It changed for the better for me in the last couple of years since I hired Randy Bush. I didn't have an assistant GM for the first four years. He's taken a lot of the load off me. This time of year, September, I don't have a lot to do. Even if we were winning, you're getting ready for the off-season or hopefully planning for the postseason. The normal process is you try to read your daily newspapers and the Internet clips from other cities so you can keep up on the baseball rumor mill. You clear the messages during the minor league season every night from all six of your minor league teams, the game reports from the night before, the injury reports, probably about 30 voice-mails a day from the minor league system and scouting. That takes about two-thirds of your morning. The only negative of having so many day games—which are great because you get to go home at night and see your kids—is during the workday you have to make a daily choice to either bear down on the game at hand and try to get into that or take business calls during the game. By the time the game is over, you're past office hours on the East Coast. There's a little balance there, and you get into a little routine and live with it. A lot of it is phone work, a lot is working with agents, a lot is talking to your peers on a regular basis, especially in the summer before the deadline. It comes and goes, and a lot of times, I am stressfully busier in the off-season than I am during the season.

I try to go into trade possibilities with a sense of the other club. I don't think you try to hit home runs. First of all, you never know how a trade is going to work out. Some of the trades I made looked like the best deals in the world on paper. The day we got Nomar Garciaparra, I was probably the most popular guy in Chicago. We had a really good team in '04 and thought Nomar was going to be the difference-maker. He was a wonderful guy, but he just got nicked up a lot. We ended up not getting in, and the Red Sox, who were ripped for trading Nomar, ended up winning the World Series. I've learned that the splashes you make on the day of the trades don't always turn out the way you planned.

I try to feel like if a trade is good for both teams, that's what you want. You want it to work out both ways, because it makes the next trade a lot easier to make. That's why I believe in open disclosure on injuries and things like that. I've made a couple trades with Billy Beane, and we've gotten to the point to we can make them in 20 minutes some days. For example, I didn't want Sean Gallagher to leave, and I wanted him to pitch well for the A's when we got Rich Harden. There has to be that kind of mutual respect. If you're always trying to beat the heck out of the other guy in a trade, you won't be making too many trades with him.

Over time, you build relationships the way you want to off the field. You try to be truthful. You be blunt. I've found I've probably spent more time with players than other GMs. That was a good thing, because I had a lot of them coming up through the system, or drafted them, or traded for them, so I have my hands in almost all of them in some way. At the same time, even when they're here and playing well, you have to remind yourself your decisions have to be based on what's good for the Cubs first and the player second. I try to do always do that, especially when I see something coming that might be an exit for that player, whether it's the budget, payroll, trade possibilities, I try to be up front and tell them that day may come. I'm certainly not the smartest GM who ever lived, but I think over time I'll be proudest that the players always got it straight and honest from me on a daily basis. I don't treat them better or worse based on how they played yesterday. I think if you're fair and honest with people, even if they don't like the decisions you make, they respect your honesty.

The 2008 postseason was really a shame. I really thought we had as good a team as anybody in the league. I thought we and the Phillies would have a battle. It's a shame the way it ended. It's such a fragile three-out-of-five series. If we would have won the first game here, I thought we would have beaten the Dodgers. But it kind of snowballed, and we kicked the ball around the second game and were up against it then. In the same sense, in '03, I'm sure Bobby Cox would say that was one of the best Braves teams he ever had. Woody pitched two gems, Prior pitched one, and we upset the Braves, who'd won more than 100 games that year and really had a better team than the Marlins. It's a strange thing—the best team doesn't always win. It's kind of who gets hot at the right time and who gets a break here or there. I was really disappointed because we had a really good team with a really good bunch of guys, and we just got swept.

278

I try to stay the same guy all the time, because obviously we've been through some big ups and downs. It's hard to win, and nobody likes coming in second. We had a disappointing year in 2009, but it wasn't a disaster. You do the best you can. We had won 97 games and lost six straight playoff games, so I was trying to find a solution to get us to a championship. It didn't work then, but if I stop trying to get us to win the whole thing, I shouldn't be sitting in my chair.

I feel a huge responsibility to win. I think that's probably one of the things that's allowed me to stay around awhile. Dennis FitzSimons gave me another chance when Dusty and Andy left in '06. I think people know my heart is in the right place. I don't take it lightly. I would tell Tom Ricketts the same thing. I expect us to be in the World Series in the next couple of years, or I think Tom should get somebody else. I don't take it lightly, and that's enabled me to roll with the punches. I get a lot of credit and get talked about very favorably when we're doing well. I take a lot of grief when we're not, and I understand that. That never downplays the importance of what I feel we owe our great fans—not only in Chicago but all over the country—and the responsibility that I have of trying to somehow, some way, win this thing one time.

Jim Hendry was named the Cubs' general manager on July 5, 2002, after holding a variety of front-office positions since joining the team in November 1994. Under Hendry's guidance, the Cubs have reached the postseason in 2003, 2007, and 2008. He is known as one of baseball's most aggressive GMs as well as one of the game's straightest shooters. Prior to his time with the Cubs, Hendry was head baseball coach at Creighton University and spent three years with the Florida Marlins as a minor league manager, scout, and special assistant to the general manager.

DERREK LEE
FIRST BASEMAN
2004–Present

I WAS EXCITED TO BE TRADED HERE. Playing here, especially in the playoffs on the opposing team, you could just see the excitement of the fans and how much they had a passion for this team. Chicago was one of the places I always wanted to play just for that reason, having a sellout every day and the excitement in this park.

As a player, it's a great place to come play. The atmosphere is unbelievable. Every day you've got a sellout. It's a lot of excitement, just a lot of energy in the ballpark. It's great as a player.

The great thing about WGN is we have fans all across the country. I know growing up, I watched the Cubs in California because most of the time they were the only game on. It was the Cubs or the Braves. So we have a lot of fans, and it's nice when you go on the road to have some support. I do get some calls from other players. Guys will be sitting around in the daytime watching us on WGN because we're the only game on. But I think it's just cool that my family, wherever they may be in the States, can usually watch our game. That's a pretty cool thing.

These fans are unbelievable in their support. If they recognize that you're giving all you have on the field on a daily basis and you perform well, they really take you in. I've had some off-the-field issues, and they have really shown their support in that area, too, so these fans have been great to me, and I really appreciate it.

Cubs first baseman Derrek Lee rips an RBI single
against the Pittsburgh Pirates during the
first inning of a 17–2 win at Wrigley
Field on August 14, 2009.
Lee had seven RBIs
on the day.

I try to play the game the right way. I grew up watching my father play, and he always told me to just play the right way and respect the game. I don't take it for granted that I wear this uniform, so I try to go out there and play the game the right way and give it my all every day.

The thing I love the most about Wrigley is the game. I love the three hours on the field playing the game, the crowd is going crazy. It's just the part I like the most. It seems like lately, the wind has not been good to us. It's blowing in every day it seems like. I haven't looked today, but hopefully it turns around and starts blowing out for us.

I don't know if Cubs fans will like this, but for now celebrating here at Wrigley as the opposing team after we won to go to the World Series is my biggest memory. I really don't know if I want to remind them. That playoff series was probably the most fun I have ever had playing baseball because it was such a great series, and there was so much excitement in the city. It was a lot of fun to play in.

I hit my first grand slam as a Cub off the Reds, and I had been struggling a little bit when I first got here. I hit that grand slam, and the fans called me out for a curtain call, which was pretty special for me.

That's the thing about our fans, they're ready to go. They want to root for you. If you're doing badly or they don't like the way you're playing, they're going to get on you. But they want to root for you, that's the basis of it. So if you give them something to cheer about, they're going to cheer you.

We do talk about what it would mean to win it here. Yes, all the time. All off-season, every day. We talk about it in the clubhouse. This city would just go crazy to win here, so that's what we're striving for, and it's definitely a motivating factor. Someday, we're going to get it done. We're going to do everything in our power to get it done, and we want to see these fans go wild.

The Cubs acquired first baseman Derrek Lee from the Florida Marlins on November 25, 2003, for Hee Seop Choi and Mike Nannini. He had 32 homers and 98 RBIs in his first season on the North Side, then followed with a career year in 2005, when he hit 46 homers, drove in 107 runs, and won the NL batting title with a .335 average. A broken wrist sidelined him in 2006, and his power numbers declined. But in 2009 Lee bounced back with 35 homers, 111 RBIs, and a .306 average. He won Gold Gloves in 2005 and 2007 and was an NL All-Star in those years, as well.

RYAN DEMPSTER

PITCHER
2004–Present

MY FIRST BIG-LEAGUE START was at Wrigley Field as a member of the Florida Marlins. I struck out Brant Brown on three pitches and thought, *Boy, this game is easy.* I walked the next guy, and Sammy Sosa took me deep. Then I walked the next batter, and Henry Rodriguez took me deep. Then it was, *Okay, I guess it's not that easy.*

First and foremost, I'm not just a player, I'm a fan of baseball. I've always been a fan of Wrigley Field and the Cubs because they were on WGN, so I could sit back at home and watch. I think it is a very special place to play, where you have 40,000 fans every day—and not just in the park, but around the park, whether it's people having a barbecue in the neighborhood or playing beanbags or at all the bars around here. It's a very unique and special place, unlike any other in the big leagues. For me, I always wanted to play here, and now that I'm here, I never want to play anywhere else.

When I was a free agent in 2004, it was a thing that weighed heavily on my mind. Obviously, my choices weren't a lot, but I did have the chance to go other places. To me, the one place I always wanted to come to was here, and I always wanted to feel what it was like to be a home player at this park. Since I came, it's been nothing but great things. I've had my ups and downs, some good games, some bad games, but there's not a day I don't enjoy coming to this ballpark.

Ryan Dempster came to Chicago in 2004 and earned 85 saves as the Cubs' closer from 2005 to 2007, before entering the starting rotation in 2008, when he went 17–6 with a 2.96 ERA.

It's been a unique place to play. I want to be comfortable. I don't want it to be a place where I don't feel like I can walk around with my family. I know I'm a Cubs player, and a lot comes with that. You get recognized a lot of places you go. But at the same time, I want to make it feel like my own neighborhood, just like I would if I were growing up. I have a family now and want it to be the same. I enjoy getting to know all the people, whether it's at the grocery store or the coffee shop or at the firehall or meeting the cops. That's important, because it makes life easier when you are living here.

One of my biggest games as a Cub was when I was closing and we were in St. Louis. I came on in the eighth inning for one of the few times in my career. The bases were loaded, and I struck out Preston Wilson and got Adam Kennedy on a groundout. I thought for me to strand those guys in that situation in a one-run game was a pretty cool feeling, and I remember being very proud of that game.

We were in Cincinnati in Lou Piniella's first season with us, and it was the second game of the year. I was closing at the time, and I think we were up about 8–1. We'd had some time off at the end of spring training, and he wanted me to get my work in, so he put me in to pitch. I struck out the first guy, walked the second guy, then Ken Griffey Jr. came up. I threw him ball one, and Lou came out of the dugout. He came out to the mound, and I thought he might be protesting something. I wasn't sure what was going on. He came up to me and said, "Son, what's the problem?" I said I didn't know what he meant. He said, "It's 30 degrees out, we're all freezing. We're up 8–1, so throw the ball over the middle of the plate, and let's get out of here." He turned around and headed back to the dugout, and I threw ball two, but he didn't see it because he wasn't back in the dugout yet. I'm glad he didn't see that one.

When I went into the rotation in 2008, I thought it would go well but didn't know it would go that well. I know I enjoyed the four days off between starts! It's a different animal, and I built up my legs to be able to pitch more innings. I found myself ahead in the count a lot and was able to put guys away. Being healthy the whole year was key in being able to pitch over 200 innings. That was as much fun in a season as I've ever had.

Having been a starting pitcher in the past, I kind of knew what I had to do, or at least what I thought I had to do, to get ready. I was very lucky to be a teammate of Greg Maddux and watch him go through everything he went through in how he prepared for a game. I just try to do the same. I try to work real hard on my days in between and mentally and physically prepare to do what I need to do to give us a chance to win that day. Luckily, for the most part, every fifth day I've given us a chance to win, and hopefully I can continue to do that.

One thing I learned from closing was inning management. You're always one pitch away from getting out of a big inning, and for me, just realizing that no matter how loud it gets or how crazy the situation is, just calm yourself down and worry about trying to execute that pitch at that time. Hopefully, that's enough to get the job done, and you don't worry too much about everything that's going on around you. Just realize that it's the same thing—60′6″ away from the plate, and make your pitches.

The Dodgers beat me in Game 1 of the '08 playoffs. If I weren't prepared, I would have been more upset as far as going out there and being ready to pitch in that game. You're never going to forget it, and I'll always remember what happened. It depends on how you deal with it. Do you let it get you down, or do you use it as motivation to push you even harder? That's what I've done. As a team, we picked a bad time to have a three-game losing streak.

I started shaking my glove as I go into my windup because I was tipping my pitches. I hadn't really thrown out of a windup in a few years, because I had been in the bullpen. I was pitching to Tyler Colvin in spring training, and he told me he could tell when I was moving from a split to a different grip in my glove. I thought, *Wow, no wonder I've been getting hit around this spring.* I went home that night and was with my friend, Kevin Millar. He suggested I just wiggle my glove around a little bit. I tried doing it, and it felt comfortable and maybe distracts a hitter here or there. It became second nature, and I don't even realize I do it anymore.

286

One day at Wrigley, I got the game time mixed up. It was supposed to be at 3:00 PM on Fox, but they didn't show it, so it was moved to noon. I was at home making pancakes at about 10:10, and the phone rang. It was Tim Buss, our strength coach. He said, "You know the game is at noon, right?" Luckily, I only live about four blocks away, so I said I'd be there in two minutes. I didn't have any breakfast, ran over the to the field, and got out there. I was out on the mound in the first inning and felt like Mark Fidrych, all wound up, and I had no food in me. Soto came out and asked me if I was all right. When I said I didn't think so, he asked me if I wanted to go to dinner that night. I said sure, then went seven innings and only gave up one run. That was the best pitching advice I got all day.

I'm a big hockey fan and, of course, I loved the Winter Classic at Wrigley. The day they announced that game, I said, "I have to go see this game." I brought my brothers and five of my buddies in for that, and we had a great time. A couple days later, we all got to skate on the ice, which was perfect.

I'm waiting for the day I hit my first home run. I just need the wind at Wrigley Field to blow a little bit harder, maybe 70 or 80 mph, and then I'll get one. I cannot wait until that day. I have this thought, maybe I don't believe it, but I stand there and watch the ball, throw my bat, run around the bases slow, and give some fist bumps, because it's probably only going to happen once. Probably the way it will go is that I'll hit it, think it's off the wall, and go around the bases as fast as I can. Then people will say I didn't enjoy it. I will catch one, though. Somebody will hit my bat, and I'll get lucky.

I try to go out there, not change, lead by example, and most important, have fun. I take my job seriously, but at the same time I realize we're playing a game. If I can use stuff that I've learned along the way from other pitchers and coaches, then it's great if I can relay it to other people; that helps. I try to play the game the right way, and your responsibility as you get older is to teach that to guys who are coming up.

Cubs fans are extremely passionate, and it's as close as you can come to the fact that the fans want to win every bit as much as the players do. It provides a unique and special atmosphere at Wrigley Field. They are all quasi-karaoke singers, because everyone wants to wait and sing "Go Cubs Go." The pressure will always be there, whether we are on the road or at home in front of our 41,000 fans. You forget that stuff during the game. Our fans do make us feel so truly welcome, though, and you don't forget that.

It's not about contracts or personal stats or those kind of things. It's about going out there and trying to help us do what we're trying to do here, which is get in the playoffs and win a World Series. I enjoy the success I've had and I feel like I've learned to pitch, but I want to get better all the time. That's my motivation.

Ryan Dempster signed with the Cubs as a free agent on January 21, 2004. He had undergone Tommy John surgery in August 2003 and was able to return to the mound as a Cub for 23 games in 2004. Dempster won the closer's role for the Cubs the next year and earned 85 saves over the next three years. He returned to the starting rotation in spectacular fashion in 2008 by going 17–6 with a 2.96 ERA and was named to the NL All-Star team. Dempster pitched 200 innings for the Cubs in 2009 and posted an 11–9 record.

BOB BRENLY

BROADCASTER

1990–1991 ★ 2005–Present

AFTER I LEFT WGN RADIO, I stayed in touch with John McDonough in the Cubs' marketing department over the years. When I got fired as the Diamondbacks' manager, I happened to have some tickets for Blue Man Group in Chicago that we were planning to use when the D–backs came to town that year but were now not going to need anymore. I called John and said, "Hey, I've got these tickets if you want to use them for Cubs charities or donate them to somebody who can use them." We just got to talking, and he asked what I was going to do now. I told him I was unemployed, so I was available to park cars, sweep up the stadium, or sell popcorn if they were looking for somebody. It just so happened that fall the Cubs were looking for a new TV color guy. One thing led to another, and before you knew it, I was at Wrigley Field for a press conference, announcing that I was going to be the new analyst for the team. I think sometimes it helps to keep those relationships with people you meet earlier in your career, and this was one case where it really paid off.

When you take this job, you have to be ready for the passion of the Cubs fans. It's unlike any other. People talk about the Red Sox and the Yankees as two franchises that have a similar fan base, but they haven't suffered the way Cub fans have suffered. You have to understand going in what it means to the fans of Chicago and what it means to be a player on a Cubs team in Chicago.

After a brief stint doing Cubs games for WGN Radio in 1990–1991, Bob Brenly went into coaching and in 2001 managed the Arizona Diamondbacks to a World Series victory. In 2005 he became the color analyst for Cubs games on WGN-TV.
Photo courtesy of Bob Vorwald

I think my days as a visiting player and manager, along with my two years in the WGN Radio booth in '90 and '91, all helped prepare me for living with Cubs Nation on a daily basis.

I think my first year here on TV was a feeling-out process for all of us. Len and I were new together in the booth, certainly we were new to the fans, and I think we probably treaded a bit lighter that first year than we have since then. We had to establish our credibility, that we knew what we were talking about, that we had a relationship with the players on the field, and that we understood what the fans in the stands felt. Once I felt we were at the point where the fans understood where we were coming from, then we could be a little more vocal and a bit more outspoken in our criticism of the team, and I'd say we've reached that point.

The game is so much faster on the field than in the booth, and the example I like to give is the double switch. Lou might want to take a pitcher out of the game, but his spot is coming up in the next inning. Up in the booth, I can take half an inning to describe why you make a double switch and why you use particular players. In the meantime, Lou has had to make 10 more decisions while I'm describing that one double switch. I think sometimes fans who don't have an intimate knowledge of the game don't understand that. The game at field level moves lightning quick. It can be a very slow-paced game for fans or us in the booth, but for the guys down on the field, making decisions that can alter the course of the game, it moves like lightning. You have to make decisions, make them quickly, and be prepared to make them on the spot.

My game routine is pretty simple. I like to talk to catchers, because they can give you some good insight about the pitchers, the guy who is throwing that day, and who is likely to be used out of the pen late in a ballgame. I like to talk to the pitching coach of the other team if I can just to get an idea of who is available and who's not on a daily basis. Certainly, we talk to the managers, but a lot of times we catch them in their regular media hump with all the guys, and all you get there is a lot of clichés. If possible, it's nice to talk to the opposing manager one on one just to get some insight about his club. More than anything else, it's just being around the players and judging their moods. When I was managing, we called it taking their temperatures. You can walk through the clubhouse some days and, just by how a guy is putting on his uniform, you can tell if it's going to be a good day or a bad day.

Cubs fans consider us family, and that's great. The most frustrating thing for us is, because they see us every day and are so familiar with us, they do feel like we're part of their family. We can't know all the millions of people who follow the Cubs. Sometimes fans will come up and start venting or praising, whatever the case may be, and they feel like they are talking to a friend. Now I'm talking to a perfect stranger, and I have no idea who he is, but that being said, I understand his feelings and why he's saying the things he's saying. Even though I might not know the man or woman or child's name, I know their feelings and what they are talking about with the Cubs.

Len and I may be a little closer to their family, and we're trying to adopt them into our family!

The expectations of Cubs fans have changed to a certain extent. The play-off runs in '07 and '08 have ratcheted up expectations a bit, but I think Cubs fans have always wanted to win. I don't think that's really anything new. I think because they've had a little taste of the postseason, they might be hungrier, but they are always hungry to win. There's no question about that.

My relationship with the managers since I've been here has been great. I think the perceived relationship because of what's been written in the papers and talked about on talk radio has been completely blown out of proportion. When Dusty was here, well, we played together with the San Francisco Giants, and I coached under him there. I've known Dusty most of my professional life. He didn't feel threatened by me up in the booth. A couple of times when things were said and got blown out of proportion, we sat down and talked about it. I don't think he ever had a problem with anything I said in the booth. The same thing goes for Lou. There have been a couple of instances where my name has been brought up as a possible replacement and some of my criticisms of players have created a situation he had to deal with. Every time that happened, I've made it a point to go in and talk to Lou about it. In some instances, I've apologized for things I said if they created a problem for Lou, because it was never my intention to create a rift with the club or the manager. We're all in this together.

I always say Len does everything in the booth and I just follow it. In that respect, I'm a little *laissez faire* when it comes to preparing for a game. I like to hang around the batting cage and the clubhouse. Len does his homework. He's on the Internet and takes immaculate notes with everybody he talks to. Len has enough information that, if we ever play an extra-inning game that goes 10 hours, he will never run out of things to say, he's that prepared. He's a little more statistically minded that I am. I'm more about the feel and rhythm of the game. I think the combination of the two things has worked out pretty well.

When I was hired, I called my view from the broadcast booth "the greatest view in sports," and nothing has happened to change my mind. There's some days we have to pinch ourselves up there, because you look out and there's a full house of crazy Cubs fans ready to watch a ballgame. The sun is shining, the grass is green, you can see the lake out there, the rooftops are filled—I can't imagine any place in the world where you go to work and have a view like that. Plus, you get to watch the game and talk about it. It's got to be the greatest job in the world.

After a nine-year playing career with the San Francisco Giants and Toronto Blue Jays, Bob Brenly joined the Cubs' radio booth on WGN Radio along with Thom Brennaman and Ron Santo for two seasons beginning in 1990. In 1992 he was added to the Giants' coaching staff where he spent four seasons before taking an analyst position with the Arizona Diamondbacks' television team. In 2001 Brenly took over as manager and led the Diamondbacks to a World Series championship in his first season. He followed with two winning seasons, but was replaced midway through the 2004 campaign. Brenly was hired as the color man for Cubs television in November 2004 and immediately endeared himself to Cubs fans with his baseball knowledge, frank approach, and sense of humor.

LEN KASPER
BROADCASTER
2005–Present

WHAT I THINK ABOUT when listening to baseball on the radio as a kid are the West Coast games when I was supposed to go to bed by 9:00 or 9:30, and the pregame show would be on with a game starting at 10:00. I'd get under the covers with a transistor radio on and listen to Ernie Harwell until I fell asleep. I would say I learned a lot about baseball and certainly about broadcasting. That's kind of what whetted my appetite for this business. At that time, not all the games were on television, so radio had a bigger place in my life at the time than maybe it would for a young kid who could watch all the games on television.

The biggest thing for me with Ernie was—and not every broadcaster is like this or was like Ernie was—when you listened to the game, you never knew if the Tigers were ahead by 15 or down by 15. He always treated every play and every inning the same way. There was always that consistency. You always knew he was rooting for the Tigers, but sometimes you turn on a game, and you can just hear by the tone of the announcer's voice that this game is probably over. I don't ever want, even if the Cubs are losing, for people to turn their TV off because they hear that I'm down. This is not a funeral, it's not a bummer. You can still have fun, even though the game may not being going the way you want it to go.

When I heard about the Cubs' television job opening up on the last day of the 2004 season, I never thought in my wildest dreams that I would have the

Len Kasper was hired as the television voice of the Cubs in 2005 and, along with his booth partner Bob Brenly, has become a fan favorite. *Photo courtesy of Bob Vorwald*

opportunity to even be considered for the job. It took me a couple of weeks to actually apply when I started to hear I might have a shot at it. I think my Midwestern roots probably helped a little bit, and I just thought I had a great job in Florida, but this was the best job in baseball, and in sports, so I had to go for it. I just told myself, "Be yourself, and hopefully that's good enough." It worked out.

That winter was a blur. I told myself before the season started that it was going to be the most interesting baseball season of my entire life. You're going to have some ups and downs, hear some criticism, and you're going to try and learn about 500 names at the ballpark. Your head's going to be spinning, but try to take it all in and enjoy the roller coaster. I think I did and that I learned a lot about myself in the process. I toughened up a little bit, because this is such a huge stage on WGN. You're going to hear the good and the bad all the time, and I don't shy away from it. From that moment on, I gained a little confidence as a broadcaster and maybe as a person.

It's unbelievable to sit where Jack and Harry sat. I had broadcast many games in this ballpark sitting 10 feet away in the visitors' booth, but it's about 100 miles away in the figurative aspects of doing a game at Wrigley Field. To come into this booth and sit in this chair has been unbelievable. It's a huge honor. I think my first year I had to sublimate that a little bit, because it was overwhelming to think about it, and I was just trying to do the job to the best of my ability. As the years have gone on and I've gotten to know Jack Rosenberg, who worked with both Jack and Harry, I've really had the history soak in. I pinch myself all the time and I do think about the incredible amount of history in this booth. We had the "Throwback Game" in 2008, where we went back to 1948, and I got a chance to do Jack's "Hey Hey" call in the ninth inning on a home run. Now I can sit back and remove myself from the job a little bit and think how overwhelming it is. It's a good feeling.

It's hard to explain to non-broadcasters, but home runs by the other team are sometimes easier to call, because you're just calling the play and you don't build in the excitement factor. Calling a home run for the Cubs is more difficult because I don't want to get too excited if it's not going to go and want to make sure it's out. I think the worst thing is to get too excited about a ball that's not going to go out. It doesn't happen sometimes, and that's fun, too, when people get excited with you and then go, "Oooooh!" When it goes out, that's when you can really open up the throttle. The Aramis Ramirez home run at Wrigley against Milwaukee in 2007 was one people ask me about a lot. My voice cracked, and that's a moment when you become a fan. You're still trying to broadcast the game, but you still have that fan inside you that comes pouring out. I'm very proud of that call because I had no idea at the time what I said. I went back later and thought, *Wow, that sounded okay*. I'm my own worst critic, but that one seemed to work out.

A home-run call has to develop naturally, and I want every home run to have its own unique characteristics. If you start to use a call that has "high fly" in it when it's a line drive, you can get caught a little bit. Harry had such a great home run call and Jack had the "Hey Hey," which was great. That became his signature. But it's a natural progression, and maybe down the road something will happen. I've used "Oh, baby!" which is certainly not unique to my calls, but it fit on the Ramirez homer. I've used it a couple of other times, so maybe that will creep in once in a while.

I think you have a general idea of how big the Cubs things is, but until you're actually in it, you don't really know. I can honestly say, when I call games with Bob and something good happens, I feel Cubs Nation get excited. I can say when it's gone the other way, we've had a lot of those moments, too. There's a collective "aaaahhh," where the weight of the world is on everyone's shoulders. I look at it as a good thing, because what happens to the Cubs means so much to the people listening and watching. It's a huge part of their daily lives. They care so much, have such passion, and are allowed to ride that roller coaster. I think Bob and I sometimes have to give you a little bit of the even keel with some of the highs and lows, but we want people to think and know that we're going to be with you every day, whether the Cubs win their 10th in a row, lose their 10th in a row, or have five straight rainouts. We're going to be here every single day. We're going to be excited about being at the ballpark. We're going to root for the Cubs, but if bad things happen, we'll tell you why they happened.

Wrigley Field and Fenway Park were always more unique to me than Yankee Stadium. After Yankee Stadium was renovated, the ballpark looked very much like the other parks from the '60s and '70s. It was the atmosphere there that everyone always talked about. The atmosphere here at Wrigley Field is why people come here. I hope Wrigley Field is here forever. At some point, whether it's 100, 200, or 300 years down the road, I think the Cubs are going to play in a new ballpark. I think the fandom and the fan base here will transfer over to that new place. We talk all the time about how people show up for the first pitch and stay until the last pitch, and nobody wants to leave, because it is such a special place. Everybody acts like they are part of a big family. It may be a dysfunctional one, but it's a big, huge Cubs family, and I'm fortunate to be part of it.

There is a lot of trust involved in being around the team every day. I think you earn that trust over time. There is no real manual on how to do this job or for what you can and can't use on the air. It's more of a feeling-out process, and sometimes, if somebody tells me something pretty compelling in just a casual conversation, I'll ask, "Can I use that?" Or, when I go into a conversation, I'll say, "Okay, for air, tell me this." Once that's done, I'll say, "Now tell me what's really going on!" Most people at home do understand that there are times when things do need to stay private. There are other occasions when I don't even want to know the real story, because having information sometimes can color how you call the game. I'd rather just not know and just call the game as it happens and let the papers report the other stuff. We're not here to scoop anybody, we're here to tell them what's going on in terms of the daily news stories and call the game.

For lack of a better term, I play traffic cop quite a bit. I like that. Television play-by-play is a lot different than radio play-by-play. TV is an analyst's medium. You can see what's happening. You want your analyst—in our case, Bob Brenly, one of the best in the business—to tell you why something happened, how it happened, and what might happen next. My job is to stay out of his way and lead him into situations where he can shine. If I can fill in a tidbit here or there and obviously call the big plays, that's great. I want to make sure he has the opportunity to do his job. The better he sounds, the better I sound. He makes me better every single day.

The seventh-inning stretch is totally unpredictable, especially when you have first-time singers in the booth, whether it's a huge star like Tim Robbins or a relative unknown like a local athlete. You don't know if they are going to be a great guest or a terrible guest, a great singer or a bad singer, or how nervous they are going to be. Generally, most people are pretty nervous, whether they're huge stars or have never been in the spotlight before. I didn't know Erik Estrada's interview would go down as such a memorable one, or Bobby Hull in 2008 in the middle of a six-run rally as the Cubs came back. That, to me, is the fun of it—the unpredictability and the big-time challenge to not only do the interview, but to keep your focus on the field, which is the number-one priority. I know people talk about it when things go badly and we have those fun moments. I know people talk about it each day, and I enjoy doing it.

I really enjoy Sunday mornings coming to Wrigley Field, sometimes on getaway day. I get here early, drop off my suitcase, head to the booth, and all you can hear is what's actually going on around the ballpark, maybe a car horn honking on Waveland. It's totally peaceful, it's a neighborhood setting. Then, over the course of the next three hours, the ballpark fills up. You think to yourself, *Three hours ago, there was no one here, and now there are 41,000.* It's just a completely different atmosphere.

What do I do for a living? The easy answer would be that I'm living a dream. The more complicated answer would be that I get to do what a 10-year-old kid does. When I was 10 and 11 and 12, I would sit in my living room or bedroom with a card table and a tabletop dice baseball game and have the Cubs and Giants or Mariners and Indians. I would play the game,

297

I'd be the manager, and I'd be the announcer. In my head, I would announce big-league baseball games. I'm doing the same thing now, except there are no dice and there is an actual game going on. I can honestly say that I got as big a thrill when I was 10 doing what I'm doing now, but I'm also having the same thrill now that I got when I was 10, and I don't think a lot of people can say that about their jobs.

Len Kasper grew up in central Michigan, listening to Ernie Harwell on the Detroit Tigers' radio broadcasts. He broke into major league baseball as a fill-in announcer for the Milwaukee Brewers, then landed a full-time position with the Florida Marlins in 2002 as their television voice. Len was hired along with Bob Brenly to form the Cubs' television broadcast team before the 2005 season. He teams with Brenly each winter to put on "The Len & Bob Bash" concert for Chicago Cubs Charities.

RYAN THERIOT
SHORTSTOP
2005–Present

IT WAS A BIT OF A BUMPY ROAD for me early in my career. I started off trying to learn to switch-hit while playing pro ball, which was difficult. For the better part of four years, I was in the minor leagues. Once I quit switch-hitting and trying to hit left-handed, that was the year I got called up. It was a trying time for me a little bit, but it finally worked out, and I learned a lot. I knew a decent amount about the franchise when I started, but I didn't know the passions that the fans bring here throughout the city. That was a big surprise for me and my family.

My first game at Wrigley was a breath of fresh air. I went from minor league stadiums, came up here, and thought this was where I belonged and where I needed to be. The intensity level was off the chart, which is something that, as an athlete, you want. We were playing Cincinnati, and it was a lot of fun. It was a really good time for me.

I always felt like I could compete and produce here. The secret is not getting too comfortable or feeling too confident. You can't be too comfortable in your job. That way, you stay sharp and on your toes.

As the shortstop on the team, you're kind of like the quarterback on the football field. I definitely take pride in the fact that my first two years here I was starting and playing every day when we won the division. That's something I am proud of, to say that I was part of that. It makes you feel good. Obviously, the postseason didn't turn out the way we wanted it to those two

Cubs shortstop Ryan Theriot connects with a pitch in a game against the Reds at Great American Ball Park in Cincinnati on August 4, 2009.

years, but we were there. We were knocking on the door and had a chance. We had an opportunity, but we didn't play well.

I feel like I am constantly learning. This game is built for that. If you get complacent and stop trying to get better, you're only going to get worse. For me, every day is something new. I try to watch other players I look up to and mimic what they do. I think you get never get slowed down with that.

Wrigley is unique in that the infield grass is a lot thicker than anywhere else, so you adjust your positioning on defense. The wind here is weird, and it swirls. Sometimes you'll look up at the flags, and the wind is blowing out. The ball goes up, and all of a sudden, it's blowing in. You really have to be on your toes when it comes to the wind.

This is what I expected. It's what I planned on from day one and what I hoped would happen. It's bigger than just baseball. It's been a blessing and a great opportunity for me to be able to come up here. WGN and all the coverage we have has opened up avenues for us as athletes to affect so many lives in a positive way. I really enjoy that. It's refreshing each day to know that if you do something good in the field, you are making people's day. That's really cool.

It's awesome to be playing with Mike Fontenot. To watch his journey and see how he persevered into having success now and finding a niche makes me proud of him. We took a lot of the same steps: playing little league baseball in Louisiana, winning the College World Series at LSU, and now playing together here with the Cubs. We didn't think it would ever happen that way, especially since we played the same position. I feel like I know where he wants me to throw it on a double play, because we've been together so long.

Hitting the ball to right field is something I've done since I was very young. My dad taught me my swing, and it evolved from there. I try to keep pitchers guessing, and one thing I've continued to work on each off-season is being able to hit a ball middle-in the other way. I feel if I can get that to the opposite field, there's not a pitch they can get me out with.

"The Riot" I've heard here and there, but never as much as now that I'm in Chicago. I think Len Kasper and Bob Brenly have something to do with that, when they use it on the broadcast. It's cool to have a nickname and hear them saying it on *SportsCenter*. I guess that means you're doing something right, if you get a nickname.

Cubs fans are diehard, intelligent, intense, and they know the game, unlike other fans across the country. They understand the small things—I guess they have to after putting up without a World Series all these years. I know they want it. It's not all on our shoulders and we can't put the burden on one team. It's going to happen, and we will give them the effort every single day. That's one thing I think we've done is play hard for ourselves, the fans, and the city.

The thing I love about Wrigley Field is there is nothing else going on but the game. There's no flashing signs, jumbotrons, train in left field, or anything jumping out at you. There's no distractions. People come to watch the game, and because of that, I feel they know the game better than most. One thing that always sticks out in my mind is that at many places on the road, we outdraw the home team. That is impressive, it really is. WGN has had a lot to do with that, and the product we've put on the field has, too.

A year after leading LSU to the College World Series title, Ryan Theriot was drafted by the Cubs in the third round of the 2001 amateur draft. Theriot played five seasons in the minors before making his Cubs debut in 2005. He grabbed the everyday shortstop job in 2007 and led the Cubs with a .307 average in 2008. "The Riot" hit .284 with a career-high 54 RBIs in 2009 and has stolen 28, 22, and 21 bases in his three full seasons with the Cubs.

LOU PINIELLA

MANAGER

2007–Present

M Y FIRST MANAGER WAS HANK BAUER, when I came up with the Orioles in 1964. He was a big, old, gruff ex-Marine who was scary to a young guy, not that he was a bad guy, because he was a nice guy. He had that big, old, gravelly voice and smoked Camels. It was really fun to see what the big leagues were like and play with Brooks Robinson, Luis Aparicio, and Boog Powell. I only got one at-bat, but it got me started. It took me three years to get back.

Chicago is a wonderful sports town and a wonderful baseball town. The White Sox and Cubs are supported very well. The city of Chicago loves their Cubs. We're trying like heck to do the best we can as a team and an organization to take this team where everybody wants us to take it. Hopefully, we'll be able to do it.

The Cubs are a unique team, playing in this old, antiquated ballpark that reminds me of a *Field of Dreams* type of situation. It's fun for me to come to Wrigley and manage a ballgame. This place gets electric during the course of a game. The fans are really into it. There's a uniqueness here with the ivy, the hand-run scoreboard, people watching from the rooftops. The clubhouses are small, and it reminds me more of Fenway than anything else. It's wonderful with the Bleacher Bums and the beautiful sky. It's such a nice place to watch a baseball game.

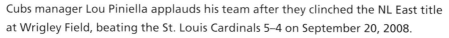

Cubs manager Lou Piniella applauds his team after they clinched the NL East title at Wrigley Field, beating the St. Louis Cardinals 5–4 on September 20, 2008.

You try to insulate yourself from all the talk about how long it's been since we won the Series. Cubs fans are wonderful. They are the best fans in baseball, but when things don't go their way, they can be a little fickle. Things haven't gone their way for a while, and they tend to get worried. If you're playing well, you're the best team in baseball, but boy, if you get in a little bit of a losing streak, you're one of the worst teams in baseball. As a player, manager, or coach, you dwell on the game or the series at hand. You're going to have peaks and valleys in the course of a baseball season, and the secret is not to get too high or too low. Stay as even-keeled as possible.

When you look at what happened in 2009, you have to stay healthy, and we didn't. The amount and length of physical problems we had to key people hurt us. Coming out of spring training, I said we weren't very deep, and it was important to stay healthy. It didn't happen, and we had some guys who didn't have the years they were capable of. In 2008 it was easier to win and harder to lose. In '09 it was harder to win and easier to lose. Over .500 and second place isn't what we wanted, but we have to take it.

Sometimes I look at this place, and it reminds me of the British Open. The weather can change from day to day, where sometimes the wind is blowing out and it's warm, then the next day the wind is blowing straight in and it's cold. You've got to have an athletic team here that can adjust and play in all types of environments. Good pitching and good defense are the cornerstones of any ballclub.

It's a fun place to come to, driving through a neighborhood, probably like Ebbets Field in Brooklyn. I never had the good fortune of being there, but I saw a lot of games on television from there back in the '50s. You drive through the neighborhood, and you see everyone in their Cubbies T-shirts, then get into the cramped parking lot, then to the office, and then the fun starts.

The fans are right on top of you, and they're really into it. These fans really know their baseball. They've been long-suffering and long-waiting. But each team has to stand on its own merits and can't change what has happened here. We've tried to get the hundred years, goats, and all that stuff, and throw it out the window and just concentrate on winning each day. Let each team stand on its own merit, win, lose, or draw.

I take pride in my job. These have been three really good years. It's been very exciting for me. It's been all I've bargained for and more. I've been very happy and very appreciative. I take winning very seriously and want to see us

305

BRICKHOUSE · ANDY PAFKO · VINCE LLOYD · ERNIE BANKS · BI

ENBERG · KEN HOLTZMAN · BILL HANDS · RANDY HUNDLEY · FE

TNER · JOSE CARDENAL · RICK REUSCHEL · BILL MADLOCK · MIKE

N DURHAM · JODY DAVIS · LARRY BOWA · KEITH MORELAND · R

RY MATTHEWS · RICK SUTCLIFFE · SHAWON DUNSTON · ANDRE D

RY PRESSY · MARK GRACE · DAN PLESAC · GLENALLEN HILL · JIM

DRY · MICKEY MORANDINI · KERRY WOOD · CARLOS ZAMBRAN

ER · LOU PINIELLA · JACK BRICKHOUSE · ANDY PAFKO · VINCE LL

N BECKERT · JACK ROSENBERG · KEN HOLTZMAN · BILL HANDS

MONDAY · LARRY BIITTNER · JOSE CARDENAL · RICK REUSCHEL

DMAN · LEE SMITH · LEON DURHAM · JODY DAVIS · LARRY BOWA

REY · BOB DERNIER · GARY MATTHEWS · RICK SUTCLIFFE · SHAV

DUX · DOUG DASCENZO · GARY PRESSY · MARK GRACE · DAN PI

WN · PAT HUGHES · JIM HENDRY · MICKEY MORANDINI · KERRY V

· BOB BRENLY · LEN KASPER · LOU PINIELLA · JACK BRICKHOUS

O · DON KESSINGER · GLENN BECKERT · JACK ROSENBERG · KEN

ONE · MILT PAPPAS · RICK MONDAY · LARRY BIITTNER · JOSE CA

BILL BUCKNER · STEVE GOODMAN · LEE SMITH · LEON DURHAM ·

Y · STEVE TROUT · JIM FREY · BOB DERNIER · GARY MATTHEWS ·